INSTITUT FÜR AFRIKASTUDIEN

The peer-reviewed series "Bayreuth Studies in Politics and Society in Africa" publishes research about socio-political processes and structures in African societies. The editors welcome innovative monographs and guest edited volumes in either English or German which discuss historical and current transformations in African countries with an empirical or theoretical focus. The series is open to case studies and comparative research from the social sciences and related academic disciplines.

Bayreuther Studien zu Politik und Gesellschaft in Afrika
Bayreuth Studies in Politics and Society in Africa

is edited by

Institut für Afrikastudien (IAS) der Universität Bayreuth
Dr. Antje Daniel
Prof. Dr. Alexander Stroh

Volume 6

Sarah Böllinger | Carsten Mildner
Ulf Vierke [eds.]

Diversity Gains

Stepping Stones and Pitfalls

Nomos

The Deutsche Nationalbibliothek lists this publication in the Deutsche Nationalbibliografie; detailed bibliographic data are available on the Internet at http://dnb.d-nb.de

ISBN 978-3-8487-6874-5 (Print)
978-3-7489-0970-5 (ePDF)

British Library Cataloguing-in-Publication Data
A catalogue record for this book is available from the British Library.

ISBN 978-3-8487-6874-5 (Print)
978-3-7489-0970-5 (ePDF)

Library of Congress Cataloging-in-Publication Data
Böllinger, Sarah / Mildner, Carsten / Vierke, Ulf
Diversity Gains
Stepping Stones and Pitfalls
Sarah Böllinger / Carsten Mildner / Ulf Vierke (eds.)
234 pp.
Includes bibliographic references and index.

ISBN 978-3-8487-6874-5 (Print)
978-3-7489-0970-5 (ePDF)

Onlineversion
Nomos eLibrary

1st Edition 2020

Contents

From Critical Intervention to Trademark – and Back! Diversity Gains in Discourse and Praxis

Introduction by Sarah Böllinger, Katharina Fink and Carsten Mildner

Diversity is virtually everywhere. It has made a career from a revolutionarily claim of advocating for social justice to a buzzword in strategic managerial strategies. In contemporary political discourse, diversity and its social implications are highly controversial. As such, it is of no difference to many other concepts with a radical zest in late capitalism. The simultaneousness of the rejection of diversity in right-wing discourse, its sometimes uncritical praise on the political opposite, and the depolitization through mainstreaming calls for a book project that assembles diverse contributions that tackle the field from a multiplicity of perspectives.

We wish to coin this a time of diversity gains, understood in – at least – two ways. In a lecture[1], Ann Fox reflected on *disability gain*, inspired by Baumann and Murray's work on *Deaf Gain* (2014). Their idea understands deafness not as hearing *loss* but a *gain* in Deaf[2] identity and culture (see also Young/Temple 2014: 18; Harmon 2010). Fox argues that disability opens new perspectives for the person themselves and for society to move on (see also Reid-Cunningham 2009: 106-107); for an example she referred to Yassine Balbzioui's work on broken porcelain (see Fox this volume, also Böllinger 2019 for disability aesthetics). We understand *diversity gain* as a gain like this: Diversity enriches the lives of everybody, it

1 Ann Fox (April 7, 2016): The Importance of "Fabulous Invalids": Or, Why Representing Disability in Mainstream Theater Matters. A BIGSAS (Bayreuth International Graduate School of African Studies) Diversity Lecture on the occasion of the International Conference on Beauty and the Norm: Debating Standardization in Bodily Appearance at the University of Bayreuth, www.beautyandthe norm.uni-bayreuth.de (19.11.2019).

2 In referring to themselves as Deaf instead of deaf, Deaf people claim an identity as a cultural and linguistic group (Napier: 2002). There are thus deaf people and Deaf people, depending on which idea they identify with and the given social context (see also Mildner in this volume, McIlroy/Storbeck: 2011).

challenges gridlocked discourses and practices, it ignites social progress, creativity and innovation.

But we also understand diversity gain as a descriptive term: In a globalizing world, diversity increases – and so do the discussions around it. More and more people claim and create new and fluid identities in reference to gender, sexual orientation or religious beliefs while others engage to deconstruct confining identities that were based on racism, ableism or sexism. The social world plays out its variety and variation, thereby reducing 'normality' to absurdity. The *Gains* in the title of this collection shall thus be read in two ways:

- as a plural of gain – referencing the increase of diversity as such as well as the increasing reactions, confrontations and oppositions it causes. We will reflect on some of these in this introduction.
- as a verb – diversity gains victory and prevails over uniformity and monotony, stagnancy and regression.

In a TED talk (Technology, Entertainment, Design), one of the iconic formats of the mesh of capital and societal movements in the early 21st century, Janet Stovall, manager of executive communications at the logistics company UPS (United Parcel Service), advocated for single-mindedness in making diversity a strong tool of dismantling exclusion in the workplace (Stovall 2018). The talk is of interest as it first links to the entanglement of language and action, and secondly because it links to the character of diversity as a process, which finds its echo in political theorist Chantal Mouffe's "agonistic pluralism" (2000). Agonism, as explored in her work with Laclau (Smith 1998), keeps democracy alive as it requires a constant discussion of diverse positions. The agonistic notion of diversity requires the tolerating of difference and the translation of it into a productive form. It says: There will not be a society that has reached the perfect state. As such, it is necessary to stay in communication, in contact, as an exchange of equals. It takes away the illusion that a trademarked version of diversity, one that finds cultural capital in the imagery of superficial heterogeneity, will help in creating a diverse, accessible society that lives by unity in difference. Audre Lorde, a writer surely to re-read as a companion to this reader, puts it as a punchline: "The master's tools will never dismantle the master's house" (1984: 110). Neither will "diversity™", as we dub the commodified version of a discourse that, by means of its mainstreaming, loses some of its radicality to challenge structural exclusion.

This is apparent in applications of diversity where human and civil rights and the social value of plurality do not seem to be sufficient enough. Instead, the value of diversity is measured in economic terms when consultancy firms argue that higher rates of diversity in boards and businesses correlate with higher profits (see Frost 2014, 2016, 2019). While this rather shortsighted motivation may pave the way for a more diverse and inclusive neoliberal society, it seems risky: What if a company that is less diverse makes even more profit – will diversity fall back to a nice-to-have ideology? And what about the nonmonetary gains, what about health, solidarity, mutual learning, creativity and innovation?

As a shapeshifting concept, meandering between appellation, emancipatory project, depoliticized surface and rhetorical topos, diversity has been at the heart of social scientific interest of inquiry for centuries. Herbert Spencer acknowledged the heterogeneity of societies that needed to be faced and managed to create a system for harmonious coexistence (Spencer 1862), while disapproving of interethnic relations (Salzbrunn 2014: 15). Georg Simmel did not condemn diversity but identified it as a challenge for social organization (1890: 101f). Pierre Bourdieu has critically analyzed the processes of differentiation and distinction in various works (e.g. 1984, 2007). The list could be endlessly prolonged, but already here it becomes clear that precursors, founders and figureheads of sociology were continuously curious about how societies develop and manage their diversity; even though it might not have been termed like that until recently (Salzbrunn 2014: 13).

The current dynamics around diversity is best described as a mainstreaming. What this mainstreaming does to the potential of a concept as a "critical category" (Arndt 2018) can be best studied in the field of gender mainstreaming (e.g. Bacchi/Eveline 2010). Diversity went from being regarded as a problematic challenge for society as Simmel saw it, to social justice discourses, to possibly being considered an asset (Michaels 2006; Salzbrunn 2014: 8, 53; Friedner 2015; Frost 2019).

Looking at diversity in action, we identify the following four levels of denotation, which are paired with quotations from the vast realm of public discussion of diversity:

- Factual understanding: On the actual state of things, our societies, cultures, nations are diverse, meaning we "inhabit a universe that is characterized by diversity" (Desmond Tutu 2001).
- Ethical understanding: As a path of good life and conduct, where accepting and promoting diversity is the right (or only) way to live, as Jacqueline Woodson emphasized when arguing for more diversity in children's books: "Diversity is about all of us, and about us having to

figure out how to walk through this world together" (Jacqueline Woodson in Kirch 2014).

- Entrepreneurial understanding: As a goal in economics and politics, where diversity is a subject of rational valuation. "There's a pure and simple business case for diversity: Companies that are more diverse are more successful" (Mindy Grossman in Goudreau 2011); or as Canadian Prime Minister Justin Trudeau has been quoted saying, "Diversity isn't just sound social policy. Diversity is the engine of invention. It generates creativity that enriches the world" (Foster 2016).
- Visionary understanding: As a path towards a better future: How can we use each other's differences in our common battles for a livable future? Audre Lorde's position about difference as a tool for a radically different society that is based on equal access while not being naïve about mechanisms of exclusion lives on in the genderqueer understanding of diversity as proclaimed by South African performance artist and writer Goldendean. In their work *Plan B* (2017), a "gathering of strangers" is proclaimed, leaning on Sara Ahmed's notion of strangeness, as discussed in her work *Strange encounters* (2000). They offer a postcolonial, queer understanding of difference that builds on the queer-feminist tradition.

These four layers allow just a small glimpse into the panoply of praise diversity continues to receive. Diversity is every step: the current state of things, the way we need to go, the goals and results we seek, and the utopia we might be dreaming of. To rhetorically exaggerate: Diversity is the problem, the solution, the process and the result. So, all the praise raises suspicion. Is it not, by being celebrated on so many fronts, losing its significance and specific edge? And is this positive reflection and assumed appraisal of diversity in academia making us too comfortable with presumably achieved and overcome struggles? When looking at the current state of affairs it is obvious that the political reality does not necessarily go along with the academic consensus.

In Poland, the political party *Prawo i Sprawiedliwość* (Law and Justice) is winning local and national elections with a clearly national orientation, just as *Fidesz* (Fiatal Demokraták Szövetsége, Hungarian Civic Alliance) is in Hungary. Xenophobia was mobilized to win over voters in the Brexit referendum in the United Kingdom. In Germany, the *Alternative für Deutschland* (AfD) (Alternative for Germany), *Christlich-Soziale Union* (Christian Social Union) and the extraparliamentary movement *Patriotische Europäer gegen die Islamisierung des Abendlandes* (PEGIDA, Patriotic Europeans against the Islamization of the Occident) are competing to dominate the right-winged discourse and blur the lines between right-of-center and radical-right in the political landscape. In the United States, Donald Trump convinced his voters with a simplistic *America First* logic, assuming this *America* to be essentially white and Christian, assailing ethnic and religious groups as well as women and people with disabilities (see also Ann Fox in this volume). Marine Le Pen had a realistic chance to take her political party the *Front National* into the presidential office. In Denmark, Italy and the Netherlands, right-wing parties have been shaping the political scene for years. And the attack of right-wing parties and initiatives in Germany against the "gender ideology", as the Alternative for Germany calls it (AfD Landesverband Baden-Württemberg, regional association Baden-Württemberg, 2016), is an assault against diversity discourses. All these examples of political movements and discourses are rooted in their respective social, historical and political background but have in common that they do not share the academic praise for an inclusive future.

It can thus be of no great surprise that the academic program of diversity is the target of many conservative or new right-wing movements. In Hungary, Viktor Orbán signed a decree to remove gender studies from the list of accredited master programs (Redden 2018). The political party website of the Alternative for Germany (AfD 2017) describes diversity and gender mainstreaming as a mere mind game, far from reality, and gender studies as ideology instead of an academic, scientific undertaking.

The scrutiny and open repudiation of diversity is linked towards a "retreat into ethnic units, a sort of nationalist backlash, as we can witness in Europe and the United States today" (Philipps 2018: 3), a reactionary desire of "imagined communities" (Anderson 1991) for homogeneity. Comedian Stephen Colbert picked up on this illusory nostalgia in the title of his book *America Again: Re-becoming the Greatness We Never Weren't* (Colbert 2012). But jokes aside; where does this burning desire to return to a nationally and ethnically homogenous past – that never actually was – come from?

Wilhelm Heitmeyer identified national identity as an anchor in times of uncertainty that people repeatedly turn to when they face economic, political and social exclusion and decline – or just the fear thereof (Heitmeyer 2018, see also Waldmann/Elwert 1989: 11). The resulting negative mental states, Julijana Ranc argues, lead to resentment and prepare the ground for populism and the new right movements we witness today (Ranc 2019: 208, see also Elwert 1989: 54). As a consequence, the fight against xenophobia and the fight for acceptance of diversity are linked closer than one might think at first. The answer lies in the social, economic and political inclusion of all. Diversity and inclusion (or inclusivity) are therefore inevitably linked – although the concepts are not congruent in what they mean and where they come from.

Diversity and Inclusion – false friends but good friends?

The relation between diversity and inclusion is not as simple as it seems at first sight. One might consider an inclusive society one that cherishes and, quite importantly, enables diversity to thrive. Yet more than the field of diversity, inclusion involves a future – or utopian (see Becker 2016) – perspective; a demand for an accessible world grounded in basic human rights. It is vital to look not just at the terms *diversity* and *inclusion*, but at the politics embedded in both. Diversity and inclusion here are certainly no longer synonymous nor can one be subsumed under the other. Rather their relation is dialectic or can be turned into a productive relation, even an agonistic one, as Fink and others (this Volume) will explore further.

Diversity politics ascribes a positive value to diversity of cultural and social entities and tries to enhance diversity, for example by trying to privilege certain minorities. In order to be able to do so, one has to identify the elements that make situations, teams and settings diverse – for example by identifying what the markers that define a minority group are. As such, diversity focuses more on the situation as it presents itself, and on a productive understanding of difference, e.g. regarding gender, religion and culture. That these discourses have the tendency to flatten into depoliticized praise for differences considered stable is perhaps best expressed by the necessity to add the adjective "critical" to academic programs[3] and conferences on diversity.

Inclusion on the other hand assumes diversity on the micro level as a given, without necessarily having to identify certain criteria. Instead, the focus is on adjusting the conditions of equal access for everyone – physical, functional, structural, socioeconomic, political, cultural, etc. These meta conditions are to be changed to get rid of as many barriers as possible.

3 See, e.g., the MA-program in Critical Diversity Studies at the University of the Witwatersrand, Johannesburg, South Africa.

Regarding practices of diversity, the concepts of inclusion and diversity intertwine. The debates in Germany (e.g. in the context of education that the editors work in) are dominated by the concept of inclusion, as enforced by the ratification of the United Nations Convention on the Rights of Persons with Disabilities (UN 2006). While affirmative diversity politics aims at appreciating and enabling minorities within a diverse society, the intention (or utopia) of inclusion is that nobody needs affirmative practices because society is as open and equal so that every person can partake from the beginning.

Let us give an example from the editors' work at becks (Büro des Beauftragten für behinderte und chronisch kranke Studierende), the administrative department for disabled and chronically ill students at the University of Bayreuth. As a matter of fact, becks practices *integration*, that is to say, by means of adjustment measures becks enables students with disabilities to study in the same way as students without disability do. At the same time, the claim and aim of becks is to reshape the university into an inclusive space where those measures are not necessary anymore, and where *disability needs* are not considered as such. This idea of practicing diversity and inclusion presents itself as a process of constantly readjusting perceptions of individuals and groups. As much as it became clear that our own concepts of diversity might have been somewhat callow, it also encouraged us to map the multiple field of diversity concepts.

Publication and Lecture Series

This publication is a result of the Diversity Lecture series of the *Bayreuth International Graduate School of African Studies* (BIGSAS), of which the editors are fellows[4]. At the same time, the editors work for becks and

4 We want to express our gratitude to the authors for their presentations in Bayreuth and their contributions to this book, as well as for their patience during the process of publication. Jennifer Rasell, Gabriele Edelmann, Moritz Wohlgenannt, and Thomas Hughes supported us in editing the articles and the manuscript, Renzo Baas translated the article by Sarah Böllinger and Ulf Vierke. The organization of the Diversity Lecture Series and our work at becks would not have been the same without our cherished longtime student assistant Linda Ilona Rohmann. The Lecture Series as well as the edition of the book was realized in cooperation

BayFinK (Bayerische Forschungs- und Informationsstelle), a research and information platform for inclusive universities and cultural institutions across Bavaria based at the University of Bayreuth. This crossroads inspired the intersectional take of the BIGSAS Diversity Lectures. They create a forum for voices that reflect on the theoretical or conceptual character of diversity, and provide case studies, examples and empirical notes for further discussion. The context in which these lectures and conversations took place, BIGSAS, is itself home to a diverse community of fellows from a wide range of disciplines, each person with their own unique identity shaped by faith, race, sexual orientation, gender identity/expression, age, ability, and socioeconomic class that is a gain for research and teaching. The community challenges assumptions, tests ideas, and broadens the understanding of the human experience and contextualization. However, diversity is more than the aggregate of different individual backgrounds, personal identities, and various worldviews. It is also the acknowledgement and deconstruction of discursive and institutional barriers and the accessibility of space that allows individuals to fully engage in academic life. While we position ourselves among those who appreciate diversity, liberty, human rights and an inclusive society, true diversity implies taking into consideration the uneven distribution of power and opportunities and to create mechanisms to address and resolve existing inequalities. BIGSAS faces these challenges with a *Diversity Program* that focuses on affirmative politics and adjustments to suit individual demands; individual measures and new labels are easier to create than to spark, implement and monitor bureaucratic and social change.

More than anything, diversity is a processual concept. It requires decision and dedicated action. To stress this, let us give attention to a very real struggle: The one for funding for academic work in the context of our graduate school. A *Diversity Grant* was on the table, and immediately heated discussions arose about who could or should be eligible for the new grant: All women? All Africans? Only Black Africans? All junior fellows with disabilities? Who's diverse *enough* for the grant? And how to define these groups and identify individual eligibility? It seemed not to be that easy to define what the *requirements* of diversity were in practice. In the end the funding body DFG (Deutsche Forschungsgemeinschaft, German

between different units of the University of Bayreuth, led by becks and the BIGSAS Diversity Program with support from BayFinK and Nomos Verlag.

Research Foundation) decided that only individuals who identify as 'female' would be eligible for the disability grant.

We faced a similar question about the criteria for diversity beyond the trademark when we started organizing the Diversity Lecture series. We scrutinized the task, asking ourselves: What is diversity? What is diverse? Who shall we invite? What is in the interest of the Lecture Series? We gave ourselves a simple answer, which allowed us a quite inclusive approach to start with and also to open up a debate on what diversity in an academic context could be. We invited friends and colleagues who are working on exciting topics or have published interesting works in the very broad field we would somehow see as fitting the label *diversity*. We found that in an international and pluricultural surrounding it has to be taken into account that the term *diversity* means different things in different places. Here appears already a lesson to be learned on the diversity of diversity. As, for example, Thomas Hughes argues in his chapter in this volume, diversity and multiculturalism in the United States of America and in Denmark are far from having the same significations due to historical difference. Denmark has – at least until recently – never been the kind of melting pot that the United States claims as its founding myth (Parrillo 2005: 8ff). Diversity has thus to be seen differently respective to its different contexts.

In this volume we wish to unfold how questions and challenges of diversity matter to those who usually are considered to make societies diverse. While academics may tend to appreciate diversity, the individual experience is at times not as merry as the discursive praise suggests. The proclamation of unity in diversity is often a charade for the people belonging to minorities of whichever kind. Since decades, minorities argue for their rights and their place within society. They get active to claim what is theirs. After all those decades we are still talking, but what are we achieving (see Windisch in this volume) – particularly given the current dynamics in politics introduced above? Marlon James takes this frustration one step further and asks, facing the often occurring reality of an all-White diversity panel: "why do we need a black person on a panel to talk about inclusion when it's the white person who needs to figure out how to include?" (James 2016). In a comparable vein Tom Humphries wonders why Deaf people continuously need to argue for their Deaf culture, while Hearing culture is taken for granted (Humphries 2008). Is diversity something foreign that the able, hearing, white, Christian male appreciates as a mere decoration of a paternalistic world, the status quo we want to defend? Is it a given gift that is there and therefore, teleologically, is good?

Or is it something we need to work on, that we need to figure out how to manage? Is it something we accept and tolerate, only to then feel more comfortable behind our desks and in our positions? Or do we need to work on being more open to change, on unlearning implicitness and hidden norms? And do we perhaps need to make space? Regarding gender diversity politics, Ann Fox critically remarks that "while laudably trying to get more women represented in boardrooms and other positions of power, [we] don't question the very structures of power that are being infiltrated" (Fox et al. 2019: 110, see also Haraway 1991 and Audre Lorde above). Part of those structures are the profit maximizing logics of late capitalism, as it plays out in the neoliberalism university.

Thus, taking diversity discourses seriously, it is revolution that is called for, not reform. As the art collective The Strategic Radicals, a temporary collective emerging from a discussion about the entanglement of arts and society in Windhoek, Namibia[5], demand: "The present system will fall. But in the time it takes to crumble, we will be radically engaged. We must accelerate" (The Strategic Radicals 2018). In an unapologetic contribution to dismantling the diversity™-discourse as camouflaging continuing structural inequality, South African students achieved a radical shift in the education system with the *#feesmustfall*-movement initiated by South African students that asked for the decolonization of institutions of higher education; and pushed for a thorough discussion of the underlying concept of exclusion and Whiteness. Now, the fight is on to keep their struggle going and protect it against being claimed by political parties.

The imperative of decolonization is transferred to other realms and lives as well. The "anticolonialist discourse" engages in "dissolving the 'West' and its highest product – the one who is not animal, barbarian, or woman; man, that is, the author of a cosmos called history" (Haraway 1991: 156). Sounds good? Sounds exciting? These radical shifts inflict disorientation and fear as well; especially by those who hold power – and those who fear to be marginalized in the future. Those who do hold power manage to mobilize some underprivileged groups against others (Salzbrunn 2014: 17), mobilizing fears of change in order to maintain the status quo (Heitmeyer

5 In the context of the exhibition "FAVT: Future Africa Visions in Time", a travelling exhibition conceptualised by Nadine Siegert, Storm Janse van Rensburg and Katharina Fink, which manifested as an edition in Windhoek, Namibia, in January 2018.

2018). Creating a broadly supported understanding that diversity brings people together in their common struggle for a better living – instead of being played off one against the other – is one of diversity's many challenges.

Neither ignoring nor supporting fear, we take it into account and demand to face it with courage and curiosity. As is the point in Deaf gain and disability gain, diversity gain shall be a gain for all. And what the diversity debate shows clearly is that societies need formats for agonistic debate.

The contributions

By inviting fellows from different disciplines and backgrounds, all labeled diversity scholars by grace of our choice, to share their ideas and thoughts on diversity with us over a few semesters, we were sure to find a great variety of contributions. This makes the collection not only diverse in content but also in writing style. Some are purely academic, some are more essayistic, even motivational, one is poetic. What this collection of articles seeks to do in this discussion is give food for thought and reflection. As mentioned above, there was no set agenda of the lecture series apart from exploring the topics that may be grouped within the scope of diversity.

Claiming identity

Having presented her thoughts on disability gain in the Diversity Lectures in Bayreuth, Ann Fox uses her contribution to draw conclusions from an art exhibition by contemporary artist Yassine Balbzioui. In reflecting the manifold shapes of his ceramics, Fox enhances Tobin Siebers' and others' groundbreaking thoughts on disability aesthetics. Disability is still dominated by the medical field and not recognized as an identity, an aesthetic, and a way of being in the world. Fox argues that Balbzioui's work can help us shape a world that cherishes diversity and equity, starting in contemporary art as well as in academia. That the criticism of inspirational or sentimentalized images of disability is also a question of context, however, is seen in the contributions by Emmanuel Sackey and Ras-I Mackinzeph. Based on his research in Ghana, Sackey studies the way the disability rights movement incorporates discourses of good governance and the role of civil society in promoting the rights of persons with disabilities. Sackey concludes that the disability rights movement in Ghana has benefitted from foreign financial and technical support and internal dynamics alike. Ras-I Mackinzeph introduces us to the current situation of people with disabilities in Cameroon where he himself is an activist. In a very personal account, he shares a perspective from the south that is different from an institutional study or a discourse analysis. With references to philosophical and theological discussions, he shares examples and experience of barriers and disability while also highlighting abilities and the potentials of those often called disregarded as incapable. The inspiration porn criticism Fox refers to is appropriate facing the experiences of demotion of the disability communities in the United States and beyond. Sackey and Mackinzeph show us, though, that in Ghana and Cameroon, inspirational and maybe inevitably reductionist role models appear to be necessary subjects of identification that enable the creation of communities and the realization of the individual's potentials.

The different glance – and what we can gain from it

Taking Rosemary Garland-Thomson's work on "how we look" seriously, Sarah Böllinger and Ulf Vierke take a close look at how Tanzanian photographer John Kiyaya depicts persons with disability working in a rehabilitation center. In the setting of a quite normative and normalizing space, Kiyaya's work appears to be interested in portraying the person rather than in a display of disability. Meticulously analyzing some of Kiyaya's photographs through the lenses of art and disability studies, Böllinger and Vierke explore how a Tanzanian "freestyle photographer" who is far from being involved in disability discourses looks, represents – and makes us look. Katharina Fink discusses participatory art and cultural projects in South Africa and Germany. Curatorial work is creative and can therefore profit from participation, diverse input and a do-it-yourself approach – a process that she terms as "synchronizing". In advocating for an inclusive take, Fink shows the potential that involving and including holds for a re-politization of the museum space.

Intermezzo towards experience

Kevin Mwachiro participated in the diversity lectures by reading from his book *Invisible: Stories from Kenya's Queer Community* (2014) in which Kenyans tell their stories of queer life, of acceptance and exclusion. Instead of an article, he contributed his poem "In the Dead of Night" to this collection.

Diversity within

Diversity, often understood as a descriptive term for a collective consisting of various groups, runs the risk to imply a certain homogeneity within the respective groups. Neubert and Stoll, within a research project by the Bayreuth Academy of Advanced African Studies, discover the diversity within a group discussed as the middle classes of Nairobi, Mombasa, Kisumu and Eldoret on their way to understand this group by quantitative and qualitative terms. Reflecting that diversity is usually understood to describe difference from the mainstream, the authors apply the term to have a closer look at the inner differentiation of a group. Based on an explorative research on deafness in Uganda, Carsten Mildner assembles three accounts of deaf people who live in the same town with the same impairment and yet experience their dis-ability very differently. He argues that looking at being deaf from a perspective that has diversity in mind opens more ways to appreciate identities and experiences while claims of unity, similitude and Culture can be limited in scope and reach.

Individual pluralities

Sociological approaches to human phenomena can never be cut loose of context. Thomas Hughes and Monika Windisch focus on exactly these constellations when multiple belongings are at stake and new questions emerge. Hughes' research participants navigate the categories of being disabled and being immigrants in the Danish welfare state. The account of Abuukar, a disabled immigrant from Somalia, reflects the experience of not being welcomed by Danish disability organizations and feeling equally excluded from the Somalian community due to his disability. Abuukar finds himself at the margins of both those groups and consequently experiences a doubled lack of belonging that Hughes terms "hypermarginality". Windisch takes the discussion of intersectionality and mainstreaming to another level, going beyond country specific questions and debates that place either impairment effects *or* social barriers to the fore. Instead, she adds a fresh analysis of how intersectionality could work in the context of disability and how intersectional experiences of gender and disability are accounted for in European antidiscrimination policies.

All the contributions, in their assembly, inspire to reach beyond a superficial reading of diversity. What we would wish for as editors is at the same time easy and a lot: That this book invites for a close reading of one's own personal and institutional practices; to continue the discussion – and potentially get the tools or links needed to work with the complexity of diversity *at home*.

Abbreviations

AfD	Alternative für Deutschland, Alternative for Germany
becks	Büro des Beauftragten für behinderte und chronisch kranke Studierende, administrative department for disabled and chronically ill students
BayFinK	Bayerische Forschungs- und Informationsstelle – Inklusive Hochschulen und Kultureinrichtungen, Bavarian Center for research and information – inclusive Universities and cultural institutions
BIGSAS	Bayreuth International Graduate School of African Studies
CSU	Christlich-Soziale Union, Christian Social Union
DFG	Deutsche Forschungsgemeinschaft, German Research Foundation
Fidesz	Fiatal Demokraták Szövetsége, Hungarian Civic Alliance
PEGIDA	Patriotische Europäer gegen die Islamisierung des Abendlandes, Patriotic Europeans against the Islamization of the Occident
TED	Technology, Entertainment, Design
UN	United Nations
UPS	United Parcel Service

References

AfD Landesverband Baden-Württemberg (2016): "Gender Mainstreaming". Available at: https://afd-bw.de/partei/resolutionen/gender-mainstream (19.11.2019).

AfD (2017): "Programm für Deutschland: Kurzfassung des Wahlprogramms der Alternative für Deutschland für die Wahl zum Deutschen Bundestag am 24.09.2017". Available at: www.afd.de/wp-content/uploads/sites/111/2017/08/AfD_kurzprogramm_a4-quer_210717.pdf (19.11.2019).

Ahmed, Sara (2000): Strange encounters: embodied others in post-coloniality. London.

Anderson, Benedict (1991): Imagined communities: reflections on the origin and spread of nationalism. London.

Arndt, Susan (2017): Dream*hoping memory into futureS: reading resistant narratives about Maafa by employing futureS as a category of analysis, in: Journal of the African Literature Association, 11:1, 3-27.

Baumann, H-Dirksen/Murray, Joseph, eds. (2014): Deaf Gain: Raising the Stakes for Human Diversity. Minneapolis.

Becker, Uwe (2016): Die Inklusionslüge – Behinderung im flexiblen Kapitalismus. Bielefeld.

Böllinger, Sarah (2019): Broken Beauty, Broken Cups: Disabled Bodies in Contemporary African Art. Claudia Liebelt/Sarah Böllinger/Ulf Vierke. Beauty and the Norm. Debating Standardization in Bodily Appearance. Hampshire, 127-152.

Bourdieu, Pierre (1984): Distinction: A social critique of the judgement of taste. Cambridge.

Bourdieu, Pierre (2007): La misère du monde. Paris.

Colbert, Stephen (2012): America Again: Re-becoming the Greatness We Never Weren't. New York.

DSW (Deutsches Studentenwerk) (2012): "beeinträchtigt studieren – Datenerhebung zur Situation Studierender mit Behinderung und chronischer Krankheit 2011". Available at: www.studentenwerke.de/sites/default/files/Beeintraechtigt_Studieren_Datenerhebung_01062012_0.pdf (19.11.2019).

Elwert, Georg (1989): Nationalismus, Ethnizität und Nativismus: Über die Bildung von Wir-Gruppen. Waldmann, Peter/ Elwert, Georg. Ethnizität im Wandel. Saarbrücken/Fort Lauderdale, 21-60.

Foster, Lauren (2016): "Best of 2016: Diversity Is the Engine of Invention". Available at: https://blogs.cfainstitute.org/investor/2016/12/20/best-of-2016-diversity-isnt-just-sound-social-policy-diversity-is-the-engine-of-invention/ (19.11.2019).

Fox, Ann/Krings, Matthias/Vierke, Ulf (2019): 'Disability Gain' and the Limits of Representing Alternative Beauty. Claudia Liebelt/Sarah Böllinger/Ulf Vierke. Beauty and the Norm. Hampshire, 105-125.

Friedner, Michele (2015): Valuing deaf worlds in urban India. New Brunswick. New Jersey.

Frost, Stephen (2014): The Inclusion Imperative: How Real Inclusion Creates Better Business and Builds Better Societies. London.

Frost, Stephen (2016): Inclusive Talent Management: How Business Can Thrive in an Age of Diversity. London.

Frost, Stephen (2019): Building an Inclusive Organization: Leveraging the Power of Your Diverse Workforce. London.

Goldendean (2017): Plan B, A Gathering of Strangers (or) This is not Working. Bayreuth.

Goudreau, Jeanne (2011): "HSN Chief Mindy Grossman Talks Women And Shopping". Available at: www.forbes.com/sites/jennagoudreau/2011/05/27/hsn-chief-mindy-grossman-talks-women-and-shopping/#4a453dbf21c6 (19.11.2019).

Harmon, Kristen (2010): Addressing Deafness: From Hearing Loss to Deaf Gain, in: Profession, 1, 124-130.

Haraway, Donna Jeanne (1991): The Cyborg Manifesto. Haraway, Donna. Simians, cyborg and women. The re-invention of nature. New York, 149-181.

Heitmeyer, Wilhelm (2018): Autoritäre Versuchungen: Signaturen der Bedrohung. Berlin.

Heitzmann, Daniela/Klein, Uta, eds. (2017): Diversity konkret gemacht. Weinheim Basel.

Humphries, Tom (2008): Talking culture and culture talking. Baumann, Dirksen. Open Your Eyes. Minneapolis, 35-41.

James, Marlon (2016): "Why I'm done talking about diversity. Or, why we should try an all-White diversity panel". Available at: http://lithub.com/marlon-james-why-im-done-talking-about-diversity (01.12.2016).

Kirch, Claire (2014): "BEA 2014: Jacqueline Woodson: Remembering a Brown Girl's Childhood". Available at: www.publishersweekly.com/pw/by-topic/childrens/childrens-authors/article/62630-bea-2014-jacqueline-woodson-remembering-a-brown-girl-s-childhood.html (19.11.2019).

Lorde, Audre (1984): The Master's Tools Will Never Dismantle the Master's House. Lorde, Audre. Sister Outsider: Essays and Speeches. Trumansburg, New York, 110-114.

Löw, Martina, ed. (2014): Vielfalt und Zusammenhalt: Verhandlungen des 36. Kongresses der Deutschen Gesellschaft für Soziologie in Bochum und Dortmund 2012. Frankfurt.

McIlroy, Guy/Storbeck, Claudine (2011): Development of deaf identity: An ethnographic study, in: Journal of Deaf Studies and Deaf Education, 16:4, 494-511.

Michaels, Walter Benn (2006): The Trouble with Diversity: How we Learned to Love Identity and Ignoire Inequality. New York.

Mouffe, Chantal (2000): "Deliberative Democracy or Agonistic Pluralism, Political Science Series, Vienna: Institute for Advanced Studies". Available at: www.ihs.ac.at/publications/pol/pw_72.pdf (19.11.2019).

Mwachiro, Kevin (2014): Invisible: Stories from Kenya's Queer Community. Nairobi.

Napier, Jemina (2002): The D/deaf-H/hearing debate, in: Sign Language Studies, 2:2, 141-149.

Parrillo, Vincent N. (2005): Diversity in America. Thousand Oaks.

Philipps, Joschka (2018). A global generation? Youth studies in a postcolonial world, in: Societies, 8:14, 1-18.

Ranc, Julijana (2019): 'Ich fühl' mich so verweigert' Das Ressentiment als ein Modus des Umgangs mit negativen Befindlichkeiten, in: Eigmüller, Monika/Tietze, Nikola. Ungleichheitskonflikte in Europa: Jenseits von Klasse und Nation. Wiesbaden, 187-210.

Redden, Elizabeth (2018): "Hungary Officially Ends Gender Studies Programs". Available at: www.insidehighered.com/quicktakes/2018/10/17/hungary-officially-ends-gender-studies-programs (19.11.2019).

Reid-Cunningham, Allison-Ruby (2009): Anthropological Theories of Disability, in: Journal of Human Behavior in the Social Environment, 19:1, 99-111.

Salzbrunn, Monika (2014): Diversity/Vielfalt. Bielefeld.

Simmel, Georg (1890): Über sociale Differenzierung: Soziologische und psychologische Untersuchungen. Leipzig.

Smith, Anna Marie (1998): Laclau and Mouffe: The Radical Democratic Imagery New York.

Spencer, Herbert (1862): First Principles of a New System of Philosophy. New York.

Stovall, Janet (2018): "How to get serious about diversity and inclusion in the workplace". Available at: www.ted.com/talks/janet_stovall_how_to_get_serious_about_diversity_and_inclusion_in_the_workplace (08.08.2019).

The Strategic Radicals (2018): The Strategic Radicals' Manifesto. Bayreuth/Johannesburg.

Tutu, Desmond (2001): "On glorious diversity: Why we should celebrate difference". Available at: www.tutufoundationusa.org/2016/07/11/glorious-diversity-celebrate-difference/ (05.12.2018).

UN (2006): "Convention on the Rights of Persons with Disabilities". Available at: www.un.org/development/desa/disabilities/convention-on-the-rights-of-persons-with-disabilities/convention-on-the-rights-of-persons-with-disabilities-2.html (01.01.2019).

Waldmann, Peter/Elwert, Georg (1989): Einleitung. Waldmann, Peter/Elwert, Georg. Ethnizität im Wandel. Saarbrücken/Fort Lauderdale, 7-20.

Young, Alys/Temple, Bogusia (2014): Approaches to Social Research: The Case of Deaf Studies. Oxford/New York.

Claiming Identity

Why Do Disability Aesthetics Matter? A Lesson in Porcelain

Ann Fox

Disability: A Diversity Identity?

Chicago-based painter Riva Lehrer has taken disability as an impetus for and subject of her work for decades. In works such as her series *Circle Stories*, she has emphasized the history and beauty of disabled people and disability culture through a series of exquisitely-wrought portraits of artists and activists.[1] And yet, as she pointed out while speaking to a disability arts symposium in the United States in 2017, despite the current interest in the figuration of identity in the world of contemporary art, there is still little interest in the disabled body. Queer bodies, women's bodies, the bodies of people of color – all find a place within major exhibitions on identity. And yet, still, for all that: not disability.

Convincing others to care about disability as an identity in and of itself feels like a similarly arduous battle at the local level as well. For example, in the almost two decades since my first introduction to disability studies, my home institution of Davidson College, a small liberal arts college in the southeastern United States, has set as a high priority understanding how to make the work we do more accessible to increasingly diverse student populations. This has particularly included first-generation college students, students with limited financial resources, and students of color; queer and transgender students also proudly claim visibility and culture on our campus, doing advocacy work that was certainly much, much less visible when I first arrived. But we (faculty, staff, and students) still struggle with claiming disability, for some fairly typical reasons.

Many (though not all) members of our community still understand disability only as the province of science, medicine, or policy rather than identity. Still others have internalized the perfectionism of our high-achieving environment and therefore the unspoken sense that accom-

1 See Lehrer's website for the full range of her work, including Circle Stories, available at: www.rivalehrerart.com (04.04.2018).

plishment and disability are at odds.[2] Some think of disability only in terms of research to be done in the lab, or service and charity work. And most, I suspect, simply do not spend much, if any, time thinking about it. 'Wellness' and health are states of being assumed to be universally desired and shared in an environment in which bodily privilege carries a great deal of cultural capital, and yet ability privilege goes largely unremarked upon. Disability still remains an individual problem to be accommodated, rather than an identity our campus fully celebrates in the way we speak about diverse identities or create inclusion.

I do not mean to suggest by any means that this is a conscious exclusion, or that it is particular to Davidson College (indeed, my disability studies work receives terrific support from the students and administration as an academic enterprise). But my larger point here is not to grouse, but rather to suggest that my campus experience is a microcosm for a larger reality that Riva Lehrer's experience also underscores. One of the great diversity fights left in the United States, and globally, is to think about disability as multicultural identity, and its inclusion as a diversity issue. This is a more difficult proposition than it seems. Layer on top of it the deep cultural resistance to reading disability representation politically. Layer further on top of it our present cultural moment and the 2016 United States presidential election, for example, in which the open mockery of all kinds of 'others' became normalized. It is a time when the then presidential candidate Trump could clearly mock disabled *New York Times* reporter Serge Kovaleski, repeatedly deny he was doing so, and suffer no apparent effect on his chances for election. Under the Trump administration, disabled and poor people are increasingly the objects of funding cuts in the name of austerity. And so, the importance of attending to the precarity of vulnerable populations and bodies has never been more urgent, more literally lifesaving.

---

2 We are a campus that is regularly ranked in the top ten liberal arts colleges in the United States of America by sources from Forbes to the United States News and World Report. In addition, while our student body is diversifying, we still heavily emphasize physical fitness as an aspect of being a well-rounded student. This happens through the emphasis on student athletics, of course, but also in the way so many non-accessible social rituals (especially at first-year orientation) are arranged around athletic and sporting events. In this way, disability is still ignored as a diverse identity to be valued and acknowledged (rather than only accommodated in the classroom).

Disability Representation: A Diversity Issue for All?

Indeed, in the face of such local and national resistance, in the face of more pressing issues facing disabled people (such as, in the United States, the seemingly inevitable revocation of the Affordable Care Act), why do work like mine, which is directed at understanding and questioning how disability is represented in the cultural imagination?[3] It's certainly true that parsing representation can feel somewhat like something an unnecessary luxury when policy needs such radical change. One could argue, of course, that activism and advocacy happen along many fronts, and for me they happen in the study of representation. In the teaching of how to read disability depictions and the attitudes encoded in them, it is my hope that eventual change happens. Literary disability studies scholar Michael Bérubé reminds us that while our work may not make immediate, material change, it does not follow that it is without value or important long-term implications. He critiques, for example, how the intellectually disabled character Lennie in John Steinbeck's *Of Mice and Men* has been used as an evaluative measure for who should and should not be subject to the death penalty in Texas. To understand the construction of such a character and what negative perceptions about intellectual disability it perpetuates means that

> disability studies will never be *only* about the textuality of texts. The question of what Lennie knows about the narrative he inhabits is a formal question; it is also a social question. (Bérubé 2016: 194)

So on one level, it matters very much to look around us and be able to identify the ubiquitous tropes, memes, rhetorics of charity, encoded language and so-called *inspirational porn* (widely circulated inspirational or sentimentalized images of disability) that do nothing but reinforce ableism. By the same token, it matters very much to be able to look at disability arts and culture and understand them as an aesthetic that is at once nascent and long term. It matters to understand that in dance, visual arts, and curation, for example, disability culture has for a long time established itself as a vivid and important presence, staring back in the face of the

3 The Patient Protection and Affordable Care Act, often referred to as the Affordable Care Act or Obamacare, was signed into law by then-President Obama and was meant to extend health care to millions of low-income and uninsured Americans. The nonpartisan Congressional Budget Office estimated in January 2017 that the 'repeal and replace' plan proposed by the current administration would result in 32 million Americans losing health insurance by 2026.

ableist gaze, and "dismantling the institutions that would silence [them] first and kill [them] later" (Ewing 2017: no page).

But most of us don't spend our lives questioning representation and the audiences for wonderful events fed by critical disability studies remain comparatively small. But here's the thing: an observer and participant in culture need not become a specialist in disability culture or art to be influenced in exciting and novel ways by disability representation. In fact, disability studies scholar Julie Avril Minich believes that the future of critical disability studies lies in taking an approach to disability studies that emphasizes its mode of analysis rather than its objects of study. As disability scholars have long noted, there is an immense body of scholarship about disabled people that few in the field recognize as disability studies: work that objectifies disability; places it under the medical gaze; pathologizes it; deploys it as a device of characterization; or uncritically treats it as a metaphor for decay, decline, or failure. At the same time, there is also an enormous body of scholarly and activist work that has until recently gone unrecognized by disability scholars as critical disability studies, despite advocating a radical politics of corporeal variation and neurodiversity: protests against racialized disparities in health, education, and policing; struggles for environmental justice and reproductive freedom; HIV/AIDS and fat activism; the writings of Audre Lorde on blindness and cancer and of Gloria Anzaldúa on early menstruation and diabetes (Minich 2016).

And I would add to Minich's list representations that might not seem, on the surface, to be even tangentially linked to disability. This means that to consider disability representation does not only mean pursuing a hide-and-seek of literal representation, as we *spot the crip*; instead, it means seeking out the ways in which a disability presence informs representations we might not overtly think of as having anything to do at all with disability itself.[4] Tobin Siebers models a way to do this relative to modern art in his landmark study, *Disability Aesthetics*. In it, he posits that

> modern art continues to move us because of its refusal of harmony, bodily integrity, and perfect health [....] because of its distinct embrace of disability as a distinct version of the beautiful. (Siebers 2010: 5-9)

4 By *crip*, I use a term of disability identity adopted by disability rights activists in the United States. A shortened version of the pejorative *cripple*, it is an insider term that seeks to reclaim that word with verve and zest, akin to how LGBTQ activists have reclaimed and proudly use the term *queer*.

As he makes clear, this appreciation of the more interesting quality of bodily variation is not the only way disability aesthetics has made its influence felt; it is also enmeshed in regard to the broken or damaged art object, reconsideration of who we consider to be the *suitable* practitioner of art, and a reconsideration of the metaphorical value of images of decay or deconstruction in art.

Inspired by ideas such as that advanced by Siebers, I recently published an essay entitled: “Fabulous Invalids Together: Why Disability in Mainstream Theater Matters” (Fox 2015). In it, I argue that disability in mainstream drama is highly interesting from a disability studies perspective, since it can be a site of subversion that we might not expect, specifically because a disability presence informs its representation. More typical depictions of disability in drama so often tend more toward stereotypes: the twisted villains, the shy wallflowers, or the melodramatic or monstrous mothers; the list goes on and on. But what, I have asked, if we consider not just what the characters are themselves like, but also what they bring to light around them? This moves us past an accounting of onstage crips and assessing their political utility according to whether they are authentic, appropriate, or adequately activist.[5] As critics like Bérubé, Minich, and Siebers have pointed out, to think this way is to imagine disability as a series of beliefs that organize our world and determine our social relationships, not simply as an individual image of bodily difference. Examined in that way, it is also then possible to reimagine our understanding of disability’s presence in a broader sense, and how it might even allow us to see the generative possibility in embodied difference. So even if we do not consciously look for it or *see* it at first glance, how *can* understanding the search for disability representation in this more expansive manner help us reimagine the world around us? How can it help us imagine diversity in a broader, richer sense? Where can we find it in areas where we might not expect it – and what are the lessons it instills?

5 And let me be clear: it is absolutely a good thing to evaluate these portrayals, particularly when we question the repetition of old patterns. For example, the in-process documentary *Code of the Freaks* takes a careful look at the reinscription of ableist beliefs through the continual use of negative disability tropes across the history of film. A working version of the documentary project can be accessed at https://vimeo.com/20531038 (01.04.2018). At present, this is the only version of the film publicly available, but updates on production progress can be found on the film Facebook page at: www.facebook.com/CodeOfTheFreaks/ (01.04.2018).

Finding Diversity through Disability Aesthetics: A Lesson in Porcelain

As an answer to the questions I raise above, let me offer a case study: the story of two visits to porcelain exhibitions. When I traveled to Bayreuth, Germany, in April 2016 to give one of the two keynote lectures at the *Beauty and the Norm* Conference, as well as present as part of the University of Bayreuth's Diversity Lectures Series, I was fortunate enough to spend time exploring the city a little bit. As often happens in the serendipity of scholarship, I happened to visit two museum exhibitions that deeply related to one another in ways their creators could not possibly have anticipated. My first visit was to the imposing and beautiful New Palace (Neues Schloss) in Bayreuth. On my way out of this majestic castle, having surfeited on its stunning design, I glanced down a hallway and saw row after row after row of porcelain organized carefully in shining, parallel glass cases. I later learned that this was an exhibition of the porcelain for which Bayreuth is famous, largely from the 18th century. Somewhat later, at Iwalewahaus, a center for the study of contemporary African culture at the University of Bayreuth, I toured a very different set of exhibitions, featuring work by present-day African artists. And I was stopped in my tracks when I viewed the installation by Moroccan artist Yassine Balbzioui, called *Porcellanographie: Future Traces*.

Collaborating with craftspeople at the Walküre porcelain factory, Balbzioui designed dishes, pots, cups, and other vessels that are clearly differently figured from traditional porcelain (one might even say *deformed*, though I'm purposely choosing to eschew the inherently pathologizing nature of that term). The installation's heavy use of porcelain, albeit seemingly misshapen and definitely broken (there were also smashed teacups layering the ground as part of it) was an homage to the heritage of Bayreuth as a porcelain-making center. But more than that, these disabled vessels were a strong and delightful reminder to me of what disability representation can do – even when it's not obviously or self-consciously called that. Working from the example of these vessels and how radically they differed from more traditional pottery, what can recognizing a disability presence (or what Tobin Siebers might call *disability aesthetics*) in them do?

First, it can make disability visible, bringing the idea of this kind of human variation out into the open. The invisibility of mistakes from our purview, the fact that we never see pottery as far as this is from what we might expect normally, is an echo of the ways in which disability has been and continues to be rendered invisible culturally. This is not only because of the absent histories of those who have been or continue to be invisible in nursing homes, hospitals, or private residences; it is also because we don't consider disability an identity that we want to make visible in the first place. Indeed, there are echoes here of the *cure or kill* trope in film, in which the introduction of disability means the disability has to be cured or erased by work's end. Porcelain is either perfect, or it never appears on store shelves (although I suppose it might have a second life clearly marked as a *factory second* – but even then the intrinsic symmetry of these vessels would be preserved, the so-called *defects* largely minor and cosmetic.) But Balbzioui's objects are neither discarded nor reshaped: they are brought into visibility, just as they are, for what they are.

Second, disability representation can make processes in the formation of bodies and contingency in their lived experience visible as well. Not only are the disabled vessels Balbzioui has crafted made visible as disabled; in the process, so is their malleability and breakability. We are reminded: things can go in a different direction than the typical when a body is formed or moving through the world. That bodies are subject to their environments is rendered on the surfaces of these porcelain objects, where we can see the intentional shaping and sculpting of material that have come from unseen hands: labor rendered invisible when the vessels appear more *normal*. We have valued such different directions when they seem a fortunate or utilitarian *error* (such as in evolutionary theory), but more often than not, we are likely to see them as defects to be corrected.

Fig. 1: Exhibition detail of "Porcellanographie: Future Traces" (Yassine Balbzioui, 2016, photo by Ann Fox, 2016)

Certainly some anomalies must be fixed in order for survival (one thinks of a congenital heart defect, or a cleft palate that would otherwise inhibit eating); but what of those disabilities that represent embodied – but not life-threatening – difference?[6] And just as a piece of porcelain can *fail* either in warping or breakage, so too can other contingent objects, like bodies. Tobin Siebers even goes so far as to find a disability value in vandalized or broken art, noting that

> the art vandal puts the art object to use again, replicating the moment of its inception when it was being composed of raw material and before it became fixed in time and space as an aesthetic object. (Siebers 2010: 10)

Third, disability representation can make us question what we think is received knowledge about the function of a body. The porcelain of *Porcellanographie* is not functional in the ways we expect: It cannot hold liquid or food. We are compelled, in looking at it, to consider the question: why *isn't* this a perfectly legitimate form for this porcelain to take? It may not be a way that makes it conventionally useful, but must the porcelain be functionary to exist?

Does its relevance depend only on the extent to which it is a vessel? The unusual aspect of the curvature, the folds, and the drooping of the porcelain renders it beautiful. And yet it is no more *useless* than the more normate porcelain in the New Palace, which while seemingly able to function in the way intended, almost certainly has not, kept instead as a decorative, curated collection of objects. Ironically, the so-called deformed porcelain aggressively insists on the lack of utility it holds in common with the most sublime and perfect of its normate counterparts (that is to say, porcelain that fits the ideals of what porcelain should look like and do, perhaps to the point of being precious and decorative rather than being for everyday use).

---

6 Chun-Shan (Sandie) Yi's Re-Fuse Skin Set is an example of disability art that resists cure or fixing. Yi creates prosthetics for her hands that have no other purpose than to re-fuse the fingers that were surgically separated when she was younger, and in so doing, refusing to see them as defective. Instead, the *refuse* of that surgery is reinserted to return her fingers to the state they were in when she was born.

Fig. 2: Exhibition detail of "Porcellanographie: Future Traces" (Yassine Balbzioui, 2016, photo by Ann Fox, 2016. Original photograph in medium format.)

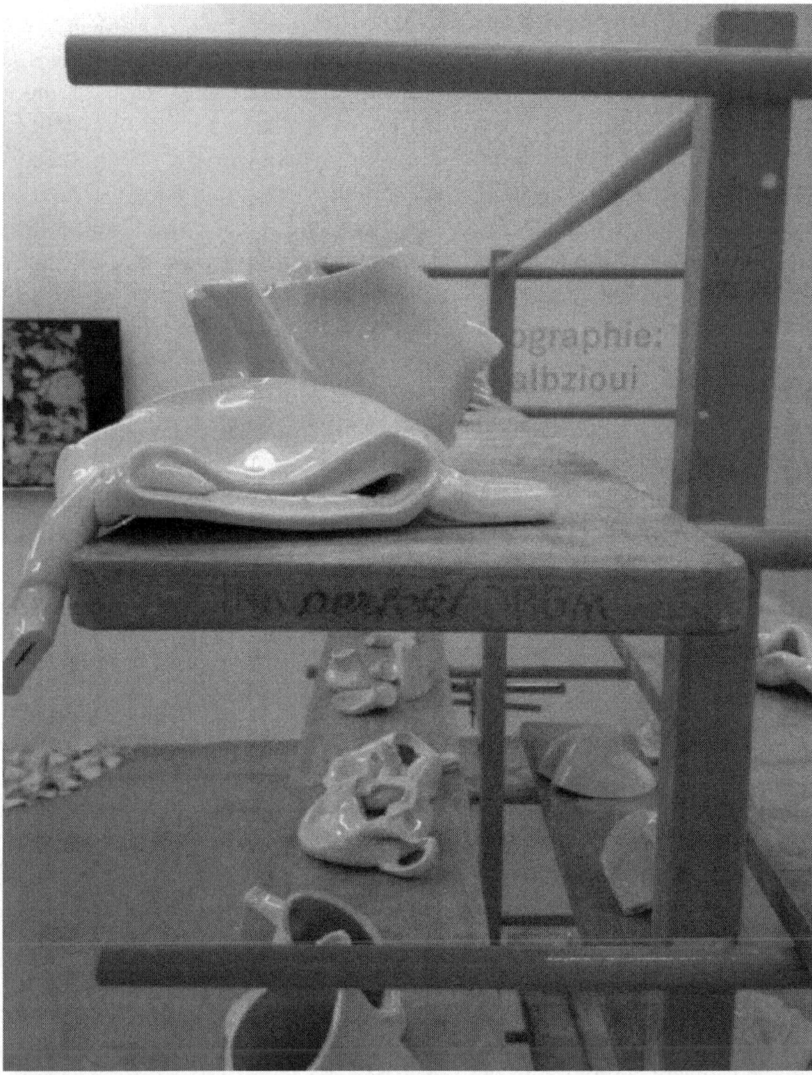

Fig. 3: Exhibition detail of "Porcellanographie: Future Traces" (Yassine Balbzioui, 2016, photo by Ann Fox, 2016)

Now, we are compelled to acknowledge how strongly and stridently we insist on that normalcy, even if it makes an object superfluous. Indeed, the variant vessels in *Porcellanographie* stand in sharp relief to their more *normal* and normed counterparts. The faience collection in the New Palace is exquisite, and of course there are lovely, varying patterns within the collection. But it only varies so much within its kind, and indeed can start to look the same after a while (although I am sure a true expert would take me to task on such an assertion!) The teapots in *Porcellanographie* catch our interest simply because they are so radically and even antagonistically different. Some pitchers lean back, as if quite at their ease, while the spout of a flattened teapot droops lazily over the wooden board of a rack. (That board is, with unintentional irony, labeled with the logo *perfekt* at one end.) In our being caught off guard by these vessels, we are reminded of that from which they deviate. Certainly, one way to read them is as defective relative to that idea of teapot, pitcher, and plate normalcy. And yet that is so one sided; how much more interesting to read them together as points on a continuum, rather than set in a hierarchy or a one-sided value judgement. Disability reminds us of the limitation of normalcy, and conversely offers the pleasure in variation and possibility.

Fourth, finally, and perhaps most significantly, these disabled vessels spark imagination. What could you do with a disabled teapot? Could you eat off of it? Admire it? Use it in some other way? What would we lose, imaginatively, in terms of thinking about how to appreciate and even use variation, if we did not have this example of difference? Rosemarie Garland-Thomson has called one version of this concept *disability gain*, that is, understanding what knowledge is accrued by the particular presence of disability.[7] In the case of these teapots, they even invited the bodies of the workers and artists who made them to think differently about the objects they are shaping. And we are, in our turn, invited to hold, touch, and encounter the object differently because in many cases the *normal* way to use it literally eludes our grasp. But in turn, what new ways of thinking, creating, or conceptualizing the world can we then seize because of disability's presence before us?

---

7 I first heard Garland-Thomson use the phrase *disability gain* in a 2013 talk given at the conference *Avoidance and/in the Academy* at the Centre for Culture and Disability Studies, Liverpool Hope University, Liverpool, UK. In it, she expanded upon the concept of Deaf Gain, one itself discussed at greater length in *Deaf Gain: Raising the Stakes for Human Diversity* (Bauman/Murray 2014).

Conclusion

While I was at Bayreuth, I was asked, quite understandably, whether the concept of disability gain was nothing but a luxury. And in an age where austerity budgets in the United States and United Kingdom specifically target the resources on which many disabled people have survived, to argue for the significance of representation in the way I have above seems disingenuous at best, perhaps even callous at worst. Isn't disability gain something that can only come into being in that imaginary place where all other needs have been met? To be sure, existing in a place where we can discuss disability gain assumes a certain level of privilege and offers little comfort to those disabled people without employment, resources, or independence. Yet it still matters.

Why? It offers a different, deeper way to understand what disability has to offer rather than the old, romanticized trope that disability simply exists to make nondisabled people better by teaching them moralistic lessons in charity, patience, or grace. As Minich points out,

> the methodology of disability studies [...] involves scrutinizing not bodily or mental impairments but the social norms that define particular attributes as impairments, as well as the social conditions that concentrate stigmatized attributes in particular populations. (Minich 2016: no page)

When disability is still a stigmatized or oppressed identity, making those pejorative attitudes visible and replacing them with possibility costs nothing, and changes everything. Disability is relevant to all of us: we live in contingent bodies, and disability is an experience immediately and inevitably available to all of us in a way no other identity is. But while embracing disability representation and the gain that results from it is about correcting oppression, it is also about creating new kinds of community. Scholar Catherine Kudlick writes that before she came into her disability identity, she and other disabled friends had been brainwashed in the same well-meaning society that still fails disabled people. We sat through tear-jerking movies where helpless blind girls groped and stumbled. Our heart-strings were pulled by fundraisers showing blindness at its worst to raise money for cures that could be many years away. Images like these isolate people with disabilities not just from society but also from one another.

And yet, when she refused "disability denial", Kudlick discovered the true power of disability community:

> Once freed from prejudice and shame, they can teach the largest class of all – society – to imagine people with disabilities as innovators, problem-solvers and true agents for change. (Kudlick 2017: no page)

And so, fittingly, this lesson in porcelain exposes the truth: in actuality, norms are more brittle than the resilient bodies that have borne their weight for far too long. New configurations of what has been seen as *broken* instead create dynamism and possibility, not because they either eschew disability or overcome it, but because they foreground it and dare a viewer to fire their own innovation and imagination. That is a lesson worth learning.

List of Abbreviations

LGBTQ — Lesbian Gay Bisexual Transsexual Queer

List of Figures

References

Balbzioui, Yassine (2016): Porcellanographie: Future Traces. Exhibition in Iwalewahaus, University of Bayreuth.

Bauman, H. Dirksen/Murray, Joseph J., eds. (2014): Deaf Gain: Raising the Stakes for Human Diversity. Minneapolis.

Bérubé, Michael (2016): The Secret Life of Stories: From Don Quixote to Harry Potter, How Understanding intellectual Disability Transforms the Way We Read. New York.

Ewing, Eve L. (2017): "Why Authoritarians Attack the Arts". Available at: www.nytimes.com/2017/04/06/opinion/why-authoritarians-attack-the-arts.html (06.04.2017).

Fox, Ann M. (2015): Fabulous Invalids Together: Why Disability in Mainstream Theater Matters. Bolt, David / Penketh, Clare. Disability, Avoidance, and the Academy: Challenging Resistance. New York, 122-32.

Kudlick, Catherine (2017): "The Price of 'Disability Denial'". Available at: www.nytimes.com/2017/05/24/opinion/disability-denial.html (04.05.2017).

Lehrer, Riva (1997-2004): "Circle Stories". Available at: www.rivalehrerart.com/circle-stories-1 (10.04.2020).

Lehrer, Riva (2017): Presence and Absence: The Paradox of Disability and Portraiture.Grand Rapids.

Minich, Julie A. (2016): Enabling Whom? Critical Disability Studies Now, in: Lateral Journal of the Cultural Studies Association, 5.1, no page.

Nussbaum, Susan/Sandahl, Carrie/Chasnoff, Salome/ Rose, Jerzy/Patsavas, Aly (2011): "Code of the Freaks". Available at: https://vimeo.com/20531038 (23.05.2017).

Siebers, Tobin (2010): Disability Aesthetics, Ann Arbor.

Good Governance, Civil Society and Rise of the Disability Rights Movement in Ghana

Emmanuel Sackey

Introduction

For many countries in Africa, the political reforms of the 1990s mark the onset of an enabling environment for civil society organizations to participate in the development process. These reforms were partly induced through the initiatives of international development agencies, particularly the World Bank which "linked the idea of civil society to its promotion of accountability, legitimacy and transparency of government" (Whitefield 2003: 382). The objective of this article is to examine the extent to which Ghana's disability rights movement appropriated the good governance dispensation and the medium of civil society to promote the rights of persons with disabilities (PWDs) in the country. The article is based on the outcome of a fieldwork conducted in Ghana between 2014 and 2015 as part of a doctoral research at the Bayreuth International Graduate School of African Studies.[1] While it has been noted that internal and external factors account for the rise of the disability movement (Downing, 2011), the emphasis in this paper is on domestic factors. I identify the democratization of the Ghanaian state and the opening of political spaces for civil society organizations as a major domestic factor that created an enabling environment for the rise of the movement. Three cases that show the extent to which the movement has been able to influence national development policies will be discussed as evidence of its progress. The current status of the movement regarding its relations to the state and the unprecedented social mobility of prominent individual PWDs in politics, the media, and sports have also been emphasized. The terms movement and federation are used interchangeably in this article.[2]

---

1 A summary of this paper was presented at the Diversity Lectures of Bayreuth International Graduate School of African Studies (BIGSAS) at Iwalewahaus, Bayreuth on 22.09.2015.

2 McCarthy and Zald make a distinction between a social movement and a social movement organization. They define a social movement as "a set of opinions and

Overview of the Civil Society and Good Governance Debate

It has been emphasized that the resurgence of the idea of civil society was accompanied by a "lack of conceptual and terminological clarity" (Forbrig 2004: 10). This concern is shared by several scholars (Edwards 2009; Maina 1998; Cohen/Arato 1992). Indeed, the meaning of the concept has evolved over time. The contemporary literature on the civil society debate indicates two broad contending schools of civil society theory, represented by a neoliberal and a neo-Marxist conception. The neoliberal version conceives civil society as a realm of voluntary associational life autonomous from the state, which seeks to check the excesses of the state in order to guarantee the fundamental freedoms of citizens.

This conception assumes that the prevalence of a strong civil society would ultimately enhance participatory governance. The contemporary proponents of this position include Gellner (1995), Seligman (1992), Putnam (1993; 1995), Shills (1991), Diamond (1994), Keane (1998) and a whole host of other liberal thinkers. These scholars consider civil society as the basis of civility and a fundamental prerequisite for a liberal democratic governance. Putnam for instance postulated that a vibrant civil society characterized by a dense network of voluntary associations generates *social capital* (i.e. norms of trust and cooperation) which is perceived to facilitate good governance and lubricate a healthy economy.

According to this perspective, civil society is able to resist, check or prevent the state from encroaching on the rights of citizens. A major premise of the neoliberal thesis is that as rational beings with parochial interests, there is no guarantee that political elites would always pursue the public interest or adhere to the rule of law without any authoritarian tendencies. On this basis, neoliberals conceive civil society as an autonomous sphere inhabited by a plurality of voluntary associations whose major function is to hold the state to account in order to safeguard the free-

---

beliefs in a population which represents preferences for changing some elements of the social structure and/or reward distribution of a society" and a social movement organization as "a complex, or formal, organization which identifies its goals with the preferences of a social movement or a countermovement and attempts to implement those goals" (McCarthy/Zald 1977: 1217-1218). Thus, the Ghana Federation of Disability Organizations which brings various organizations together under one umbrella is a movement organization.

doms and rights of citizens. It is considered that without such autonomy civil society cannot "make demands on the state, to improve the structure and functioning of the state, and to hold state officials accountable" (Diamond 1997 cited in Tar 2014: 260).

On the other hand, the neo-Marxist variant conceives civil society as a sphere of struggle for hegemony. In contrast to the contemporary neoliberal conception of civil society, the neo-Marxist version views civil society as a sphere of social conflict and struggle between dominant and subordinate groups (Gramsci 1971). This perspective holds that, far from being an intermediary for cooperation and liberal democratic governance, civil society remains a medium for hegemony and counter-hegemony. In simple terms, neo-Marxists think of civil society as a sphere of social conflict because it remains both the domain through which the ruling class imposes its ideals on the rest of society as well as the channel through which the subordinate classes could resist or counter the hegemony of the ruling class.

With the participation of civil society organizations as its central component, the contemporary notion of good governance was first used in development discourse by the World Bank in 1989 (Abrahamson 2000: 47-48; World Bank 1989). Since then the work of Putnam (1995; 1993) regarding the extent to which the prevalence of voluntary associations and networks could generate social capital has given further recognition to a vibrant civil society as a fundamental prerequisite for democratic governance. The core tenets of the good governance discourse include adherence to the *rule of law, transparency and accountability,* and *participation* of the representatives of civil society in the formulation of national development policies. As part of the *conditionalities* for development assistance, countries that went to the World Bank and the International Monetary Fund (IMF) for support were required not only to liberalize their economies but to democratize their political system in order to pave the way for the participation of civil society. In this regard, civil society organizations were expected to participate in the formulation of national policies, provision of social services, and monitoring, in order to serve as checks and balances on the state.

Despite the laudable assumptions it invokes, some critics have pointed out that the mere proliferation of civil society organizations would not necessarily lead to good governance and development (Abrahamson 2000; Foley/Edward 1996; Igoe/Kellsaw 2005; Cooke/Kothari 2001; Forbrig 2004; 2002). They argued that any conceptualization of civil society that does not acknowledge the blurring of boundaries between the state and civil society is unrealistic (Edwards 2009: 60). The projection of a civil society as always opposed to the state without due consideration for the inevitable blurred boundaries was deemed problematic (Edwards 2009; Bratton 1989). Secondly, some critics argue that the role assigned to civil society organization could be played better by political parties since they are directly represented in parliament and have the mandate to form government (Edwards 2009; Foley/Edwards 1996). Another contested point is that the new policy agenda was a ploy to impose western sociopolitical values on the global south (Tar 2014; Hearn 2001, 1999; Abrahamson 2000). Despite these contentions, the neoliberal notion of civil society forms a salient part of the notion of good governance promoted by the international development agencies.

The Rise of the Disability Movement

As pertains to other social movements, the prevalence of an enabling political environment (McAdam et al. 2008; Tarrow 1998; Tilly 1995), the availability of resources (McCarthy/Zald 1977), and the use of collective framing processes (Snow/Benford 1988) have enhanced the mobilization of disabled people at both the local and global level. The social model of disability discourse (Oliver 1990) has been crucial in providing such framing for PWDs. Contrary to the conventional medical notion of disability, the social model views disability in terms of barriers created by society, rather than only the functional limitation due to a person's physical and sensory impairment. The implication of the social model is that instead of PWDs having to strive to fit into the way society is organized, the state and society are under an obligation to make all sectors of social life accessible to PWDs. This obligation includes the provision of appropriate technological devices and an enabling environment that could enhance the participation of PWDs in societal life, including access to education, employment and political participation. Advocacy based on this model has been influential in securing inclusive policies and disability specific legislation at both national and global levels.

At the global level the advocacy initiatives of organizations such as Disabled People International (DPI), the World Blind Union (WBU), the World Federation of the Deaf (WFD), Rehabilitation International (RI), Inclusion International, and International Disability Alliance (IDA) contributed to the formulation and adoption of the United Nations Convention on the Rights of Persons with Disabilities (UNCRPD) in 2006. Prior to the promulgation of the UNCRPD, the advocacy initiatives of the international disability movement also contributed to the formulation of the Standard Rules for Equalization of Opportunities for Persons with Disabilities (UN 1993)[3], and adoption of the World Program of Action Concerning Disabled Persons in 1982.

As is the case in other sectors of civil society, the need for a stronger front has stimulated the establishment of coalitions and networks by Disabled People's Organizations (DPOSs) that previously operated in isolation. In Ghana there was no umbrella organization in this sector prior to the establishment of the Ghana Federation of Disability Organizations (GFDO), which is referred to as the Federation in the rest of the paper.[4] The federation was established in 1987 by three founding member organizations, namely the Ghana Association of the Blind (GAB)[5], the Ghana Society of the Physically Disabled (GSPD), and the Ghana National Association of the Deaf (GNAD). The federation is currently composed of eight organizations. The other DPOs that joined later are the Ghana Association of Persons with Albinism (GAPA), SHARE CARE (an organization of persons with auto immune ailments), the Mental Health Society of Ghana (MEHSOG), Inclusion Ghana (IG) which promotes the rights of children with intellectual disability, and the Ghana Burns Survivors Foundation (GBSF).

---

3 The Standard Rules for Equalization of Opportunity for Persons with Disabilities and the World Program of Action Concerning Disabled Persons served as bases for technical cooperation between member states of the UN but were not legally binding. The UNCRPD becomes legally binding upon signing and ratification by member states.

4 The name of the federation has changed over time. It was originally called Federation of Disabled Associations (FODA). The name then changed to the Ghana Federation of the Disabled (GFD). In 2015 it was renamed the Ghana Federation of Disability Organizations (GFDO) to emphasize that it is a network or umbrella body representing organizations rather than individual persons with disabilities.

5 In 2010 the Ghana Association of the Blind merged with the Ghana Society of the Blind to become the Ghana Blind Union (GBU).

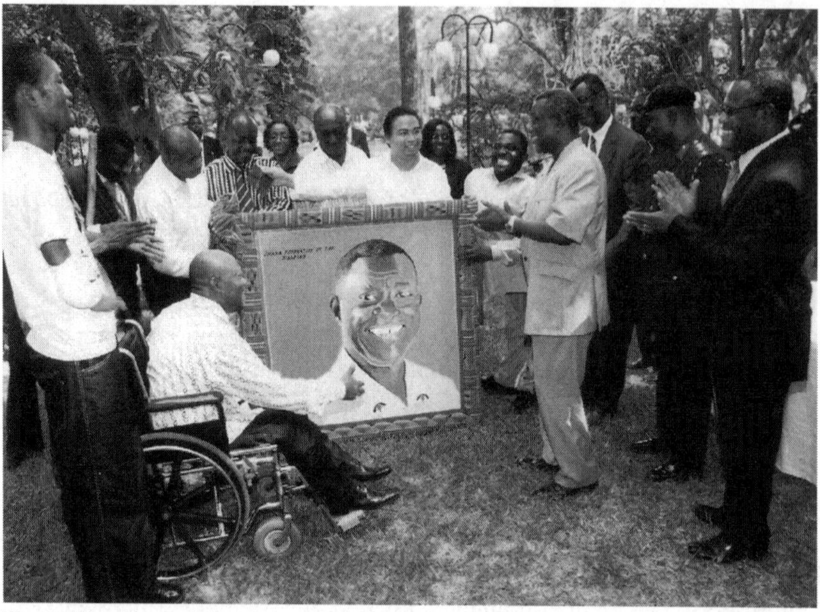

Fig. 1: The Ghana federation of the disabled handing over a portrait of former president John Mills by the disabled artist Benjamin Nyameye. (Photo by Emmanuel Sackey, 2009)

In accordance with its constitution, the federation acts as an umbrella body which engages the state and society on general disability matters through advocacy, while the individual member organizations pursue the specific needs of their members through service provision and advocacy. Apart from disabled people and their respective associations, nondisabled entities also form part of the disability movement. Even though such organizations and individuals may neither be exclusively focused on disability issues nor composed of PWDs, they either share the concerns of PWDs or their work has some impact on the lives of PWDs. The following sections provide three clear cases that demonstrate the extent to which the disability movement in Ghana has taken advantage of the medium of civil society to advocate for the mainstreaming of disability aspects into national development. I will discuss the promulgation of disability laws, political inclusion of PWDs, and the inception of a Common Fund for PWDs.

Promulgation of Disability Laws and Policies

Since Ghana's return to democratic governance in 1992, the advocacy initiatives of the disability movement led to the promulgation of a National Disability Policy in 2000. Following the formulation of the policy, the movement advocated for the passage of a National Disability Law in accordance with the provisions of the 1992 National Constitution (Government of Ghana 1992). While the constitution contains a general declaration to protect the rights of all citizens, including PWDs, Article 29 (8) makes provision for the promulgation of specific disability laws, and Article 11 (7) confers power on parliament to enact special legislation to complement the constitution. Following initial difficulty, a persistent advocacy initiative comprising of dialogue with government, parliament, media campaigns, and street protests achieved that the National Disability Act (715) was ultimately passed in 2006.

Among other statutory obligations the law seeks to protect PWDs against stigmatization and discrimination. It seeks to promote employment through formal education, special rehabilitation programs, accessible transportation, healthcare, sports, and recreation. In order to ensure its implementation, the law makes provision for the establishment of a National Council for Persons with Disabilities (NCPD). In accordance with Article 42 (1) of the Disability Act, the Council is mandated to formulate policies that will ensure the mainstreaming of disability aspects into national development (Government of Ghana 2006). The Council was subsequently inaugurated in March 2009. Despite the passage of the law in 2006, as of 2018 it has not seen any implementation. This setback has been attributed to lack of a comprehensive Legislative Instrument (LI) to guide its implementation.[6] In 2012, the advocacy role of the federation contributed to parliament's ratification of the UNCRPD, which is considered more comprehensive than the National Disability Act.[7] The federation is currently advocating for parliament review of the National Disability Law to make it compatible with the statues of the UNCRPD.

---

6 Personal Interviews, Executive Director, GFDO, 14.04.2015, Accra.

7 Unlike previous international protocols, the UNCRPD puts legal obligations on member states that ratify it (United Nations 2006).

Political Participation of PWDs

Following the federation's engagement with the government, there has been a significant increase in the appointment of the number of persons with disabilities currently serving in the decentralized local government units, often referred to in Ghana as district assemblies. In June 2012 there were 216 assemblies. The number of members that compose each assembly depends on the categorization of a given area, i.e. whether a local government unit is classified as a district, municipality, or metropolitan area. In accordance with Article 1 (4) of the Local Government Act 462 a district has between 75,000 and 95,000 residents, whereas a municipality has a population of over 95,000 and metropolitan areas over 250,000.

Irrespective of whether a decentralized area is deemed a metropolitan area, a municipality or a district, 70 percent of assembly members are supposed to be elected, whereas the remaining 30 percent are appointed by the government. In 2014, as part of the advocacy for political inclusion, the federation urged the president to appoint a minimum of two PWDs to each of the 216 assemblies as part of the 30 percent appointees mandated by the Local Government Act. The federation argued that the appointment of PWDs to the assemblies was necessary because it would increase the number of representatives of PWDs from 18 to 432 out of an estimated 8,160 assembly members across the country (Daily Graphic 2014).

In making the case for political inclusion, the federation based its arguments on factors such as historical marginalization, stigmatization and discrimination as well as the higher cost required to break such barriers (Sackey 2015). The president of the federation for instance stressed that

> a person with a hearing impairment (deafness) who is contesting in a local election will need a sign language interpreter throughout the campaign, which will be too costly to bear, these difficulties, among others, are impediments for PWDs interested in serving their communities.[8]

Similarly much of the physical environment is not accessible for political aspirants with severe mobility impairment. Following the aforementioned advocacy engagement, the government appointed 79 PWDs into the district assemblies in 2015, whereas 25 PWDs contested and won.[9] This increased the number of PWDs in the district assemblies from 18 in 2012 to

---

8 Daily Graphic: Give Us Better Representation in Assemblies-PWDs, 26.11.2014, available at: www.graphic.com.gh/news/general-news/give-us-better-representa tion-in-assemblies-pwds.html (18.03.2016).

9 Ghana News Agency (2015).

104 by 2015. The improvement in the representation of PWDs in local governance is unprecedented and became possible through the advocacy of the federation.

The Inception of the Common Fund

Another major stride attained by the disability movement in Ghana has been the inception of a disability fund that supports PWDs in every district. In 1994 the government established a fund to support local development as part of the country's decentralization program. The scheme which became known as the District Assembly Common Fund (DACF) remains a very important source of revenue for the assemblies (Banful 2011). In accordance with the 1992 constitution, up to 5 percent of the total income of the country can be disbursed to the various assemblies. Since 1994 the criteria for allocating the fund has evolved. During the funding period 2005-2006 a disability component was introduced as part of the criteria for the disbursement.

It seems likely that the inclusion of the disability component was partly due to the involvement of representatives of the federation in the formulation of the second Ghana Poverty Reduction Strategy Paper (GPRSP II). The first phase of GPRSP (2002-2004), which was a requirement for concessional lending and debt relief under the Heavily Indebted Poor Countries (HIPC) initiative of the World Bank and the IMF, did not emphasize the relationship between disabling barriers and poverty reduction. The federation campaigned for the inclusion of disability aspects in the second GPRSP. Thus, the participation of the Federation in the formulation of the second GPRSP contributed to the inception of the disability component of the DACF.[10] In accordance with the regulations of the fund, two percent of the DACF is to be spent on supporting persons with disabilities in every district. The common fund has since remained the major financial grant for PWDs in the country.

10 Interview, Former Coordinator. GFDO, 12.03.2015, Accra.

Social Mobility of Individual PWDs to Prominence

Another indication of the rise of the disability movement is the improved social and political status of individual persons with disabilities and the relative contribution of the movement to this development. I cite cases from three sectors, namely politics, media and disability sports.

The Case of the First Disabled Minister of State

Following the election of John Mahama as President of Ghana in December 2012, he nominated his first batch of ministers in January 2013. For the first time in the history of the country the president included a person with disability among the ministers. Dr Henry Seidu Danaa, a lawyer with visual impairment, was assigned as the Minister for Chieftaincy and Traditional Affairs. The appointment of the blind lawyer was met with protest by some local chiefs, who maintained that aspects of the tradition and customs in certain local communities did not allow a person with disability to hold such a high office (Sackey 2015). In its response, the federation emphasized that the appointment of a disabled person to a ministerial position was in accordance with the principles of inclusive governance and that there was no Ghanaian law restricting PWDs from such public positions. The Federation argued that the appointment was based on the competence of the candidate who had previously served as the director of research at the same ministry. Consequently, the appointment committee of parliament approved the nominee as the substantive minister for chieftaincy and traditional affairs.

It is imperative to note that the appointment of a PWD to such a high political office did not occur by chance. It was the outcome of consistent advocacy by the disability movement. For instance, during the presidential debate that preceded the 2012 elections, the advocacy officer of the federation urged the presidential aspirants to include PWDs in their government[11]. Prior to the presidential debate, the federation lobbied the national parliament, the government and various political parties for the promulga-

11 The presidential debate was held in Tamale, the capital city of the Northern Region of Ghana, on 30.10.2012. It was broadcasted live on the various TV networks.

tion of an affirmative legislation that would guarantee the political inclusion of PWDs.

The First Ghanaian Presidential Candidate with Disability

The December 2016 general elections witnessed the highest number of candidates with disabilities that Ghana had ever seen. This included 16 parliamentary aspirants and one presidential candidate, Ivor Greenstreet, a lawyer and businessman who became disabled through a motor accident. He ventured into active politics in the early 1990s. In 2004, Greenstreet contested the national elections as the parliamentary candidate of the Conventions People Party (CPP) for the Ayawaso West Wugon constituency (a suburb of Accra, the national capital city) but lost, despite an impressive performance.[12] He became the General Secretary of the CPP in 2007 and carried out this function until 2015. On January 30, 2016, Greenstreet was elected presidential candidate of the party.

Even though neither Greenstreet nor any of the 16 parliamentary aspirants won a seat, the successful nomination of Greenstreet as the presidential candidate of the CPP was the first time that a person with disability attempted contesting for the presidency. While not all candidates identified themselves with the disability movement, they drew inspiration from the advocacy of the movement.[13] For instance in March 2016 a delegation of the Ghana Disability Forum, paid an official visit to congratulate Greenstreet and pledged their support. To a significant extent these developments enhance the vibrancy of the disability movement.

The Rise of a Disabled Media Icon

The social mobility of individual PWDs cuts across sectors. Besides politics cases can also be found in the media and sports. With regards to the media, a few visually impaired (blind) broadcasters have recently emerged onto the Ghanaian media scene. The emergence of these disabled personalities has given further impetus to the prominence of disability issues in

12 In the said 2004 elections, Ivor Greenstreet obtained 4,964 votes. This was an unprecedented increase with the CPP receiving less than 500 votes in the constituency's previous elections (Class FM online, 31-01-2016).

13 Personal Interview, Chairman, Ghana Disability Forum, 15.07.2017.

the public sphere. One of such few personalities is Paul Anomah-Kordieh, a broadcaster who works with ETV Ghana, a subsidiary of the Global Media Alliance.[14] Born in 1979, Paul holds a Bachelor of Education degree from the University of Cape Coast. He switched from radio to television in 2010 and won an honorary award at the Ghana Radio and TV Personality Awards in 2013. He has since become a motivational speaker and an icon for the disability movement.

Fig. 2: Ghana amputee football team during the African Nations Amputee Football Cup final between Ghana and Liberia at the Accra Sports stadium, Ghana. (Photo by Theodore Mawuli Viwotor, 2011)

Emergence of Prominent Disabled Sports Personalities

As noted above, another dimension of the prominence of the disability movement in the public sphere has been the rise of individual disabled athletes. All the three founding organizations of the disability federation

14 The Global Media Alliance is a South African based multi-media broadcasting company.

have sports wings. These are the sports wing of the GSPD, the Ghana Deaf Sports Federation, and the sports wing of the Ghana Blind Union. The activities of these subgroups have contributed to new trends in disability sports ranging from amputee football, paracycling, wheelchair athletics and wheelchair basketball. The GSPD sports wing in particular has produced a number of prominent disabled sports personalities such as Aleem Mumuni, Ajara Mohammed, Raphael Botsio Nkegbe and other disabled athletes. These athletes have represented Ghana at the World Paralympics and other international competitions. With regards to their achievements Aleem Mumuni was a three-time African (C2 category) Paracyclist Champion and the first Ghanaian paracyclist to have competed at the Olympic Games (London 2012) and later in the Rio 2016 Paralympics. Ajara Mohammed participated in the women's 200 and 1500 meters in the T-54 wheelchair competition at the Athens 2004 and Beijing 2008 Paralympics together with Nkegbe who participated in the men's 100, 200 and 400 meters. Both won gold medals at previous editions of the All African Games. Nkegbe also participated in the London 2012 Paralympics. As members of the disability movement, not only did they use their popularity to advocate for the rights of persons with disabilities but their exploits and the media coverage they received also contributed to the visibility of the movement.

Consultative Status as Evidence of the Rise of the Movement

Previous studies on the history of disability and rehabilitation in Ghana show that between 1961 and 1966 the relationship between disability organizations and the state was characterized by state incorporation.[15] The voluntary disability organizations were incorporated as part of the state social welfare department (Grischow 2011; Geurts 2015). According to Grischow the socialist orientation of the CPP government influenced the regime's decision to incorporate the DPOs as part of the state apparatus.[16]

15 The Ghana Society for the Blind and the Society for the Deaf were the most prominent DPOs at the time.

16 According to Grischow, after political independence from Britain, a priority of Ghana's first President Kwame Nkrumah was industrialization and thus "rehabilitation sought to integrate disabled citizens into the national economy as productive workers […]. The colonial initiative drew heavily on the British model of social orthopaedics, which equated citizenship with work. This philosophy reso-

Since the overthrow of the CPP government and the end of the socialist experiment in 1966, the DPOs have been autonomous from the state and therefore remain purely voluntary nongovernmental organizations. It is arguable that the nature of the relationship between a social movement and the state, and a movement's ability to influence state policy, can be considered a relevant indicator of its success. On this premise, I argue that the movement's autonomy from the state, under the contemporary democratic dispensation, and the federation's attainment of civil society consultative status in relation to national policy formulation is an indication of its strength.

From this perspective, the federation's success at initiating the establishment of a bipartisan national parliamentary caucus that lobbies for the deliberation of disability laws and policies attests to how dynamic the disability movement is in Ghana. The federation's special consultative status with state agencies such as the National Electoral Commission (NEC), the National Commission for Civic Education (NCCE), the Special Education Division of the Ministry of Education (SPEED), the Ministry of Gender and Social Protection, and the National Development Planning Commission (NDPC) provides further impetus to influence development policy. In 2016, for example, the Ghana Education Service adopted a National Inclusive Education Policy that was initiated by the Ghana Blind Union. The disability movement's attainment of a consultative status with the state therefore reflects its influence within the civil society sector.

Conclusion

Ghana's disability movement has solidified as a result of both internal and external factors. The external factors include financial and technical support from foreign donors, and development agencies. For instance, since 2008 the Danish International Development Agency (DANIDA), the Disabled People's Organizations of Denmark (DPOD), and other external partners continue to provide financial and technical support. Even the formative stages of the federation's organizational development that led to a shift from voluntary management to professionalization was funded by NORAD, a Norwegian Development Organization (Geurts 2015). Other

nated with Nkrumah's vision of national development based on full employment" (Grischow 2011: 179).

external influences on the impact of the disability movement include support from allies in the international disability movement. Organizations such as the World Federation of the Deaf and the World Blind Union have supported the local DPOs. For instance, the WFD has been providing periodic advocacy training for members of the Ghana National Association of the Deaf, whilst the WBU has had similar collaborations with the Ghana Blind Union. Above all, local DPOs have adopted the social model of disability discourse from their western counterparts.

With regards to the domestic factors, the formation of the Federation in 1987 and its ability to foster cooperation among the various disabled people's associations has been a salient contribution to the rise of the movement. Nonetheless, the opening of political spaces for the participation of civil society organizations under the good governance dispensation and the capacity of the disability movement to mobilize PWDs contributed to the strengthening of the movement. As Gyimah-Boadi (1994) has emphasized, the era of military rule (1966-1969, 1972-1979, and 1981-1991) was not very conducive to the development of a vibrant civil society. Thus, to a significant extent, the disability movement has been able to influence more the content of national laws and development policy under the contemporary democratic dispensation than in any other period in the history of the country.

Hypothetically, the future of the disability movement, in terms of its potential to promote and protect the rights of PWDs, looks promising. However, there also exist potential challenges to the movement's progress. The data analysis indicates three key assets that make us hopeful about the future of the movement. The first is the significant degree of cooperation that exists among the major organizations and groups comprising the movement. As shown in the case of the passage of the national disability law, mobilization of PWDs and alliance formation for policy advocacy has been impressive. Secondly, the various DPOs have been able to strategically respond to the institutional pressures from the civil society sector. Through professionalization the DPOs managed to successfully progress from an era of voluntary management to a relatively more effective stage of organizational development.

The professionalization of the DPOs and emphasis on capacity building have significantly improved the quality of human resources for the governance and management of the federation and the member organizations. The available evidence indicates that the DPOs are committed to sustaining this trend which is encouraging for the future of the movement. The third asset is the dynamism of the advocacy strategy of the movement.

Analysis of the federation's advocacy strategy indicates comprehensive long and medium-term plans geared towards consolidating the promotion of the rights of PWDs in Ghana. To a significant extent, the internal governance structures and participatory nature of its consultative forums contribute to this dynamism.

In terms of weakness and threats likely to be potential impediments to the movement's progress, a high dependency on external donors for financial sustenance remains a challenge. In view of the competition for scarce donor resources among NGOs, this dependency syndrome sometimes compels the DPOs to align their interests to the thematic calls of donors. It however sometimes leads to undue shifts in priorities. Since the DPOs depend on donor support for both administrative expenses and project implementation it makes them vulnerable in times of scarcity of donor inflows and remains a major threat to their future sustenance.

Another threat to the vibrancy of the movement is internal conflict. While a certain degree of conflict can be positively functional, not all conflicts contribute to stability. Competition for resources among the DPOs and perceptions of domination and marginalization of certain subgroups have shown to be potential sources of tension and division within the movement. To a significant extent these tensions are exacerbated when factions within the movement link their interest articulation to their distinct (disability) identities. The following remarks from one of the leaders in the movement highlight some of these tensions:

> You know, I am a physically disabled person and I talk about issues that affect me and other physically disabled persons. You know, when I want to talk about issues that affect the blind, the blind people want to speak for themselves. I should not assume that I know what problems a blind person faces even though I am a disabled person. I am not a blind person, and I face a different challenge. I have observed that the issue of tension revolves around two issues: the issue of funding and the federation's unequal representation of challenges facing the various categories of disabled members. (personal interview, Member GSPD, 20.01.2015, Accra)

Nonetheless, the preceding elaborations show an optimistic future for Ghana's disability rights movement. This is boosted by the current liberal democratic nature of the public sphere, induced by the political reforms of the Ghanaian state. Since the adoption of the National Disability Policy in 2000, the extent of state response to the demands of the movement has been unprecedented. Thus, the current trends in Ghanaian politics with regards to state and civil society relations make the future of the movement bright. Yet, the level to which further progress could be made is contingent on the extent to which the aforementioned threats are managed.

List of Abbreviations

ANAC	French acronym for Cameroon Association for the Blind
ANC	African National Congress
BIGSAS	Bayreuth International Graduate School of African Studies
CPP	Conventions People Party
CRPD	Convention on the Rights of Persons with Disabilities
DACF	District Assembly Common Fund
DANIDA	Danish International Development Agency
DIY	do it yourself
DPI	Disabled People International
DPOD	Disabled People's Organizations of Denmark
DPOs	Disabled People's Organizations
FODA	Federation of Disabled Associations
GAB	Ghana Association of the Blind
GAPA	Ghana Association of Persons with Albinism
GBU	Ghana Blind Union
GBSF	Ghana Burns Survivors Foundation
GDP	Gender and Diversity Program
GFD	Ghana Federation of the Disabled
GFDO	Ghana Federation of Disability Organizations
GNAD	Ghana National Association of the Deaf
GPRSP	Ghana Poverty Reduction Strategy Paper
GSPD	Ghana Society of the Physically Disabled
HIPC	Heavily Indebted Poor Countries
IDA	International Disability Alliance
IG	Inclusion Ghana
IMF	International Monetary Fund
LI	Legislative Instrument
NCCE	National Commission for Civic Education
NCPD	National Council for Persons with Disabilities
NDPC	National Development Planning Commission
NEC	National Electoral Commission
NGO	nongovernmental organization
NORAD	Norwegian Development Organization
MEHSOG	Mental Health Society of Ghana
PWDs	persons with disabilities
RI	Rehabilitation International
SPEED	Special Education Division of the Ministry of Education

UNCRPD	United Nations Convention on the Rights of Persons with Disabilities
WBU	World Blind Union
WFD	World Federation of the Deaf

List of Figures

References

Abrahamsen, Rita (2000): Disciplining Democracy: Development Discourse and Good Governance in Africa. London.

Banful, Afua Branoah (2011): Do formula-based intergovernmental transfer mechanisms eliminate politically motivated targeting? Evidence from Ghana, in: Journal of Development Economics. 96:2, 380-390.

Bevir, Mark (2011): Governance as Theory, Practice and Dilemma. Bevir, Mark. The Sage Handbook of Governance, London, 1-16.

Bratton, Michael (1989): Beyond the State, Civil Society and Associational Life in Africa, in: World Politics. 41: 3, 407-430.

CitiFmonline (2016): “Who is Ivor Greenstreet”. Available at: www.peacefmonline.com/pages/politics/politics/201601/268487.php (10.04.2020).

Cooke, Bill/Kothari, Uma (2001): The Case for Participation as Tyranny. Cooke, Bill/ Kothari, Uma. Participation: The New Tyranny?. London, 1-15.

Cohen, Jean L./Arato, Andrew (1992): Civil Society and Political Theory, Cambridge.

Daily Graphic: “Give Us Better Representation in Assemblies-PWDs”. Available at: www.graphic.com.gh/news/general-news/give-us-better-representation-in-assemblies-pwds.html (18.03.2016).

Diamond, Larry (1997): “Civil Society and the Development of Democracy”, in: Estudio/Working Paper, 101: Madrid.

Downing, Andrew (2011): Power and Disability in the Global South: A Case Study of Ghana’s Disability Rights Movement, Master Thesis. Lund:

Edwards, Michael (2009): Civil Society, Cambridge.

Edwards, Michael/Hulme, David (eds.) (2013): NGOs, States and Donors: Too Close for Comfort?. Basingstoke.

Foley, Michael W./Edwards, Bob (1996): The Paradox of Civil Society, in: Journal of Democracy, 7: 3, 38-52.

Gellner, Ernest (1995): The Importance of Being Modular. Hall, John R.. Civil Society: The Theory, History and Comparism. Cambridge.

Ghana Federation of the Disabled (2008): Contextual Analysis of the Disability Situation in Ghana. Unpublished official policy document.

Ghana News Agency: "Regional Ministers Flout Directive on PWDs Appointment. 24 October 2015". Available at: www.ghananewsagency.org/social/regional-ministers-flout-directive-on-pwds-appointment-federation--96195. (17.03.2016).

Government of Ghana (1992): "The Constitution of the Republic of Ghana". Available at: www.wipo.int/edocs/lexdocs/laws/en/gh/gh014en.pdf (18.03.2017).

Government of Ghana (1993): Local Government Act 462. Accra.

Government of Ghana (2006): National Disability Act 715. Accra.

Government of Ghana (2007): Domestic Violence Act 732. Accra.

Gramsci, Antonio/Hoare, Quintin/Nowell-Smith, Geoffrey (1971): Selections from the Prison Notebooks of Antonio Gramsci. London.

Gyimah-Boadi, Emmanuel (1994): Associational Life, Civil Society and Democratization in Ghana. Harbeson, John W./ Rothchild, Donald/ Chazan, Naomi. Civil Society and State in Africa. Boulder, 125-148.

Hearn, Julie (1999): Foreign Aid, Democratization and Civil Society in Africa: A study of South Africa, Ghana, Uganda. Discussion Paper 368. Sussex.

Hearn, Julie (2001): Uses and Abuses of Civil Society in Africa, in: Review of African Political Economy. 28: 87, 43-53.

Howell, Jude/Pearce, Jenny (2001): Civil Society and Development: A critical Exploration. Boulder.

Huntington, Samuel P. (1991): Democracy's Third Wave, in: Journal of Democracy, 2: 2, 12-34.

Ibrahim, Saad Eddin (1998): Nurturing Civil Society at the Wold Bank: An Assessment of Staff Attitudes toward Civil Society, in: Social Development Papers, 24.

Igoe, Jim and Kelsall, Tim (2005): Introduction: Between a Rock and a Hard Place. Igoe, Jim/Kelsall, Tim. Between a Rock and a Hard Place: African NGOs, Donors and the State. Durham, 1-33.

International Monetary Fund (2012): Ghana: Poverty Reduction Strategy Paper-Volume II, in: IMF Country Report, 12: 204, no pages.

International Monetary Fund (2012): Medium-Term National Development Policy Framework: Ghana Shared Growth and Development Agenda (GSGDA), 2010-2013, in: IMF Country Report, 12: 203, no pages.

Keane, John (1998): Civil Society: Old Images, New Visions. Stanford.

Lewis, David/Kanji, Nazneen (2009): Non-Governmental Organizations and Development. New York.

Levi-Faur, David (2012): From Big Government to Big Governance. Levi-Faur, David. The Oxford Handbook of Governance. New York, 3-18.

McAdam, Doug/McCarthy, John D./Zald, Mayer N. (2008): Comparative Perspectives on Social Movements. Ruggiero, Vincenzo/ Montagna, Nicola. Social Movement: A Reader. London and New York, 279-288.

McCarthy, John. D./Zald, Mayer N. (1977): Resource Mobilization and Social Movements: A Partial Theory, in: American Journal of Sociology 82: 6, 1212-1241.

Oliver, Mike (1990): Politics of Disablement, London.

Powell, Walter W./DiMaggio, Paul J. (1991): Introduction. DiMaggio, Paul J./ Powell Walter W.. The Neo-Institutionalism in Organizational Analysis, Chicago, 1-38.

Putnam, Robert D. (1995): Bowling Alone, in: Journal of Democracy 6: 1, 65-78.

Putnam, Robert D./Leonardi, Robert/Nanetti, Raffaella (1993): Making Democracy Work: Civic Traditions in Modern Italy. Princeton.

Sackey, Emmanuel (2012): Strengthening the Disability Movement in Ghana, in: Innovia Foundation Newsletter, 19, 7-11.

Sackey, Emmanuel (2015): Disability and Political Participation in Ghana: An Alternative Perspective, in: Scandinavian Journal of Disability Research, 17: 4, 366-381.

Seligman, Adam (1992): The Idea of Civil Society, New York.

Shills, Edward (1991): Virtues of Civil Society, in: Government and Opposition, 26, 3-20.

Snow, David A./Benford, Robert D. (1988): Ideology, Frame Resonance, and Participant mobilization, in: International Social Movement Research, 1, 197-217.

Tar, Usman A. (2014): Civil Society and Neoliberalism. Obadare, Ebenezer. The Handbook of Civil Society in Africa. New York, 253-272.

Tarrow, Sydney G. (1998): Power in Movement, second edition. New York.

Tilly, Charles (1995): To Explain Political Processes, in: American Journal of Sociology, 100: 6, 1594-1610.

United Nations (1982): "World Program of Action Concerning Disabled Persons". Available at: www.un.org/development/desa/disabilities/resources/world-programme-of-action-concerning-disabled-persons.html (10.04.2020).

United Nations (1993): "Standard Rules on the Equalization of Opportunities for Persons with Disabilities". Available at: www.un.org/esa/socdev/enable/dissre00.htm, (22.07.2015).

United Nations (2006): United Nations Convention on the Rights of Persons with Disabilities: UNCRPD". Available at: www.un.org/development/desa/disabilities/convention-on-the-rights-of-persons-with-disabilities.html (01.07.2015).

Whitfield, Lindsay (2003): Civil Society as Idea and Civil Society as Process: The Case of Ghana, in: Oxford Development Studies, 31:3, 379-400.

World Bank (1989): Sub-Saharan Africa: From Crisis to Sustainable Growth, Washington D.C..

World Bank (1992): Governance and Development, Washington D.C..

Zald, Mayer N./McCarthy, John. D. (1979): Social Movement Industries: Competition and Cooperation among Movement Organizations, in: Center for Research on Social Organization (CRSO), Working Paper 201, no pages.

Disability and Social Breakthrough: The Cameroonian Context

Ras-I Mackinzeph

Preliminary Remarks

For some time now, I have been endlessly pondering over this anecdote which I entitle *The Nuremberg Experience.* In order to attend the wonderful BIGSAS Diversity Lectures I flew in June 2015 from Cameroon to Germany via France. On the outward journey it became apparent that Paris Charles de Gaulle airport and Airport Nürnberg are more adapted to different accessibility needs than at Yaounde Nsimalen Airport, where I had to limp with my walking stick from the control space to the foot of the plane. At Paris airport while being wheeled to my connecting flight to Nuremberg I gave an impromptu concert. The accompanying hostesses, ground control staff and other travelers were kept spellbound, not in pity of my impairment, but being stunned by the power of my "enchanting mellow vocals" as a passenger remarked. With this mindset of self-assertiveness, I have never allowed my impairment to disable me because I have transformed it into a powerful asset. Can you imagine I was held back by the check-in staff to perform for 25 more minutes after they had processed the documents for my flight? That is why I agree with Helen Keller, a great woman with multiple impairments who says, "Man creates his environment – mental, emotional, and physical by the attitude he develops" (Maxwell 2001: 76).

After such positive flight experiences I was thus shocked on the return journey when I was asked by officials at the airport in Nuremberg to either abandon my walking stick or pay 100 Euros (65600 CFA Francs) for it to be sent to the baggage hold. I protested to no avail, pointedly asking: "Did I choose this condition? Am I paid a salary, for being physically impaired, that is intended to cover such costs?" I did not really mind their concerns for the general security during the flight including mine, but I was disturbed by being obliged to pay for my walking stick, as if I reaped benefits from my physical impairment. This act, deliberately or not, tried to make me feel disabled. If you were in my shoes, what would you have done? Would you have abandoned your walking aid or pay the 65600 CFA Francs; feel psychologically battered and humiliated; or take it serenely?

All the same, life, powered by the soul which is endowed with free will for meaningful choices towards a qualitative living, is the greatest gift of God to the human race. This makes it a sacrosanct, though to an extent a frail, commodity which commands and necessitates utmost attention, care, happiness and protection by each member of the human family. In fact, the sanctity of human life and how well it should be lived has always dominated, and still does, the greatest proportion of human thought and actions. It is from this perspective of the sacredness of life that the concept of disability or the state of being disabled can be best discussed.

For analytical clarity, it is necessary to define the key terms of our topic on disability and social breakthrough. To achieve this goal, we are not going to engage in philosophical debates on the meaning of the terms concerned, but simply build up working definitions for the purpose of our investigation. Firstly, what or who is a person? In other words, what does it mean to possess the quality of humanity? Secondly, what is disability? Who are Persons with Disabilities (PWDs)? Thirdly, what is social breakthrough?

Joseph Omoregbe quotes Severinus Boethius who defines *person* as "an individual substance of a rational nature" (1996: 36). For his part, Thomas Aquinas sees a person as a "rational subsistent", that is, a being with the quality of a priori existence by virtue of its essence (Stumpf/Fieser 2008: 160, 166). Hence, *person* is a combination of both individuality (rooted in matter and avidity with a strong sense of self or ego), and personality or the substantial form – that is, interiority to self, intellect and freedom. It would be more relevant, within this context, to go beyond the rationalistic, and the Cartesian *intellective knowledge* or *self-consciousness* meaning of man, to take a dialogical view that the essence of a person is fully expressed in his/her relation to, or rapport with, others.[1]

Within the African context, the human person is seen more from the dimension of the *heart*. It is in this light that Leopold S. Senghor (1967) once said "Emotion is Negro and Reason is Hellenic" (Azombo-Menda/Enobo Kosso 1978: 29). He did not mean, like Lévy-Bruhl in *How Natives Think* (1926) earlier propounded, that the African lacked rationality or was void of logical thought, but that the African reflected and acted more from a compassionate, intuitive and humanistic point of view. Julius Nyerere (1968) underscores that a person becomes a person through the

1 Such an approach was taken by Pope John Paul II (Catholic Church 1995: 74, 75, 76).

community. This underlines the culture of the African personality wherein man is asserted through his/her communication and cooperation skills and etiquette which highlight the respect and humane treatment of the other in social communion (Tempels 1959).

Thus, being in a community is seen as the basis of social well-being in African sociopolitical thought and existence. This is what Nkrumah in his *Consciencism* refers to as "communalism" (1964), what Senghor calls "a community-based society" (1967) and what Nyerere denotes as "Ujama'a", meaning "the extended family" (1968). Even before the articulations of the abovementioned political thinkers, Belgian born missionary Placide Tempels had explicitly argued that in Bantu thought the human being is defined in terms of the community, which he describes as the "vital force" (1959). As such, the world is interpreted as an interrelationship of forces within the entire realm of existence. This relationship posits the importance of the whole community in shaping and reshaping the life of the individual.

Similarly, South African philosopher Mogobe Ramose uses the notion of "Ubuntu", which means "humanity" or "being human", to explain the African conception of community. He puts it more clearly in his maxim "umuntu ngumuntu ngabuntu" which means "a person is a person through other persons" (1999). This does not only describe human beings as "being with others", but it is also a prescription of how to relate to others; that is, how being with others should be. On his own account, John Mbiti adds more quintessence to this collective ontology by arguing that: "I am because we are; and since we are, therefore I am" (1969: 209). In a nutshell therefore, a person is a substance made of body and spirit, and endowed with autonomy in being, self-consciousness, communality, communication and self-transcendence.

At the next level of clarification of relevant terms, we can lexically define *disability* as a condition, illness or injury which makes it difficult for someone to perform the activities that other people do. Cameroon's *Law No. 2010/002 of 13 April 2010 relating to the Protection and Welfare of Persons with Disabilities* defines disability as "[t]he limitation of a person's ability, due to a deficiency, to fully participate in an activity in a given environment" (Law No. 2010/002: 3).

Within the same context, a *person with disabilities* is:

> Any person who is unable to fulfill by themselves all or part of the requirements of a normal person or social life as a result of a physical or mental disability, be it of birth or otherwise. (Law No. 2010/002: 3)

That is why *social breakthrough* within the framework of this paper can be defined as the collective removal or surpassing of obstacles for a goal driven stride towards the enhancement of individual and societal wellbeing at large.

From this perspective, our focus is to find out whether disability really does pose an impediment to the (socioeconomic and financial) enhancement of PWDs? Hence, to what extent can disability and the mindset it creates hinder the social inclusion and progress of people with disabilities?

Challenges to the socioeconomic breakthrough of PWDs

Disability is a social construct which affects the way people treat fellow humans; the way society treats the physically and mentally challenged. The images people have of PWDs are ones acquired in society through the use of language which gives messages that have a lot of expressive power. Such language usages which generally result from myths and misconceptions about disability are afferent arteries to incomplete information, mistaken perceptions and ignorance that build up to stereotypes like pitiable, baleful, retarded, physically disabled, cripple, handicapped, and incapable of fully participating in everyday life. I well remember that when I was six, about four years after a polio attack that left me disabled, one superstitious old man in our neighborhood regularly threatened to drown me in a river on the mystical grounds that I could be a vessel of the "evil spirit" that attacked me and would in turn attack his children who were paradoxically very fond of me and admired my intellectual prowess. So, throughout history, society has been constructed along the lines of such language usages, posing as condescending hegemonies and even discriminating, which have a negative bearing on the self-image of PWDs. This greatly affects the performance of not only the individuals in question, but the society at large. Such negative stereotypes reduce PWDs to a predetermined and permanently unalterable condition, parallel only to Parmenides' concept of the "changelessness of Being" (Burnet: 1930, cited in Stumpf/Fieser 2008:16-17). To Parmenides, permanence is real, while change is illusory. What is is; what is not is not. Hence all the stereotypes ascribed to PWDs by society are considered permanent and unalterable. It suggests that PWDs cannot transcend their predicament; thereby adversely affecting their self-esteem which can make them appear worthless to themselves and society at large simply because they are caused to focus more on their shortcomings than on their strengths and aptitudes. The situation is unfortunately worsened by the fact that these tags give PWDs an identity which is predetermined and closed, affecting not only the level of awareness of the intrinsic value of their personhood, but also the care and education that PWDs deserve. So, the ensuing myths and misconceptions about disability greatly influence the way people think about disability and how they consider PWDs.

One area of human life which guarantees hope and breakthrough is the legal protection of individual rights and freedoms. In this domain, the state of Cameroon has done some commendable efforts in setting up laws for the protection of PWDs. These efforts, however, are being watered down by the absence of a strong political will which results in delays in the implementation of policies promoting the rights of persons with disabilities. The situation is worsened by the fact that key provisions of the disability law specify that the conditions of their application "shall be fixed by regulation" or "shall be laid down by regulation" (Law 2010/002: 4, 8, 9, 10, 13, and 16). A so-called Enabling Act or implementing regulations are required, but no such regulation has yet been put in place. This intensifies the social stereotypes which implicitly tag these citizens not as persons with full rights, but as burdensome and meriting only a pitiable and pitiful treatment, rather than as people with inalienable rights and freedoms which must be respected. How then can one expect PWDs to progress in life?

Another aspect of social life which is fundamental to the development of every PWD and society at large is education and training, but PWDs in Cameroon benefit from this to a mixed extent. The worth of education is a pointer to the fact that the human person, whether literate or not, needs empowerment in knowledge, skills and attitudes/values summing up to competences that will not only permit him or her to be autonomous, but to know how to relate well to fellow humans. In fact, there is much substance to Aristotle's assertion in his *Nicomachean Ethics* that: "Educating the mind without educating the Heart is no education at all" (cited in Ross 1925: 67). From this, it is clear that the most powerful and dynamic economic resource is the human resource because of its auto-propelling, creative and inventive endowments. It is in this light that the Cameroon government seeks to guarantee the education of PWDs and their offspring by granting them affordable access to education at primary and secondary school levels. Unfortunately, the process is quite cumbersome and discouraging due to the resources involved (time, physical energy, and financial expenditure). This aside, there are few genuine schools for learners with special needs, given that there are very few teacher-training institutions for that purpose. Even those structures that manage to provide such services are too expensive, given the poverty level of this category of people and the society in general. As such, their right to education is confounded by a poorly developed inclusive education system which, in itself, is a product of the absence of a special status for PWDs.

That is how more than three decades ago before the advent of digital ICTs one of my visually impaired university classmates only managed to study by recording lectures on audio tapes. Considering the cost of the total number of tapes he would use per month, it is clear that without the monthly scholarship scheme initially granted to all university students at the time, he would have dropped out of school like many students today. The monthly scholarship scheme was abruptly stopped in 1992 without considering the plight of PWDs. Yet PWDs are evaluated and admitted into professional schools on the same criteria as nondisabled students when the playing ground is not level. If we agree with Francis Bacon that "knowledge is power" (1905), then it is doubtless that with the lack of proper attention, their needs and the psychologically battering stereotypes, PWDs would naturally feel abandoned, discriminated against and disempowered in a world that, to me, seems more of a jungle.

One would think the PWDs who overcame the impediments to effective training had now made it. A worse uphill task, however, awaits those who brave the obstacles with excellent results. The point, here, is access to employment. This is where real discrimination takes place since PWDs are considered more as liabilities than assets due to the strong influence of tradition and societal stereotypes. Seen as dependent and incapable of fully participating in everyday life, PWDs are often sidelined for fear of low output. So their chances of getting employed are highly jeopardized. The situation is worsened by the frail backup in terms of social security. If there was a special allowance for employed PWDs, it would reduce the psychological and financial burdens that their condition imposes on them. In fact, I would not have embarked on the rhetorical questions of *The Nuremberg Experience*. I would simply have paid for the transportation of my walking stick out of my so imagined special disability allowance. Tragically, there is no regular support scheme even for unemployed PWDs which incapacitates them financially and makes it difficult for them to survive socially and take proper medical care of their impairment, let alone have an acceptable matrimonial life. Even though section 19 (1) of *Law No. 2010/002 of 13 April 2010 relating to the Protection and Welfare of Persons with Disabilities* contains provisions for financial support of PWDs, it is limited in scope by the absence of implementing regulations as already indicated above. How then can PWDs provide quality education for their offspring with such financial limitations coupled with inadaptable access to their places of work?

Hence another hitch on the way of PWDs towards social breakthrough is their access to public, study/academic and professional environments that are not adapted to their conditions of impairment. Public gardens, leisure spaces, school buildings, workplaces and ministerial buildings are rarely constructed in cognizance of the different types of impairments. While the physically challenged are confronted with staircases, the blind battle with the difficulty of crossing roads and the absence of brail write-ups to indicate services in public places and buildings. Such glaring societal discrimination against PWDs negatively influences even the way they perceive themselves and creates barriers to full citizenship and personal achievements. Meanwhile, the United Nations Convention on the Rights of People with Disabilities of which Cameroon is a signatory emphasizes that: "products, environments, programs and services" should be designed to "be usable by all people, to the greatest extent possible" (UNCRPWD 2008: 7). My own tedious experiences of moving around the university when I was a student, having to climb stairs with my walking stick to give lectures in the school I taught before my appointment in 2017 and even access to my new office of Regional Pedagogic Inspector of Philosophy in Cameroon's capital city, Yaounde, show quite how far short Cameroon falls of this requirement. Most often, I was obliged to solicit the assistance of my students to push me on my tricycle across the uneven and either muddy or dusty campus depending on the season. On the hilly roads outside my present workplace, I ask for help from oncoming vehicles to tow me on my tricycle uphill.

Do these difficulties provide sufficient grounds to dash the hopes of the socioeconomic and financial breakthrough of PWDs? In other words, are these obstacles a closed door to our (PWD's) destiny?

Fig. 1: Ras-I Mackinzeph braving the hilly roads of Yaoundé. (Photo by Ghong Ndum née Kang Odette Ezia, 2017)

The right mindset (attitude) of PWDs for authentic breakthrough

A person's identity as a PWD is not essentially predetermined, but progressive. This is evident in the following existentialist view: "Man is at the start a plan which is aware of itself"; hence, "man will be what he will have planned to be. Not what he will want to be" (Sartre 1957: 16). Sartre argues that there is no such thing as a specific essence that defines what it is to be human. He asserts that the individual produces his/her essence because man does not possess any predetermined and fixed essence. Hence, each PWD "will be what he will have planned to be. Not what he will want to be" (Sartre 1957: 16). On this account a PWD illustrates just part of the total being or essence of the person that he/she is. This means that a person is what he or she makes of himself or herself.

This attitude of an individual persevering and making progress despite all odds can be likened to the evolution of society as illustrated in Auguste Comte's philosophy of social evolution, progressing from the "primitive stage to the *positive stage"* (Comte 1830;1842). Just as nothing is fixed permanently, so also must PWDs make considerable strides of mental and physical evolution so as to meet the challenges of time. Hence as society grows in complexity, PWDs have to move with the times, as much as the society has the moral obligation to accommodate their needs accordingly.

The early Greek thinker, Heraclitus, recognized this around the 5th Century BC when he propounded that the only permanent thing is change. To explain that "All things are in flux", he uses the analogy of a river, stating "you cannot step twice into the same river, for fresh waters are ever flowing on upon you" despite the presence of huge rocks along the riverbed (cited in Stumpf/Fieser 2008: 12). With the understanding that the human person is a continuous project in adversity, PWDs should work relentlessly to create an essence for their lives by perpetually fine-tuning their positive qualities in the face of all arduous hurdles. As Jean Paul Sartre puts it, "existence precedes essence" (Sartre 1957: 15). Inferring from these views, I think without any doubt that PWDs have the capacity to develop a sublime personality that is capable of impacting their lives and the lives of others. To achieve this, PWDs need the right attitude and commitment.

So, instead of sowing seeds of discord and rivalry as is the case with some associations of disabled persons in Cameroon, it is imperative for us to synergize our various skills and resources in a common platform (like a Cross-Disability Alliance) so that we can advocate for our rights and well-being with consistency. This will enable us to brainstorm, share information and network in a bid to market what our potentials can offer, be they mental or physical. Unnecessary contradictions will be minimized, and state institutions and civil society organizations will take us seriously. As the adage goes, "divided we fall, united we stand." Analogically, a broomstick breaks with little effort, but a bundle of broomsticks is unbreakable.

Working in synergy or combining efforts results in greater empowerment and bearing on society. In such a context, which is unity in diversity, our differences will instead be harnessed into a powerful asset. In fact, the African conception of communalism which projects "togetherness", "brotherhood", and "the extended family" should be our driving force. To buttress this point, it is worth citing the example of the Baptist Mission that, in cooperation with CBM International, runs an inclusive education scheme in 18 secondary schools across the North West Region of Cameroon. In the same vein, the Cameroon Association for the Blind, better known by its French acronym ANAC, has set up an inclusive education scheme in four public schools in the South West Region in Bokwaongo, Muyuka, Fiango, and Mbalangi. Imagine if a few other specific disability associations joined a project like this – what a federation of ideas it would be; what an impact it would have! Julius Nyerere makes clear that such collaboration is crucial through defining his "Ujama'a socialism" as "the belief that a community should be based on cooperation …the advancement of the whole is the foundation for each individual's existence" (Nyerere 1968:18). Hence, the thrust towards progress and an improved quality of life must be as a team.

In another vein, and with such united forces, the challenges facing PWDs can be better surpassed through advocacy for a sincere public-private partnership like ANAC is currently doing in the South West Region of Cameroon. This will more expediently bring pressure to bear on the government for relevant legislation to be put in place. Secondly, the value of PWDs in the progress of society will be felt and recognized, permitting us to get the profits of our input into the national economy. Thirdly, the various derogative social constructs against PWDs in general will gradually die out, creating a more psychologically, emotionally, professionally and socially conducive environment for a better self-realizable, self-transcending, self-determining, and dignified life.

As we all know, freedom is not given, but taken. In the same light, education which is the source of the greatest power (knowledge) does not simply come our way; we grasp it. So, a strong advocacy for inclusive education, taking care of the specific needs of the various impairments within the same study space with the physically fit, should be the major concern of the whole confederation of PWDs. The advantage is that the PWDs will then not feel desolate, but will have the opportunity to interact, develop faster and easily integrate into society. Educational advocacy should be the greatest goal of PWDs (literate or illiterate) because education or knowledge is the greatest power without which even economic, political, military or any other power is impossible. It is knowledge that permits humanity to cajole nature and discover its secrets for the improvement of the human condition. It is nothing other than knowledge that dispels ignorance and prejudices or even social tags against PWDs. It is only when PWDs begin advocating from the platform of knowledge and wisdom that the collegiality of their voices will constitute a force to be reckoned with. They will not only be persuasive, but as convincing as the deductive thinker, such that their social insertion and breakthrough will come by necessity. This means that when associations of PWDs begin achieving inclusion through strategized, concerted efforts, the government and civil society will have no choice but to become partners.

Given that life is a continuous project, PWDs need a vision of epistemic empowerment which will serve as the dynamo of their aspirations for autonomy and job qualifications. This implies that PWDs, literate or illiterate, should do their best to develop personal skills and the ability to preempt any sort of discrimination. This is because they are generally pushed into a state of inferiority not only by the aforementioned societal tags, but equally by the lack of requisite talent, skills, self-confidence and hope for the future. But what are the aspirations of PWDs? Are they comfortable with their condition? If simply considered as the nature of things or unchangeable, such a psychological complex can lead to perpetual dependence and anguish. My fellows should know that it took an unknown Rosa Parks who refused to relinquish her seat in a bus to a white person for the civil rights movement to gain great impact throughout the United States. By this act, she turned inferiority into equity and provoked the rise of visionaries like Martin Luther King Jr. whose famous "I have a dream" vision brought a new turn to civil rights legislation in the US. In the same vein, my personal experience has taught me that one can possess all the right attitudes it takes to exist or execute a project, but when he or she is void of the capacity to conceive solutions, predict possible obstacles/difficulties and preempt the right actions, his or her passion for success will lack a sense of direction. That is why I can still hear Kwame Nkrumah echoing from his grave that "Practice without thought is blind; thought without practice is empty" (Nkumah1964: 78). So we need not necessarily be famous, but carry along with us a proactive winning mentality at all times. That is why I wish to call on us all, including you reading this chapter, to join the chorus with Abraham Lincoln as we say, "Always bear in mind that our own resolution to succeed is more important than any other one" (Maxwell2001, 8).

As concerns the society in all its ramifications, it is time to valorize every aspect of its potential and actual human resources, because disability is not merely a physical reality, but equally a social construct which generally ensues from impairments of any sort. Davis L. says:

> An impairment is a physical fact, but a disability is a social construction…lack of mobility is an impairment, but an environment without ramps turns that impairment into a disability (cited in Harris 2006, 12).

The story of Pastor Nick Vujici of Australian birth is very inspiring. Born without arms and legs, he was sustained by true love and care of his parents to the point that he decided not to commit suicide when he saw just how much he was loved. Parental love equally prevented Nick from seeing his impairment as a disability. Today, he runs a nonprofit ministry, Life Without Limbs, and is inspirational to many, even the physically fit. He once declared that he has never had the opportunity to either embrace his wife or carry his two children, but that he carries and embraces them with love. He equally professed that if he were given a second chance to be born into this world again, he would choose to be in the same physical condition. As such, society can benefit much from what it makes of people with impairment. U.S. citizens will confirm that the impairment of his two legs never limited President Franklin Roosevelt in taking the U.S. out of the worst economic crisis of its whole history and empowering the U.S. for its crucial role in ending World War II. This suggests that disability is not necessarily deterrent to the dreams and exploits of a person. In fact, the American electorate saw more of an asset than a liability in Roosevelt and offered him an unprecedented and never equaled four presidential terms. Let us also consider the therapeutic power of the artistic works of Stevie Wonder (United States of America), Talla Andre Marie, Angelina Tezano and the late and much lamented Kotto Bass (all from Cameroon), among others. These are visually and physically impaired musicians, whose exceptional skills in musical composition and rendition overpowered their impairments, thereby establishing themselves as role models over and above the usual attributes like *derisory* and *pitiable*. Therefore, the society, especially the state, should build strong institutions to guarantee the empowerment and protection of PWDs.

For instance, the state should ensure that all laws are promulgated simultaneously with implementing regulations or what is commonly known in Cameroonian parlance as "texts of application". It follows that PWDs need love, care, solidarity, justice, equality and equity for them to demonstrate their power of productivity for personal and social progress or else the ensuing societal tags will produce negative boomerang effects on the very society which sources them. For as Immanuel Kant propounds, we need the goodwill to do what is right and recognize the humanity of the other. Doing what is right is also a rational and autonomous will (Kant/Wolff 1969: 16).

Now, permit me to conclude alongside offering my final take on *The Nuremberg Experience*. Definitely, I refused to be a psychological victim in the whole dilemma of choosing either to abandon my walking stick or to pay for it to be checked into the hold; to feel battered and humiliated or to take it with composure. I wish to first and foremost call the attention of my fellow PWDs to the fact that in life there are situations whose course we can change or influence and there are others which do not directly depend on our competence and power. But the paradox is that we are always obliged to make choices for meaningful solutions. That is why, to end the anecdote, I immediately called my wife back in Cameroon to place an order for another walking stick worth less than two Euros (1000 CFA Francs). So, fellow PWDs, do not allow yourselves to be taken in by whatever societal stereotypes you are confronted with because even the *Holy Bible in Proverbs 23:7* says that a person is a product of his/her thoughts: "For as he thinketh in his heart, so is he". Even the "superstitious old man" finally had no choice but to become a defender of PWDs because of my positive self-image. I was more interested in my future and the redressing of my impairment which I saw more in the proper education of my mind and heart than in minute distractions. In effect, his threats and tags drove me, alongside other PWDs of the little community of Bolifamba, to a crazy quest for academic excellence. This created a widespread view that PWDs are naturally intelligent. Thus, disability is not synonymous with inability. Instead our various impairments should serve as great steppingstones to our destinies, because PWDs are persons with special abilities not inabilities.

We must carry along a positive mindset of self-worth and perseverance; a mindset that contains only what we are as a project or "plan" (Sartre 1957: 16). Just listen to the emphasis of General George S. Patton as you read through his lines: "Attitudes determine actions. You are not what you think you are. What you think, you are" (Maxwell2001: 65). This reminds me of a good friend, an engineer, who decided to commit suicide on the pretext that life was unbearable because for more than ten years he had been applying for jobs to no avail. Curiously, one day after the attempted suicide he received a phone call offering him employment in an international company that he had earlier contacted. The job offer included a service car, a residence paid for by the company and a salary of over one million CFA Francs (about 1524.49 Euros). On this account, I wish to call on all of my fellow PWDs to always look ahead with optimism and bear in mind that hope should never be lost.

My good friend's remorse over the attempted suicide, his zeal to live again, and the asset he has suddenly become to his community makes it compelling for us to take to heart Roberta Flack's words that "The situation you live in doesn't have to live in you" (cited in Maxwell 2001: 83). We are not liabilities, but assets and persons with special abilities that require only to be ignited. Yet, no one else can start this process but us, given that introspection is internal and personal. So, as Albert Schweitzer says, "Man must cease attributing his problems to his environment and learn again to exercise his will" and determination to make more out of life (Maxwell 2001: 37). In this light, introspection serves as the gateway to self-examination which constitutes a powerful instrument for the transformation of any form of impairment to an asset that can be of great value to humanity as a whole. Hence we must pay attention to what we carry in our minds because “You are where you are and what you are because of the dominating thoughts that occupy your mind” (Maxwell 2001: 82).

List of Abbreviations

PWD	persons with disabilities
CFA Francs	Franc de la Coopération Financière en Afrique

List of Figures

References

Aquinas, Thomas (2012): Summa Theologiae. Lander.

Azombo-Menda, Soter/Enobo Kosso, Martin (1978): Les Philosophes Africaines par les Textes. Paris.

Bacon, Francis (1905): Novum Organum. Spedding, Ellis/Spedding, James. The Philosophical Works of Francis Bacon. London, 259-387.

Boethius, Anicius M. S. (1897): The Consolation of Philosophy. James, Henry R.. The Consolation of Philosophy of Boethius. Adelaide.

Burnet, John (1930): Early Grek Philosophy, 4th ed.. London.

Cameroon (2010): “Law No. 2010//002 of 13 April 2010 Relating to the Protection and Welfare of People with Disabilities, (Law No. 2010//002 of 13.04.2010, RPWPWDs)”. Available at: www.un.org/development/desa/disabilities/wp-content/uploads/sites/15/2019/11/Cameroon_decree-of-application-2010-law-english-version.pdf (10.04.2020).

Catholic Church (1995): Post-synodal apostolic eyhortation, Ecclesia in Africa, of the Holy Father John Pual II to the bishops, priests, and deacons, men and women, religious … evangelizing mission towards the year 2000. Nairobi.

Comte, Auguste (1830): Cours de Philosophie positive, Vol. 3. Paris.

Harris, James C. (2006): Intellectual Disability: Understanding Its Development, Causes, Classification, Evaluation, and Treatment. Oxford.

Kant, Immanuel/Wolff, Robert Paul (1969): Fundamental Principles of the Metaphysics of Morals. Indianapolis, 16.

Lévy-Bruhl, Lucien (1926): Les fonctions mentales dans les sociétés inferieures. Clare, Lilian A.. How Natives Think. London, 392.

Maxwell, John C. (2001): The Power of Attitude. Benin City.

Mbiti, John S. (1969): African Religions and Philosophy. London.

Nkrumah, Kwame (1964): Consciencism: Philosophy and Ideology for Decolonization. London.

Nyerere, Julius (1968): Ujama'a, Essays in Socialism. London.

Omoregbe, Joseph (1996): Metaphysics Without Tears, A Systematic and Historical Study. Lagos.

Philips, Philip E. (2012a): A Companion to Boethius in the Middle Ages. Leiden.

Philips, Philip E. (2012b) Anicius Manlius Severinus Boethius; A Chronology and Selected Annotated Biography. Leiden.

Ramose, Mogobe B. (1999): African Philosophy Through Ubuntu. Avondele Harare.

Ross, William D. (1925): The Works of Aristotle. Oxford.

Sartre, Jean Paul (1957): Existentialism and Human Emotions. New York.

Sartre, Jean Paul (1969): Being and Nothingness. London.

Senghor, Léopold S. (1967): Les fondements de l'africanité ou négritude et arabité. Paris.

Stumpf, Samuel E./Fieser, James (2008): Socrates to Sartre and Beyond, 8th ed.. New York.

Tempels, Placide (1959): Bantu Philosophy. Paris.

United Nations (2006): "United Nations Convention on the Rights of Persons with Disabilities: UNCRPD". Available at: www.un.org/development/desa/disabilities/convention-on-the-rights-of-persons-with-disabilities.html (10.04.2020).

The Different Glance – and what we can gain from it

Diverse Perspectives. Foreignness and Intimacy of the Photographic Gaze on Disability

Sarah Böllinger and Ulf Vierke[1]

In Memory of Alain Ricard[2]

Introduction

In this chapter we will grapple with the intersection between discourses around the "African" body in the arts and the discourses around disabled bodies in Africa. So far, this intersectionality has received little attention from anthropology and the pictorial sciences. Based on John Kiyaya's series titled "Usa River Rehabilitation and Training Center", we want to approach manifestations of disabled identities in Tanzania and initiate a discussion around the photographic representations of disabled bodies[3]. We

1 Translated by Renzo Baas.

2 Ulf Vierke remembers: "In 2010, during one of his many visits to Bayreuth, Alain Ricard brought along a large folder containing photos by John Kiyaya and asked us what we thought of them. They were the pieces that were published three years later by Mkuki na Nyota and are at the center of this chapter. The photos captured our imagination immediately. The question of 'why' led to a four-hour discussion and Alain nearly missed his flight from Nuremburg. John Kiyaya, on Alain's initiative, came as an artist in residence to the Iwalewahaus and presented some of his extraordinary pieces. Alain was known far beyond his scientific field, literary studies. He was a true universal scholar and mediator. Throughout the years, he helped to inspire and sharpen our seeing, thinking, and understanding of contemporary art." Alain Ricard passed away in 2016.

3 The "Usa River Rehabilitation and Training Center" (URRC) is an institution of the Diocese of the Evangelical Lutheran Church in Tanzania (ELCT) in Meru (Tanzania). The aim of the center, which operates according to the motto "We believe in your ability", is to enable a self-determined life for people with disabilities. In this sense, the URRC offers various apprenticeships. The residents can study to become carpenters, tailors, bakers, or locksmiths. The usual apprenticeship averages three years. At the end of the apprenticeship, the apprentices receive a nationally recognized degree or certificate. See for example Kaaya, Elibariki/Wollner, Thomas (undated).

will be using Enwezor's approach to photography, who speaking about it at the exhibition "Snap Judgement" said:

> This exhibition is in part devised to ask pertinent questions about the role of images in the public narration of the African self and spaces within a global image ecology. (Enwezor 2006: 19)

In a similar way we ask which self of the disabled identity does Kiyaya portray.

The representation of persons with disabilities in Africa can be scrutinized according to a twofold "Othering" (see Spivak 1985: 247-272). One does not have to search for long in order to find images, in the context of aid agencies and NGOs (nongovernmental organizations), looking down on other people and their bodies. These looks are either benevolent, the disabled people smiling up into the camera showing that they can also live a fulfilling life with the support of the organization. Or the images are pitiful and look down on a sick, ailing person, who would have to suffer a miserable existence without the support of the organization. Both image types provoke a gaze that is not founded on a reciprocal dialogue. Rather, the viewer is directly prompted to realize his/her position of power and use it for "good" (usually by donating money). The fact that the bodies, who provoke this reaction, are black and disabled reinforces the dominant gaze in these photographs. One can therefore detect a blatant gaze in them, manifest in this twofold "Othering". The disabled black body enables a colonial gaze, better known from photographs emerging from the late 19th and early 20th centuries (see Natermann 2017).

John Kiyaya's photographic oeuvre distinguishes itself overall because he succeeds in creating an alternative to the inquiring colonial gaze. His work is still documentary and seeks to portray the lifeworld of his contemporaries, yet this happens, as we will attempt to show, without exemplifying them. Kiyaya's photographs are simultaneously inquiring and subjective, comparable with an entry into a field diary, which we try to comprehend through the adjective "semidocumentary". Kiyaya, so we argue, is far from a potential "Othering" in photographs, in which Africa becomes an alien counterpart to the Global North. However, what happens when this photographer works with people with disabilities? Is he immune against "Othering" or rather an "enfreakment", which becomes apparent through the gaze on norm-deviant restricted bodies? And if yes, how does he manage this?

John Kiyaya and the Photographic Mapping of his World

The Tanzanian photographer, John Kiyaya, who was referred to as a "hidden jewel" (Kiyaya 2013: 7) of Tanzanian photography by Walter Bgoya, the head of the publishing house Mkuki na Nyota, has been known in Europe for a long time for his serial studies of the residents of Lake Tanganyika. Back home, Kiyaya, who was born around 1970, only received attention after the 2013 publication of his monograph *John Kiyaya – Mpiga picha Mtanzania na watu wa Ziwa Tanganyika / Tanzanian Photographer and People of Lake Tanganyika* (Kiyaya 2013). Kiyaya's photos recount everyday scenes, which every astute visitor to the region around Lake Tanganyika can observe, in a semidocumentary style. Kiyaya, himself a son of a fisher family (see H.B. 2000), not only photographs the residents of the Lake Tanganyika Region in his studio, his specialty is on-site photo shoots which he dedicates to certain topics and the peculiarities of the everyday:

> All along, I've been taking photographs that have particular 'themes': for example, about fishing, and fishermen's lives; about women's work, in farming, selling things, or while they're making things and so forth. (Kiyaya 2013: 7)

Until his 19th birthday, Kiyaya wanted to become a priest and attended a seminary. Once he met his present-day wife, it became clear to him that he cannot enter into the ordination of priests. It was at that time that he found a new calling in photography. He met the author and journalist Jean Rolin, who gave him his first camera. Thanks to Rolin's support, he was able to attend a school for journalism in Dar es Salam where he majored in photography (Kiyaya 2013: 13; see Bebey 2015 and African Loxo no year). He maintained his livelihood through small photography commissions, for example taking portraits of his fellow students and teachers (see Rolin 2007). Up until this day, Kiyaya still works in analog. He sends his exposed films to France to be developed in order to, as he says, achieve a better quality result than would be possible in the photo studios back home. This procedure takes much longer than normal, however, people in his hometown of Sumbawanga started talking about the unique quality of his images and he continuously received more assignments (see Kiyaya 2013: 8). Besides the offers from locals, he also received offers from abroad. At the beginning of his career, these came directly from Jean Rolin, who used Kiyaya's images for journalistic reports and thus opened doors for him to bigger assignments. Through Rolin he became known in the European art world and is able to exhibit his works outside of Tanzania; first in France[4], and later in the United States of America, in Mali, and in Germany. He had publications in a number of newspapers and magazines and won the Leopold Godowasky Jr. Color Photography Award in 2000 (see Kiyaya 2013: 15-16). His first monograph, titled "John Kiyaya – Mpiga picha Mtanzania na watu wa Ziwa Tanganyika", appeared in 2013.

John Kiyaya's career is captured in the published stories and reports of his first encounter with Jean Rolin. It is the typical story of serendipitous discovery, in which the path of an undiscovered African talent crosses with that of a discoverer and later patron from the Global North. It is a story by Europeans for Europeans. Therefore, it is all the more important to place John's own story, his images, at the center. They offer a complementary version to the written reports, one in which patronage does not feature, only the visual grappling with his own cultural and visual world.

Let us, however, begin with how other authors have read Kiyaya's body of images. From Kiyaya's monograph, consisting of short articles, an interview, as well as 85 photographs, one gets the impression that his photographs are informed by two essential elements. Firstly, his "deeply African" look on life, as Jean Rolin describes it: "Et elles [les photographies] ressemblent à l'Afrique tout entière, à travers l'œil insoupçonnable d'un Africain" (Rolin 2007) ("And they [the photos] reflect the whole of Africa, through the unsuspicious eyes of an African.")[5]. Secondly, his flair for minimal staging, which allows the viewer to believe the "authenticity" of the photo (see Kiyaya 2013; African Loxo no year). Rolin's and Kiyaya's narrative strands are explained time and again through the fortunate coincidence that the German colonial ferry "Liemba", on which Kiyaya met his patron Jean Rolin, still traverses Lake Tanganyika. Although their memories of the initial encounter and the genesis of their collaboration differ, they both swoon about the West-Tanzanian romanticism, the seclusion of John's places of activity, and their mutual love of the water. In this way, Kiyaya's photographs become soulful pieces, which offer a look into Tanzanian rural realities. This reading of Kiyaya's oeuvre is romantic and possibly even nostalgic. We will contrast this to Kiyaya's corpus, using the example of the disabled body, which appears as a documentary-orientated factual-conceptual work.

---

4 He had his first exhibition in Lectoure, France in 1992 (Rolin 2007: 18).

5 If not marked as such, all foreign quotes have been translated by the authors.

Skewed and deep Images – Kiyaya's Oeuvre

Kiyaya's oeuvre impresses through emphasis on the details in his environment. He does not portray individuals but types, similar to the German photographer August Sander in his monumental work "Die Menschen des 20. Jahrhunderts" (eng. "People of the 20th Century", 1980). The photographical spectrum of Kiyaya's monograph "John Kiyaya – Mpiga picha Mtanzania na watu wa Ziwa Tanganyika" ranges from single and group portraits to scenic and animal photographs.[6] While Sanders used black and white photography, Kiyaya only works with color film. Except for two images, all of Kiyaya's analog photos were taken outdoors, during the day, without an additional light source. For experienced observers of portraits, a certain tension is created by Kiyaya playing with the genre of studio photography by moving it outside. While most of Kiyaya's work documents the work itself, he typifies his models not only through their occupations. Rather in his photographs he follows the nature of work, as well as the nature of those who perform the work.[7] He achieves this not by looking down on those photographed, but by trying to meet them at eye level or looking up to them and engaging in a considerate dialogue. At the same time, he does not entirely recede or suggest a photographic autonomy, which objectively reports. Rather, with the help of the position of his camera as well as attention to tiny details in the scene, he focuses the gaze of the viewer on the nature of the people in front of the camera. His photos are not snapshots, often they appear constructed.

Ulf was able to shadow Kiyaya a number of times and observe the time he invests in the photographic process, which manifests itself in his work. A couple of minutes before pushing down the trigger, he assures himself of the scene without looking through the camera lens. Only then does he take the camera into his hand and again a couple of seconds pass before he presses the trigger. In this way, his photos receive an emphatic depth, not inherent in every documentary photograph, which is why we refer to his images as semidocumentary.

Long before using the film in his camera, Kiyaya spends time with the people he is portraying; they talk to each other and get acquainted. While the photo shoot is taking place, and before the moment in which the cam-

6 In his photographic career, Kiyaya has shot thousands of photos. Most of them are located in archives in Europe. (Kiyaya, 2013: 16, 202)

7 Zwlethu Mthethwa has a similar approach in his works in Mtethwa and Njami 2011.

era is positioned, he directs the scene and has the person in front of the camera disappear as an individual and reappear as a type. This is how the semidocumentary images that often appear skewed gain their emphatic depth. It is this skillfully spun emphatic texture of images consisting of foreground and background, model and landscape (rarely interiors) that make his work special. Not only are Kiyaya's works special in regard to content, but they also offer technical intricacies: If one looks at the negatives of his photos and compares them to the published images, one can detect a nearly unsettling slant. There is sometimes an incline in the horizontal lines to the left on the prints, but more often to the right. The negatives in our possession all have an incline to the right. Perhaps some photos were printed in inverse, in any case it appears that the pressure from the finger on the trigger makes the camera fall slightly to the right at the moment of exposure. This has nearly always been corrected in the publications by the editors, which was well-meaning, but unnecessary, maybe even wrong. Including a visible trace of the pressure of the finger on the trigger makes the photo tangible as a process and human. For the Western observer this may be disturbing, but for Kiyaya it is part of his photography and his collection of the work done by the people of Tanganyika.

Following Susan Sontag's assumption that "collecting photographs means collecting the world" (Sonntag 1995: 9), one can safely say that John Kiyaya has collected his world of Lake Tanganyika with thousands of images. And yet, he does not employ his camera as a weapon, as Sonntag argues often happens (1995), but rather as a calligraphy brush. He takes time when shooting, he lovingly replicates the everyday and values aesthetic contemplation. In this way his semidocumentary images are not just witnesses but also analytical instruments, as Enwezor fittingly formulates it: "photography has been adapted as a probing tool; it is as much a medium of witnessing as it is an analytical one" (Enwezor 2006: 25). It is, however, not the singular image here that is an "immutable mobile", a time constant and mobile object in the sense of Bruno Latour (Latour 2006: 275), just as important is its classification in a serialized system. Kiyaya's photographs are like a mosaic that "only becomes a synthesis when it can be shown in cluster", as Schneider wrote about the comparable photos by August Sanders (Schneider in Grebe 2016: 224). Anna Grebe's findings for August Sander's archival creative work can also be conveyed onto John Kiyaya's oeuvre: Through

> the receding of the individual markers of his referents in favor of an averageness that discloses itself to the viewer when looking through the series and connecting the individual images they convey the impression of a typological-anthropological stocktaking. (Grebe 2016: 224)

Kiyaya as a visual anthropologist

What makes the content of Kiyaya's work special, as briefly outlined above, is his relationship to his models. Seldom does he take pure landscape photographs, rather, the landscapes are used as a backdrop. Kiyaya's photos are reminiscent not only of the type studies done by Sanders, but also of photo studio shots from the 1970s, 1980s and 1990s in which the background offers further insights about the model (Keita et al. 2011, see Sidibé/Knape 2003). It is obvious that we are looking at staged images. Although, we have to invest time in Kiyaya's images in order to discover the clues of staging, for example a purposefully placed Coca-Cola bottle. Therefore, we only partly endorse Alain Ricard's statement that "[...] he could almost be an anthropologist" (in Kiyaya 2013: 38). He might be in regard to where his epistemological interests lie, but he definitely is not in regard to the claim of the documental; anthropologists are committed not to distort their observations through interventions. On the other hand, Kiyaya's detailed, slow, exact work based on observations over a long period of time could be understood as a method of visual anthropology, since his methodology seems to lean on field research. Kiyaya returns to the same places over years and decades and observes the people there. He participates in their lives, speaks to them about their wishes and photographs his and their experiences.

Visual anthropology attempts to understand the proximity between observer and observed in terms of photography. Schneider, for example, references Heisenberg's uncertainty principle to illustrate visual anthropology's agency:

> Heisenberg's uncertainty principle in German is referred to as *Unbestimmtheitsrelation* (literally 'relation of uncertainty'), but also as *Unschärferelation* (literally relation of fuzziness, blurredness, or 'out-of-focus' principle). It is this relative positioning of focus to the perceived object, to seize the basic idea, […] then, the degree of focus that visual artists apply to their chosen subject (here indigenous cultures and, more generically, the cultural 'Other') is an appropriate criterion, albeit shifting in its content, which can be used in understanding their work (Schneider 2008: 173).

As such Kiyaya's study would be relatively astute, as he is himself Tanzanian and is culturally close to his models (see above on his "African gaze", Ricard in Kiyaya 2013). Furthermore, he only experiments minimally with the mentioned additions in his works. Nevertheless, the concise headings, which he gives each photograph, as well as his relationship to the models over an extended time, point towards Kiyaya as a chronicler, whose focus is not the activity but rather the active person.

This documentation on equal footing, clearly present in the photographs in Kiyaya's monograph, will be looked for in the photographs from the disability center at the Usa River. We explore what distinguishes Kiyaya's gaze on disability and if it, like Ricard said, has something "African". We wish to analyze if he falls into the trap of "enfreakment" and dominant "staring", as Rosemarie Garland Thomson described it in "Staring – How we look" (2006), or can he correct his haziness in regard to disabled bodies with the help of the camera in order to seamlessly integrate them into his remaining oeuvre?

Even if we do not want to completely subscribe to the idea of an essential "African gaze" or "African eye", as the authors of Kiyaya's monography refer to it (see Kiyaya 2013), we appreciate these descriptions as they defy the prevailing Afro-pessimism in relation to the expectation of African photographers. Enwezor does not speak of an African gaze, but he does use the attribute "African". Being well aware of the local limitations of the term "Africa", he uses it not only to contrast art of the former colonial powers and the colonized, but also to engage with the concept of the cosmopolitan. Not in the sense of an urban identity, but in the sense of an identity grappling with the continent. Here, it does not matter if the artist was born or lives in Africa or whether he/she grapples with their African cosmopolitanism from the perspective of the diaspora. When it comes to "being African" or "seeing like an African", it is about the perspective of the gaze (see Enwezor 2006: 24-26). As mentioned above, Kiyaya's works do exactly that: they document the everyday as something exceptional, comparable with the works of Seydou Këita or Malik Sidibé. In his essay for the exhibition "Snap Judgement" (2006), Enwezor interprets their art as antitheses to the dominant narrative of Africa that "nothing good ever comes out of Africa" (Enwezor 2006: 11). Even if one cannot state that Kiyaya consciously positions himself against this neocolonial view of Africa as the dark continent, his works still have this effect. His stories of a normal day's work at Lake Tanganyika can be seen as an alternative to what Enwezor has described as the "atlas of disorder" (Enwezor 2006: 12).

Kiyaya's photographs distinguish themselves in respect that they are shaped by familiarity and proximity, but they also showcase a will to abstraction and mapping. Mapping in the sense of an inquiring gaze, which does not only replicate but also wants to comprehend. His gaze is not only documental, but also analytical, which is why we refer to it as semidocumentary. Again, using Schneider, one could speak of experimental field research, without it being parasitic[8] or condescending. While Schneider sees the uncertainty principle as a method and yardstick for the quality of traditional field research for visual anthropology, Enwezor agrees with Susan Sontag and understands the lens of the camera as a weapon: "The telescopic lens, allows the photographic hunter to act as both ethnographer and surveyor, the more to underscore the cultural distinctions between himself and the subject" (Enwezor 2006: 14).

Kiyaya's photographic documentation at the Rehabilitation Center at the Usa River is remarkable as experimental research insofar as it is the first time he is working together with people with disabilities. His access in the sense of a typological-anthropological survey is on the one hand achieved through the handicraft, which resonates with his existing archive. But he arrives at typologies also through the very personal dealing with the people in front of the camera. The disabled or norm-deviant body, however, is not subject to his visual inquiry or typologising.

An empathetic gaze on the disabled body

As mentioned above, the observers and analysts of John Kiyaya's images agree that what makes his images special is the intensive relationship between photographer, model, and scene. Kiyaya's photos are reminiscent of the works by Nontikelelo "Lolo" Veleko. In her pictures, the relation between model and photographer is of decisive importance as well:

> In these street portraits, the subjects are approached directly, frontally. Their open stances indicate a sense of ease in relation to the photographer, which might suggest to observers a form of social and ethical transaction between photographer and photographed. This is the nature of the dialectical and analytical image. The subject is never an object already predetermined, a priori, by a discourse (Enwezor 2006: 32).

Enwezor's description of the dialectic negotiation process between photographer and model is applicable to Kiyaya's method and his work. His photographs are developed in discourses, which he leads with his environment. He first captures them on film, then leaves it up to the reviewer to discuss and contextualize.

---

8 Enwezor states that photography is a "vampiric machine", which must be reflected upon as soon as one writes of photography in Africa (see Enwezor 2006: 14).

In the photo series URRC that we consider here, which Kiyaya photographed in 2012 at the Usa River, a market space at the foot of the Kilimanjaro, halfway between Arusha and Moshi (Tanzania), a similar spectrum as in his monograph can be found.

Kiyaya does not only portray, he observes and analyzes. In the URRC series, one can track this analytical step quite well. The roughly 200 small-scale negatives can be understood to a large extent as process studies, if the few group photos are ignored.

During four one-day visits, together with Ulf Vierke, Kiyaya was able to gain insight into the vocational training and work at the URRC. The result is photographs, which depict a productive identity for people with disabilities, who either work there as trainers or are apprentices. Kiyaya's special attention to work or productivity is emphasized through the high percentage of photographs that show this perspective. On average he shot just over one film roll per day. Given this limited number of photographs, it is remarkable that Kiyaya photographed the explanation by the workshop supervisor of his work of producing leg and foot prosthetics in minute detail and in high frequency, so that when they are strung together, like in a flick book, they make the whole process comprehensible. As Kiyaya did not take just one photo of the man at his turner but a whole series lets one assume that he appreciated the man's work and his explanation, so that he spent much of his limited analog film on him.

Similar to the portraits in his monograph, Kiyaya does not let his gaze wander to the details of the process (in this case the prosthetic), rather he always has the person who performs, shares and produces knowledge at the center of the picture. This focus on the person is decisive in the URRC series. He never lets the person he photographs appear as an extra. The photographed are never just referential as a signifier for a certain normative value. They never lose their self in Kiyaya's shots, rather it is they who are emphasized through these shots.

The productivity of the person is foregrounded, whereby Kiyaya also gives disability a certain meaning. Mirroring the motto of the URRC "We believe in your ability", Kiyaya concentrates on ability. His photographs emerge in the context of "ableism". The term "ableism" describes the reduction of the human body to its physical, mental, sexual, social, biological, cultural, or other abilities. As soon as a body is deviant and unable to perform its ascribed role, it is regarded as inferior and becomes marginalized. This creates power imbalances amongst people with and without "able bodies" (see Wolbring 2009; Hutson 2009; Campbell 2009).

If we now place the shots from the URRC in the context of Kiyaya's oeuvre it becomes clear that he does not pay any special attention to the disabilities of his protagonists, his focus lies in the activities of the person, irrespective of their physical abilities. Their disability is not important.

The focus on the person and his/her work is the common thread that runs through his work for more than 30 years. The people with disabilities in his pictures are not dependent victims of their own restrictions, but active participants in their lives. They work as tailors, metalworkers, prosthetic makers, they go to the hairdresser and the doctor. Their disability often only becomes visible through their aids. All protagonists appear self-reliant, not helpless.

A portrait of a young girl whose face is hidden behind a sewing machine while sewing seems emblematic[9] for his style of photography. Although Kiyaya always places the person at the center of his images, this is, however, always in relation to their activity so that the shot does not appear voyeuristic or glorified romantic. Nevertheless, it must be observed that even though Kiyaya approaches his model and also bends down to her, he is not at eye level with the young girl, whose face is just above the edge of the table. Additionally, her face is covered up by the machine. If one would only see this picture and disregard the rest of Kiyaya's oeuvre, then one could conceive of this depiction of disability as dehumanizing and anonymizing. That is why we find it vital that his depiction of disabilities and their configuration are always considered in connection to his whole corpus.

9 Refer to the section "Portraits" for the technical details of Kiyaya's photographs.

Fig. 1: untitled (Girl behind the sewing machine.), John Kiyaya, 2012

The more than 200 images of the series, all shot at the URRC, can be divided into the following eight themes,[10] of which we will discuss the first four: "On the way to... ", "In the orthopedic workshop", "At the hairdresser's", "Portraits", "At the doctor's", "In the metal workshop", "At the tailor's shop" and "Waiting in the park". If one looks at the images in a chronological order, one accompanies Kiyaya on a scouting expedition through the URRC. He gazes upon the school children's different spheres of life but does not get private or obscene, rather he encounters the children during their day's work as an interested observer.

In the orthopedic workshop

The most extensive series is dedicated to the orthopedic workshop. Here one also finds detailed shots of materials and products, in contrast to the other training areas. Kiyaya does not only document the making of a prosthetic, but also the materials used in the production, their storage and their disposal. It seems that he is not only fascinated by the processes in the or-

10 The themes were decided upon and named by the authors. We were guided by the descriptive titles, which Kiyaya gives his works otherwise.

thopedic workshop, but especially by the aesthetics of the aids (see Fig. 3). He devotes a lot of attention to them as singular objects. In contrast, none of his photos show a person wearing such a prosthetic.[11] In the image chosen for this article, one can recognize how close Kiyaya gets to the object. The shot, taken just above the workbench at eye level, showing the depth of the room, looks upon an I-shaped wooden block; in the background a screw-injection molding machine is visible. The landscape format image is overexposed. The foot in the foreground and two thirds of the picture, which shows a workbench cluttered with work tools, are very light, while the back of the room is nearly black. A close to completed dark brown prosthetic foot sticks out from the screw-injection molding machine. The wooden block and the prosthetic foot are staged in such a way through the perspective and the lighting that they give the image a certain sturdiness, which is contrasted by the "mess" on the workbench and the wooden model that half-stands on the plate. This solidity and reference to the human foot makes this photograph stand out in regard to other classic depictions of disability.

Fig. 2: untitled (Detail of the orthopedic workshop.), John Kiyaya, 2012

11 However, we do not know if there are any people at the URRC who wear such prosthetics. Possibly, these prosthetics are only produced for outsiders.

In classic depictions of disabled bodies in images, texts or music, usually a stereotypical depiction of a medical image of disability is analyzed and set against the social model of disability (for a definition of the social and medical model of disability see Shakespeare 2005, also Hughes and Mildner in this volume). Familiar depictions include portraits of people with a visible disability or depictions of a cheerful disabled person in a group of able-bodied people. Kiyaya's picture breaks with these classic depictions. It represents disability without the disabled person. Further, at first glance it is not clear from the image that it shows the production of a prosthetic. One must grapple with the image quite intently and look at the details in order to understand what exactly is being illustrated. Through Kiyaya's semidocumentary gaze on the workbench the disabled person becomes visible, however, he/she remains a referent. Because the photograph is at eye level, it does not entice to stare at the prosthetic, rather the chosen perspective allows a roaming gaze.

Tobin Siebers (2009) demands that the understanding of the disabled body, learned and perpetuated through classic depictions, be expanded upon. According to him, one cannot separate aesthetic and political judgements and subjects. The analysis of disabled bodies must be broadened to include other bodies. Focus should be put on the body politic, built structures, and works of art and move away from political and aesthetic uniformity. "Disability is everywhere in culture, as soon as the critic knows where to look – from Oedipus up until the Human Genome Project", argues Rosemarie Garland Thomson (Lutz 2003: 241). It is in this setting that Kiyaya's study of the prosthetic can be understood. It does not look at the disabled human body, but at an aid, which refers to disability. Beyond that, and this is remarkable concerning the work, it refers to the processualism of disability and the (possibly also limited) dimensions of the social model of disability. The space, in which the disabled body moves, is not only changed through the production of the prosthetic, but so is the disabled body.

On the way to...

The series “On the way to... ” is livelier and more colorful than the orthopedic series. In this case, Kiyaya photographed the school children on their way between the classrooms and workshops (possibly during their breaks). Perhaps they are done with their classes and going back to their rooms, or to the green areas that are to be found between the various building parts. Another difference to the orthopedic series is the fact that all the people in the pictures are all young and always in groups and support each other.

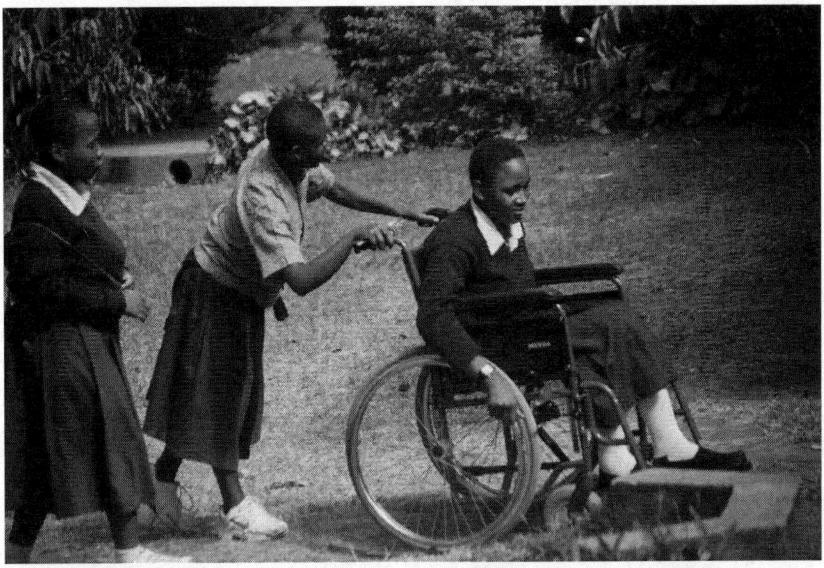

Fig. 3: untitled (Three schoolgirls from the URRC strolling around the premises.), John Kiyaya, 2012

The girls in the picture are pushing along their colleague/friend in her wheelchair and are engaged in rigorous conversation. Based on the girls' closeness, one can assume that they are not assisting each other because they are obliged to, but because they are friends or acquaintances on their mutual way (Fig. 3). We can see three girls in dark blue school uniforms moving from left to right. The girl in the middle is pushing another girl in a wheelchair, she is slightly bent forward and appears to be conversing with the girl in the wheelchair. The third girl casually has a bag hanging from her shoulder and is participating in the enjoyable conversation, the girl in the wheelchair is smiling. The triviality of this relaxed scene of three friends is emphasized by the perspective of the image. Kiyaya photographed them from the side, as if he were someone dwelling by the wayside who the trio slowly and calmly pass. Furthermore, the impaired mobility of the girl becomes trivial. Kiyaya did not photograph the disability, but the three girls who are on the way into their (possibly free) afternoon after their school day. Their identity as girls, friends, and especially schoolgirls (see the uniforms) are foregrounded. Their disability is not central, but supplementary. Kiyaya is able to stage the disability, but without dramatizing or romanticizing it. Through his gaze this profane, quotidian scene is given a believable documentation of a nonhierarchical participation in social interaction.

Portraits

Most images of the URRC-series that could be regarded portraits do not appear to be in portrait format, still the image that we wish to discuss here is in portrait format (see Fig. 4). Here, as in all of Kiyaya's other pictures, it is clear that no photo editing or lab techniques have been applied. The depth of field is remarkable. The high definition and picture sharpness from the grass in the foreground to the person in the middle ground and beyond suggests that the lens must have almost been closed completely. The almost pale green leaves in the foreground as well as the shadows behind the person and the bright reflections on her face show that a flashlight was used. The shadows and the sunlight in the background suggest that the photo was taken in the late afternoon. Given the deep depth of field, a 50mm prime lens and no zoom must have been used. For Kiyaya's praxis this means that he worked with a portable, rather small and handy camera, which allowed him to be close to the person that he portraits, just two to three meters away.

Fig. 4: untitled (Crouching woman in the park.), John Kiyaya, 2012

The picture shows a woman in full-length, squatting on the grass in a garden. The foreground (the grass and some fallen tree leaves) is in perfect definition and remarkably dominant (both in regard to light and space/quantity). In the background a path and flowerbeds are in dim sunlight and much weaker. In one sense the image is extremely symmetrical and well-balanced: The grass at the bottom of the foreground makes up one quarter of the space and forms a clear horizontal division to the middle ground, where the body and face take up two quarters, and the top section takes up another quarter. This ratio is broken up or confused if we consider the leaves in the top as part of the foreground. Grass and leaves, as elements of nature, form a stage setting. It is not only characterized by the three sections of foreground, middle ground and background, but Kiyaya creates a proscenium arch. He offers the spectator's eye a smooth gliding view onto the stage with the pale grass in the foreground as an empty proscenium, followed by the frontal full-length portrait with the body perfectly in the center of the middle ground and then from the backdrop towards the leaves or the proscenium arch. A swift gliding motion of the eye is proposed, finally leading from the proscenium arch to the face. The motion is supported by a golden ratio: The foreground and background are slightly shorter than the middle ground. The staging's highlight is the positioning of the leaves and the face. The leaves form a triangle on the top right, which clearly breaks the otherwise rather strict horizontal setup. The face and the leaves form a binary pair. The perfectly constructed stage setting allows these two elements to immediately turn the spectators' attention to the center of the portrait. And here something remarkable happens: The portrait is in immediate communication with the spectator. The young woman's agency is obvious. She chose her position, she offers eye contact, she smiles at herself and us.

There seems to be no doubt about the agency that the portrayed woman has. This is the result of a long process in which photographer and the portrayed woman got to know each other. The photograph was taken on Kiyaya's fourth day at the center. Kiyaya creates a portrait of a young woman whom the viewer might expect has a disability. However, the photo does not really give any information about the identity of the woman. She might be a worker or a patient. Her presumed disability remains invisible.

For many photographers, the caption or the title is closely linked to the image itself. Some would say that the image is incomplete without the text. For John Kiyaya, the captions are not important at all. One could take for granted that he, the photographer, would at least insist on mentioning the name of the crouching woman in the photograph, but he does not. He did not even write down the names of the people he portrayed. We would argue that he trusts his visual medium and also that he portrays humans as one, not as individuals.

At the hairdresser

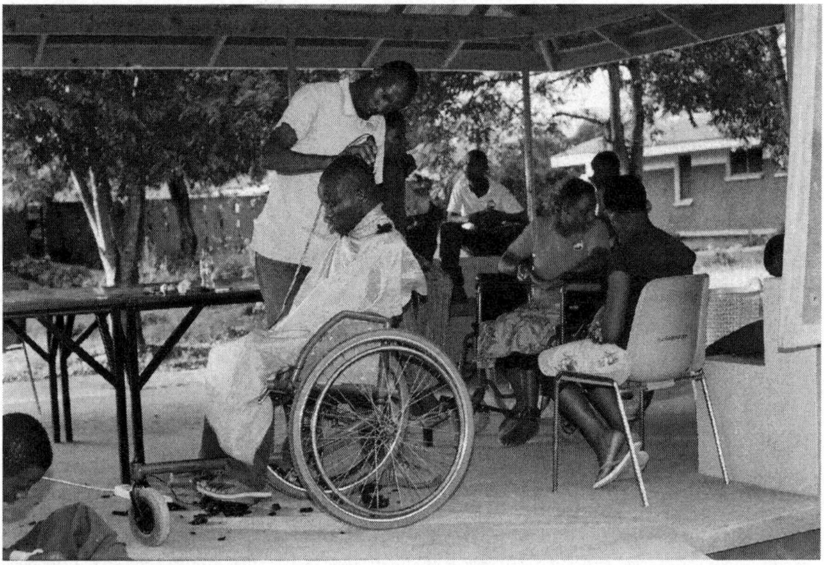

Fig. 5: untitled (Wheelchair user having his hair trimmed.), John Kiyaya, 2012

While Kiyaya's portraits captivate through their perspective and the staging of the background, his shots taken at the mobile workshop the door-to-door-hairdresser's set up one day, focus on the activity of the barbers and the apprentices as customers. On the selected photograph in landscape format we can see a young man having his head shaved. He is sitting in a wheelchair and looks downward toward his lap. The hairdresser is standing next to him and is cutting his hair with an electric razor. His head is nearly bald, fallen tufts of hair lie under his wheelchair. The whole scene takes place in the open. People, men and women, seemingly waiting their turn, linger on a type of roofed stage or terrace with tables and chairs.

The disability is visible through the wheelchair, but rather unobtrusively. The wheelchair is visible in the center of the image, but the gaze of the viewer is unavoidably drawn towards the shimmering lilac colored hairdresser's gown that the man is wearing: thus, it is the context that makes this picture so inclusive. Every customer usually sits when having his/her hair cut. The fact that this chair has wheels is a detail that has no significance. The fact that people with disabilities get their hair cut also does not seem surprising. The wheelchair user is being photographed while making use of a daily and (globally) familiar service without his disability making him special or even a victim of this depiction. Kiyaya manages to create the impression that he is looking from afar and accidentally touched upon this scene, just like in the beforementioned photograph series "On the way to... ".

When looking at the image in more detail, the wheelchair seems to reveal more about its user. It has a third wheel, which is connected to the pivot of both larger wheels and is mounted in front of the wheelchair between the legs of the driver. Thus, it appears that the wheelchair is a tricycle that can be operated with suspended handle, for better grip on uneven terrain. This detail unfolds an interesting symbolism, as the man's arms, if he has any, are not visible but indicated via the wheelchair. A closer look at the person's aid changes it from a metallic object to a transformable and possibly sensory assistive device.

In her article "The Wheelchair's Rhetoric – The Performance of Disability" Petra Kuppers describes, based on her review of the film "Murderball", what aesthetic added value a wheelchair can have:

> The scenes celebrating the materiality of the chair engaged me most. For many but not all wheelchair users the chair is an extension of their selves. Informal conversations with chair users bear out the importance of the chair's adornment and the acknowledgement of its status as a fashion accessory. For many users, frame colours, wheel decorations, and even the grunge look of heavy use are issues of aesthetics and self-definition going far beyond usability. Clearly, the wheelchair has rhetorical value in disability circles. This multivalence of potential readings of the chair in itself and of chair use and the narratives attached to specific chairs extends to the nondisabled world (Kuppers 2007: 86).

This rhetoric of the wheelchair appears in Kiyaya's picture, although very subtly. The positioning of the metallic mint-colored wheelchair at the center of the image contrasts to the vertical lines of the terrace's roof; it functions through its contrast. The wheelchair does not stay a medical aid, but becomes a fashionable accessory, whose owner is equally "glammed up" in the scene. This formal-aesthetic staging of the wheelchair most probably does not suffice to give a better understanding of the multivalence of the wheelchair to a nondisabled viewer, however, Kiyaya manages to disentangle it from its banalization as a "fetter". This is manifest in a number of formal and contentrelated aspects of the image. For example, there is a second person in a wheelchair, who we have not so far mentioned because the person is an implicit part of group. Just this implicitness or inconspicuousness is equally a remarkable pictorial statement. Furthermore, there is the staging of the colors in the picture. The wheelchair, the table's edge and the plastic basket all have the same color in an interplay with other color statements such as the flip-flops, the gown, etc. And finally, there is the wheelchair and his user: as the arms of the user are hidden, the suspended handle in the image also becomes a theme.

Conclusion

John Kiyaya, as is often said colloquially when talking of photographers who value the closeness to their images, is "always close". Initially, one might like to think that "close" refers to the people being portrayed. If we imagine his technique, he must be close to his central motif. This is a very conscious decision by the photographer concerning the camera, the lens, the aperture, and shutter speed, as well as his own position. A very specific style is visible: The compact camera with a small lens allows for depth of focus in large spaces and even to capture movements by hand. The space around the portrayed person can thus become the complete stage consisting of foreground, middle ground and background. A big show, so to speak. The theatre metaphor can be taken further because he does not portray individual subjects, but rather roles and types. Kiyaya does not create studies of the body or of individual people but portraits of agents, whose agency and actions he foregrounds. Actors showcase their roles. Kiyaya creates the stage and the connection to us, the audience. The spectacle is successful if we initially submerge ourselves in the spectacle and acknowledge that these people are genuine. At the same time, however, Kiyaya's photography leads us to the acknowledgement of our "staring". Kiyaya portraits actions, the portrayed persons enter his stage and show themselves as people.

However, Kiyaya does not use the technique of an ethnological visual inquiry, as described by Alain Ricard, because he is not sufficiently part of those he portrays. More likely, one could compare his technique to field research notes, which are manifest as not-yet analyzed observations. And even while he attempts to get up close, he is not dynamic in his photography. He does not interact with those he portrays, except if it concerns the staging of the image. He remains static and maintains the same distance, the same image detail, and the same perspective. If this stasis cannot speak for his dynamism as a photographer, at least it represents a common thread in his photographic works; the URRC series is no exception here. It does not seem important to Kiyaya that he is photographing people with disabilities. Rather, through his pictures he documents the triteness of disability and how one can live with it. The seemingly stoic semidocumentary method protects Kiyaya from engaging in "Othering" or even "enfreakment". Through his staged proximity, viewers are also brought closer to the people on the images. They can enter into a dialogue with them, without lapsing into an exploitative staring.

One should, however, note that this triteness exists in a staged setting. The URRC was created for people with disabilities. It is in itself already an exclusive space in which Kiyaya, in turn, took photos that propagate an inclusive attitude towards people with disabilities. Even if his images, merely through their authorship and the on-scene production, are part of the Tanzanian society, so are they an integrative, but not an inclusive part. It would therefore be highly interesting to see what images of disability Kiyaya would take outside such a specialist environment for disabled people.

List of Abbreviations

NGO	nongovernmental organization
URRC	Usa River Rehabilitation and Training Center
ELCT	Diocese of the Evangelical Lutheran Church in Tanzania

List of Figures

We want to thank the residents of the URRC, who allowed John Kiyaya to be their guest and to follow them through their daily routines. We will avoid individual naming because we do not see John Kiyaya's photographs as individual portraits, but as a documentation of types. Comparable to the photographs by August Sanders, Kiyaya carves out amalgams of individual and universal actions in his pictures.

References

African Loxo (no year): “John Kiyaya (Tanzania)”. Available at: www.africanloxo.com/john.kiyaya.htm (14.10.2016).

Bebey, Kidi (2105): Histoire d'un livre (2) John Kiyaya et Jean Rolin. Available at: http://xtrafrica.blogspot.de/2015/07/histoire-dun-livre-2-john-kiyaya-et.html (10.10.2016).

Campbell, Fiona Kumari (2009): Contours of ableism. The production of disability and abledness. 1. publ. Basingstoke.

Enwezor, Okwui (2006): Snap judgments. New positions in contemporary African photography; [in conjunction with the Exhibition "Snap Judgments: New Positions in Contemporary African Photography" organized by the International Center of Photography, New York … March 10 through May 28, 2006]. 1. ed. Göttingen.

Garland-Thomson, Rosemarie (2009): Staring. How we look. Oxford.

Grebe (2016): Fotografische Normalisierung: Zur sozio-medialen Konstruktion von Behinderung am Beispiel des Fotoarchivs der Stiftung Liebenau. Bielefeld.

H.B. (2008): “Albi. Photographies. John Kiyaya, portraitiste de villages africains”. Available at: www.ladepeche.fr/article/2008/05/13/453454-albi-photographies-john-kiyaya-portraitiste-de-villages-africains.html (14.10.2016).

Hutson, Chrisitane (2009): “Unverschämt. Wir im Spannungsfeld von Rassismus, Hetero-/ Sexismus und Ableism. Jenseits der Geschlechtergrenzen. Universität Hamburg. AG Queer Studies. Universität Hamburg, 13.05.2009“. Available at: www.zedis-ev-hochschule-hh.de/files/hutson_rassismus_sexismus.pdf (02.01.2018).

Kaaya, Elibariki/Wollner, Thomas (no year): The Usa River Rehabilitation and Training Center in Arusha, Tanzania. Available at: www.zoomtanzania.com/biz/The-Usa-River-Rehabilitation-and-Training-Center (11.11.2016).

Keita, Seydou/Magnin, André/Ryan, Kathy (2011): Seydou Keïta. Photographs; Bamako, Mali 1948-1963. 1. ed. Göttingen.

Kiyaya, John (2013): John Kiyaya. Mpiga picha Mtanzania na watu wa Ziwa Tanganyika. Tanzania Photographer and People of Lake Tanganyika. Dar es Salaam.

Kuppers, Petra (2007): The Wheelchair’s Rhetoric. The Performance of Disability, in: TDR/The Drama Review 51: 4, 80-88.

Latour, Bruno (2006): Drawing Things Together. Die Macht der unveränderlich mobilen Elemente. Bellinger, Andrea/Krieger David. Anthology. Ein einführendes Handbuch zur Akteur-Netzwerk-Theorie. Bielefeld, 259-307.

Lutz, Petra (ed.) (2003): Der [im-]perfekte Mensch. Metamorphosen von Normalität und Abweichung. (/Schriften des Deutschen Hygiene-Museums Dresden, 2). Köln..

Mthethwa, Zwelethu/Njami, Simon (2011): Zwelethu Mthethwa. Madrid.

Natermann, Diana M. (2017): „Koloniale Dokumente im Museum für Völkerkunde Hamburg. Afrika als Gegenstand der kolonialen Fotografie“. Available at: www.kolonialismus.uni-hamburg.de/koloniale-dokumente-im-museum-fuervoelkerkunde-hamburg-afrika-als-gegenstand-der-kolonialen-fotografie/ (01.01.2018).

Rolin, Jean (2007): "Au-delà du fleuve et sous les arbres". Available at: www.liberation.fr/grand-angle/2007/03/22/au-dela-du-fleuve-et-sous-les-arbres_88152 (14.10.2016).

Sander, August (1980): Menschen des 20. [zwanzigsten] Jahrhunderts. Portraitphotographien von 1892-1952. München.

Schneider, Arnd (2008): Three modes of experimentation with art and ethnography, in: Journal of the Royal Anthropological Institut (14), 171-194.

Shakespeare, Tom (2005): The disability reader. Social science perspectives. London.

Sidibé, Malick/Knape, Gunilla (2003): Malick Sidibé. Photographs. 1. ed. Göttingen.

Siebers, Tobin (2009): Zerbrochene Schönheit. Essays über Kunst, Ästhetik und Behinderung. Bielefeld.

Sontag, Susan (1995): Über Fotografie. 28. Aufl. Frankfurt am Main.

Spivak, Gayatri Chakravorty (1985): The Rani of Sirmur: an Essay in Reading the Archives. Barker, Francis. Europe and its others. Proceedings of the Essex Conference on the Sociology of Literature, July 1984, Bd.1. Colchester, 247-272.

Wolbring, Gregor (2009): Die Konvergenz der Governance von Wissenschaft und Technik mit der Governance des "Ableism", in: Technikfolgenabschätzung: Theorie und Praxis 18: 2, 30-35.

"When Making is Inclusive, Good Things Happen" – Really? Why *Diversity* is Problematic, and Why an *Inclusive* Practice Might Re-Politicize the Museum

Katharina Fink

"When making is inclusive, good things happen", insisted the recent, optimistic headline of an article in the magazine *Make:* (Dougherty 2016) that a friend had shared with me[1]. The author of the piece talked about the productive power of practicing *inclusion*[2] in the makers' DIY-movement. Its hands-on optimism and prefigurative vision of improvisation and owning the means of production read like a breath of fresh air in the often problem-centered academic discussion of *inclusion* in public institutions such as museums, obsessed with institutional structure and top-down solutions. So, going beyond the article: Does the same apply to the context of museums and art spaces? For curation and the day-to-day operations in the assemblage that is the museum? Do good things happen if we find informal and hands-on solutions for larger, structural issues?

I believe and will argue: Yes. Moreover, I will demonstrate citing a number of examples from recent practice that informal solutions and a certain DIY-spirit do help to open up the discourse that has lost its activist passion and power. While laden with heavy baggage, the terms *diversity*, *inclusion* and *accessibility*, I suggest, offer the chance to re-politicize the conversation around representation and the museum space, if they are developed to function as critical tools and "ports of entry"[3] for future connection.

---

1 Thanks to Prof. Michael Zöllner (Hof University) for sharing this link and starting a conversation.

2 The key terms of my discussion – diversity, inclusion, and accessibility – are written in italics in this chapter to mark their central position. Quotation marks are used if a historic case or specific case is referred to.

3 "Ports of Entry" is a festival curated by Emeka Alams, fashion designer and artist. It took place in the context of the annual festival "Grenzüberschreitungen" held at Iwalewahaus Bayreuth. The concept was the metaphorical weight of art practice in imagining and therefore creating "ports of entry" – a symbol which goes beyond a limited understanding of "access" and focusses on its potential of informality.

This, I believe, is very necessary because by mainstreaming *diversity* most of its zest and passion was lost. While proclaiming a diverse practice, privilege reigns on. So there is some homework to be done in order to make "good things happen", which can also mean working towards the irrelevance of talking about it. Marlon James recently put this very aptly in his text "Why I'm one talking about diversity" (James 2016, no page). In his contribution, he puts his finger on the problem I'd like to address by mixing discourse and empirical notes in order to present an ideally refreshing, hands-on cocktail: "It's not just that diversity, like tolerance is an outcome treated as a goal", James writes. "It is that we too often mistake discussing diversity with doing anything constructive about it." This echoes Sara Ahmed's point about the "Non-Performativity of Anti-Racism". In her paper of the same name, Ahmed identifies a disconnect of antiracist institutional programs and actions.

How I structure this chapter, following James' critique and drawing on Ahmed's points, is threefold. Firstly, I'd like to explicate my argument that *diversity* as a term in many contexts is more of a problem than a solution. I will prove this point by referring to a number of examples. Secondly, I will take a closer look at some of the examples to see what can be done to shift the discussion from *diversity* to *inclusion* as a more productive category. And finally, I suggest ways of re-entangling pragmatic and utopian strands of the debate, as a re-claiming of its performativity for museum work devoted to an ethics of accessibility – and towards its own, as James put it, "irrelevance".

In order to do so, I will focus on three stories that I noted down during my work and research in the field of museum practice, which show how the concept of diversity can be an obstacle to its own aims and how *inclusion* can be used in a productive way. All of my examples draw on encounters in the realm of the museum and exhibition spaces. In the course of the projects, which largely took place in South Africa, those spaces are turned into sites of "un/doing diversity"[4], as I will explain later. The first example from my notebook is taken from the set-up of an exhibition about photography of urban Apartheid in the 20th century. It takes a look behind the stage which shows the necessity of connecting narratives *on display* with the surrounding realities, a process that I have termed "synchroniz-

4 I draw on the concept of performativity used in order to analyze museum practice as used in my report (Fink 2015a; 2015b).

ing"[5]. In my second example, I illustrate the imaginative power of collective curating by what I termed "unlearning together" (Fink 2015b). And thirdly, as a kind of bold synthesis and speculative thought for museum practice devoted to an inclusive practice, I will draw on Bourriaud's concept of "relational aesthetics" (Bourriaud 2002), queer it and bind it together with my argument. If we as practitioners are willing to open all doors for a radically accessible, inclusive approach at all stages of museum practice, "good things" – or at least *better* things – will indeed happen.

Some conceptual remarks

The current debate around the limits of talking diversity and thereby re-enacting its underlying policies of difference in a kind of good-intentional annunciation is a prime opportunity to re-entangle discursive strands around art, representation and activism. The debate provides museums and related institutions with the chance to connect on a theoretical but also on a practical level. It is a unique discursive moment which requires following the guidelines that activist groups plotted out as well as the inclusion of queer and postcolonial theory into mainstream discourse. The inclusivity debate requires a radical rethinking of normalized practices. To try and work it out is work indeed, but it has to be playful in order to live up to the task that the discourse – largely driven by activists and now taken over by the political mainstream – around open and inclusive art and museum experiences reminds us to make cultural institutions public in the constitutive sense of the term. The shift from *diversity* to *inclusion*, and therefore *inclusivity,* is vital in that.

Some concepts have to be defined in order to avoid being imprecise. I argue from a discursive standpoint which takes *inclusion* as a critical intervention into the formation of power. An inclusive museum, art space or stage in this understanding is based on cultural models of dis/ability and access (see Garland Thomson 2004; Ha 2005). It does not follow the principle of unreflected addition but rather takes an inverted perspective throughout to dismount barriers at all stages of the process and to identity biases disguised as progress. This, though quite a lot of work in the first

5 "Synchronizing" is one of the terms used in the research project "Future Africa Visions in Time" (a BMBF-project, 2014-2017), used to express nodes in which multiples temporalities collapse into one.

place and not always comfortable, has a utopian quality to it, with "utopia" understood as a critical tool.[6]

This already explains the urge for a re-politization of museum practice that I argue for. *Inclusion*, as I outlined above, does not celebrate *diversity* uncritically. It in fact operates against a politics of multiculturalism (see, amongst others, Kros 2005) and integration in which oppressive patterns of enabling and disabling people reverberate. To make this happen, it is necessary to problematize *diversity* as a concept that often goes unreflected and still applauded – as Marlon James smirks regarding the cited "diversity-panels" of which, indeed, there are many. I suggest a turn away from diversity's normalized usage by referring to Foucault's notion of "problematizing", described as the

> […] development of a given into a question, this transformation of a group of obstacles and difficulties into problems to which the diverse solutions will attempt to produce a response, this is what constitutes the point of problematization and the specific work of thought. (Foucault 1984: 389)

And here is why it is important to "problematize" our discourses and tools of dismantling rehearsed privilege carefully: *Diversity* entails an understanding of the heterogeneous coexistence of somewhat homogeneous (cultural) entities and focusses for the most part on the past and present of the subjects declared diverse. In contrast, *inclusion* and *accessibility* allow for the un/doing of *set* futures as plotted out by a discourse of *diversity*. The direction, I argue, is different. The "not yet" (as Ernst Bloch phrased it in relation to the works of "concrete utopias") of inclusion is its driving engine.

This is a generalized statement which has to be examined carefully according to the precise context. Still, particularly in the context of South Africa, where two of my examples are situated, diversity and multiculturalism formed a politically desired and rhetorically enacted illusion of participation in the period dubbed "transition" – the 1996 "White Paper on Arts, Culture and Heritage" is an example of this. Other manifestations of such a trademarked, rainbow diversity, a relevant token in the tourism in-

---

6 Thanks to Nadine Siegert for her inspiring usage of Bloch's definition of utopia in her discussion of Angolan art (Siegert 2015) and to the introduction to the work of José Esteban Muñoz, "Cruising Utopia", by Henriette Gunkel, through which the critical potential of the utopian terminology for the inclusion-discussion became much clearer to me. And, as always, I am grateful for the discussions with Sarah Böllinger in the context of shared interests and our practical work regarding inclusive aesthetics.

dustry, are the re-naming of public holidays such as "Reconciliation Day"[7] or an "add-on"-approach (see, e.g. Witz/Minkley/Rassool 2000; Minkley 2010) to writing history, particularly in the field of exhibition-making. In the German context, the term "Migrationshintergrund"[8] is characteristic of such an approach to diversity. While it would be important to get away from focusing on the past and origin, paradoxically precisely those categories are discursively turned into registers of mapping out the future and access.

So, breaking it down further: what's the problem with *diversity*? Where is the discomfort with it being marketed as a radically transformative tool located? Since Clifford's reflections on the "contact zone", his adaptation of a concept coined by Marie Louise Pratt, the antagonistic potential of museum practice has been widely – and hotly – discussed. Besides these discussions not much happened. This is symptomatic of a connection severed by the logics of a popular academic practice, which Ahmed (2006) described as its "non-performativity." The divide between practice and theory, between speaking and acting, between the grassroots of everyday politics and social action and the discursive heights of professional academisms runs deep. This is something that has to be addressed seriously, particularly for the relevance of higher education in the future. In the museum field, this rift can often be experienced when, particularly in institutions dealing with cultural history, the displayed events, time, and context are clearly marked as unrelated to the surroundings of the very institutional practice.

Two more key terms relevant for my argument are still in need of clarification: institutions and *diversity*. I consider the institution as a set of practices. This shift to the micropolitics of representation enables us to

7 Reconciliation Day is the name introduced in 1995 for a public holiday annually celebrated on the 16th of December. The holiday has a layered history. First, the 16th of December was celebrated as the so-called "Dingaans Day" and stood for Afrikaaner-historiography. On this day, the "triumph" of the Voortrekkers against the Zulu army had been recalled. This holiday formed an important part of the arsenal building of Afrikaner Nationalism. From 1952 onwards, December 16th was dubbed the "Day of the Covenant" or "Day of the Vow". The day was also used for protest actions against White rule. In 1961, the Manifesto of uMkhonto weSizwe was launched on this day.

8 Which loosely translates to "migratory background" and is characteristic of the German debate on belonging and the nation state. On the consequences of a politics of "Migrationshintergrund" in the school system in the 2000s, see Allemann-Ghionda 2006.

discuss museum practice in the light of performativity (Bal 1998; Butler 2006; Fink 2015). I also draw on the concept of "critical diversity literacy" that Steyn (2007) suggested[9]. This is understood as looking at how "systems of privilege intersect, interlock, coconstruct and constitute each other" (Steyn 2010: 60). Indeed, *inclusion* and *diversity* are multilayered affairs with a history of exclusion and ethnicized and racialized undercurrents of monolithic understandings of culture.[10]

But actually, this is not new to the debate. In the 1980s, Audre Lorde put her finger on the shortcomings of such an approach, mapping out the elaborate task (indeed a "lifetime pursuit") of turning categories of oppression into "critical categories" (Arndt 2015).

> […] Too often, we pour the energy needed for recognizing and exploring difference into pretending those differences are insurmountable barriers, or that they do not exist at all. This results in a voluntary isolation, or false and treacherous connections. Either way, we do not develop tools for using human difference as a springboard for creative change within our lives. We speak not of human difference, but of human deviance. (Lorde 1984: 115)

Regarding the project of an open society, the very concept of *diversity* easily fools us into believing it represents just like that a tool for radical change and accessibility. But it only very rarely actually attacks constellations based on inequality. On the contrary, in most cases it rather aids in perpetuating their existence. Inclusion, on the other hand, focusses on looking closely at the system which has to be shared, and on the patterns of exclusions which hinder radical access up to now. This accounts not only for the context of disability, but also in other realms of societal restrictions of access.

Following this critique of *diversity*, "disintegration" could be a useful term for our discussion as well. Take for instance the recent "Desintegrationskongress"[11] about contemporary Jewish positions in Germany, held at Berlin's Maxim Gorki Theater. Max Czollek, organizer alongside Sasha Marianna Salzmann, found words for the subtle distinction between proclaimed top-down diversity versus the process of an active group and so-

---

9 From 2019 onwards, I have had the honor to work with Prof. Melissa Steyn and her team in the Centre for Diversity Studies (WiCDS) as an associated researcher and in the context of a DAAD-sponsored short term lectureship (2019/2020) at the University of the Witwatersrand in Johannesburg/South Africa. This has considerably deepened my understanding of the potential of "diversity".

10 See also Steve Vertovec's concept of "super-diversity" (Vertovec 2007).

11 Compare the archived program of the Gorki Theatre Berlin, available at: https://issuu.com/maximgorkitheater/docs/gorki_zeitung10_v7 (01.12.2016).

ciety constituting itself: "This is not about real-life diversity. We meet on a political level, it's about mind work for a collective constituting itself."[12] This is an important intervention into the debate around contemporary societies, beyond a flattening, nondiscursive and disputable "diversity". Foucault, I guess, would love this. Eventually, *accessibility*, understood as physical access to museum spaces, but also access to the 'means of production' of a narrative on display, is key. This access never arrives as a perfectly developed change in society but emerges as a process of mutual learning guided by the spirit of a "common cause"– such as striving for a democratic society defined by equal access and opportunities for all. In the work of Leela Gandhi this is framed as "moral imperfectionism", which she describes vehemently as "defending democracy as a shared art of living on the other side of perfection" and which "mounts a postcolonial appeal for an ethics of becoming common" (Gandhi 2014: 16). It is indeed about the attitude and passion to practice a "becoming common", a future performed in the present.

So, what I want to establish in this conversation is a shift towards conceptualizing and – most importantly – implementing an inclusive practice as a beautiful, dangerous tool of "connecting" while addressing privilege in the light of a shared human experience. This is by all means a political act, understood as the space of understanding oneself and society in relation to other forms of life, the world, resources etc. Changing the politically rehearsed claim of a stable, one-off diversity concept into a quest for inclusive societies helps us to enthusiastically develop a roadmap for a "common cause".

Some examples from the field of museum practice will outline what this means in the everyday practice of exhibition-making, and where the beauty of "developing tools" (Lorde 1980) or doing "mind work" (Czollek 2016) resides. I follow this with a paragraph on "aesthetics of relation" that will merge my arguments with art theory. Below I look at examples

---

12 Czollek, Max (2016), cited in the newspaper article Lühmann, Hannah (2016): "Wenn sich deutsche Juden zur Desintegration treffen", in: Die Welt, 11.05.2016, available at: www.welt.de/kultur/article155260858/Wenn-sich-deutsche-Juden-zur-Desintegration-treffen.html. Also recommendable concerning this debate is Elmenthaler, Sophie (2016): "Süß ist nur Rache", in: Der Freitag, 25.05.2016, available at: www.freitag.de/autoren/rotebrezel/suess-ist-nur-rache, both last access: 01.12.2016. The term machloket, translatable as disputability, seems, at least following the media debate around the congress, important in his and Sasha Marianna Salzmann's concept of radical diversity as a process of "contact", to relate back to Clifford.

from my recent practice in order to try and map out the markers of a fruitful usage of diversity and inclusion as starting points for a museum practice of the future with an emphasis on success and ideas. I will also try to be frank and open about failures and underlying challenges. I will draw on conceptual nodes in order to bundle the practice-based examples into a statement for further discussion.

Example I: "We're not in a township here": Synchronizing museum communication

One of my earliest and most revealing experiences about the superficiality of the business of representations in the context of "cultural diversity" happened when I was working with a South African museum devoted to the recent history of segregation and the disenfranchising force of Apartheid. As usual, the real work happens before the show begins, in the back end of the exhibition. During the set-up for a show dealing with the history of Forced Removals, the white[13] director was appalled at the conversation between staff members during the mounting of images and muttered under her breath: "We're not in a township here." For the director, this statement about the exclusively Black[14] colleagues was by no means in contrast to the motivation and the images of the show, which celebrated past *diversity* and the resilience of people living in nonracial constellations during Apartheid in urban South Africa, using framed black and white photographs and oral history accounts. The comment was made side-ways and en passant. It was not intended to be public, but to create a *commonality* of whiteness via citing a derogatory stereotype of a loud, unruly township life. It fell in line with other remarks in the context of museum practice dealing with cultural history, where in quite a number of cases a yawning abyss between display and message awaits. Often, the connections between a narrative on display and its seeping into the present are not drawn/carved out and made visible, which results in at times a bizarre and paradoxical disconnect, particularly around the history of Apartheid. Examples for this are manifold and can mean the presentation of exhibition contents exclusively in a colonial language, in this case being the

13 It is relevant to mention this identification of staff here to make the dimension of the disconnect and the dimension of infringement understandable.

14 See the comment above.

English language). It can also mean the resistance to tell history in an accessible way that goes beyond a multiculturalism that perpetuates difference in its flat understanding: Telling histories as separate and – consciously or unconsciously – not exploring the overlaps and the twilight zones, the entangled histories.

A nearly allegoric image for this is a scene I wrote about in an earlier thesis on the Apartheid Museum in Johannesburg: Susan Matamela, one of the museum's cleaning staff, from Pimville/Soweto, wiping a glass case filled with images and objects that, from the museum's narrative aim at representing lives in a histioric, therefore "past" Soweto. In her narration, however, the sites and sights, living conditions and structures, are very contemporary items of her lived, quotidian experience.[15] This disconnect between the story and the surrounding societal reality, understood as the embodied everyday life experienced by people, is not necessarily intentionally glaring. On the contrary, it is often made with good intentions. What it shows, though, is a disconnect on several levels, among which to me the chrono-political[16] one is the most important. It also represents a missed opportunity: Postcolonial museology working in the spirit of inclusion should be willing to ask: Does the story I tell with the object arrangements exclude relevant narratives for the very context? This is where – and why – inclusive museum work is strictly postcolonial.

The disconnection, of which the example cited is but one instance, allows for reflection and critique about this aesthetic and narrative of dismembering.[17] An approach to exhibition-making as a practice embedded in society has to consist of a multiplicity of perspectives on a shared, "common cause". Particularly but not exclusively outreach programs and the educational aspirations of an open approach to discussing representational processes are key. As important is the in-reach and the implementation of notions of accessibility and inclusivity within the own, everyday

---

15 Unpublished Magistra-thesis, Katharina Fink 2007, "The Museum as a Contact Zone? The Apartheid Museum in Johannesburg", University of Tübingen, Germany.

16 Thanks to my colleagues at the Bayreuth Academy of Advanced African Studies for the great discussions on the politics of time.

17 Compare Toni Morrison's novels, Ngũgĩ wa Thiongo's book "Re-Membering Africa" (2009) as well as the conversation "Museum. Raum. Geschichte: Neue Orte politischer Tektonik Ein virtueller Gedankenaustausch zwischen Belinda Kazeem, Nicola Lauré al-Samarai und Peggy Piesche", available at: http://eipcp.net/transversal/0708/kazeemetal/de (01.12.2016), or Kazeem, al-Samarai/Piesche 2009.

practice. This goes beyond the promises of diversity, as a brief look at a less privileged part of the audience will show.

Example II: Happy 90th birthday, Bloke!

Over the past seven years, I have had the pleasure to continuously work with young wo_men of the SoFireTown Crew, a youth organization from Sophiatown, Johannesburg. The realities of young people growing up in the city from unprivileged families differ starkly for the most part from the images of what their lives as so-called "born frees" (as the generation born after the formal departure from the Apartheid regime is called) should look like. Unemployment and structural inequality and inaccessibility are continuous factors in their lives as the *#mustfall*-movement[18] vividly highlights. In the life of young continuously disadvantaged people in South Africa, the legacies of past constructions of racialized thought and practice, colonial patterns of defining and 'doing' gender and race, continuing structural imbalances, the economic sector's resistance against transformation proper and the newly established *glass ceiling* for non-party members intersects with the hunger of young people to make the world their own, and the self-imagination of becoming *someone*. Young people, in their ways inspired by global pop culture, use the cultural archive of Sophiatown, by which I mean the narratives around a place in the shape of a largely accepted myth. They irreverently take out fragments of what I dub "heritage dispositive" (Fink 2015), a constellation which administers the past by the interrelation of modes of saying and acting. They remix, play, re-configure the cultural significations in their present, thereby complicating and re-entangling the narratives of the past and interfering with an intended linear logic of the future driven by visions of the nation state. In the case of South Africa, this is the so-called Post-Apartheid state.

William "Bloke" Modisane, an important journalist and author from Sophiatown/South Africa was, as most of his generation, forced into exile in order to live his life as a writer. He is one of the key authors of the so-called DRUM Decade from the early 1950s onwards. While never being in line with the official politics of the ANC in his time, his biography re-

18 #mustfall/#fallism is an inclusive term for a series of interrelated struggles in South Africa. The critique of the neoliberal, impermeable social matrix in South Africa started off as a critique of students at the University of Cape Town again student fees.

sists alignment with current politics of the ANC. In fact, what Modisane had plotted out as a future South Africa in his times as a young man is in parts what social movements such as #mustfall address today. His future vision for an inclusive society not tailored along the patterns of race as well as addressing the unequal distribution of land has not been achieved. This is where young people start off. In the exhibition and cultural project "(In) A Way Back Home", we[19] facilitated the move of the literary estate of the late William "Bloke" Modisane from Germany to South Africa, curating ongoing cultural encounters around the question of what constitutes a "home". Working together on this, by referring to narrated visions of the future by an artist from the 1950s, shows the danger of *diversity* which Modisane himself had warned about – when cultural recognition of "otherness" framed in terms of Apartheid, in the language of *race*, is continuously produced. We cooperated with the National Archives of South Africa but mostly tried to pull out the relevance of the writer's thoughts for a global present, while being conscious of the very context in which we interpreted his work anew.

Our point of entry was a fictive 90th birthday party for Bloke Modisane, which we celebrated at the African Freedom Station in Johannesburg, a club close to the place where Modisane was born 90 years earlier into a society transforming segregation established over centuries into consolidated Apartheid. We put up colorful banners, decorated tables, served drinks and played music, that we imagine he would have played to entertain guests, while giving impromptu tours of the estate material. This certainly was not the best way to do so, but we tried, no one was hurt, it was fun and it raised attention – more importantly, it insisted on the presence of a writer who had been writing about the dangers of *diversity* along the lines of multiculturalism half a decade ago.

A key decision we as a collective had to take was how to remember playfulness and fiction in the life of a story-maker, an author who lived by and for his words. We were sure that we needed to open up the questions Modisane, who appears as a complex, complicated personality himself, had left for us in a manner in which everyone can respond to the main concern of a writer long departed – e.g. how can we live together beyond

19 I refer to a group of youth activist and myself here as "we". I am indebted to Kabelo Tselapedi, Sipho Ndlovu, Steve Motshiping, Billy Langa and Mbali Zwane. We thank Peter Lehlohonolo Makurube for advice and enthusiasm, and Steve Kwena Mokwena for providing the space to enact our dreams. Sanza Sandile has been encouraging the ongoing project ever since.

race – if s_he wants to. An inclusive, open approach means self-representation, which is key in fractured societies where belonging is largely achieved by side-stepping the official initiatives, through nonofficial, noninstitutional grassroots and art projects. Spaces and opportunities for establishing new modes of belonging and unlearning have to be created, spaces in which representation in terms of diversity makes room for an "understanding of history as possibility rather than determination" (Freire 1992: 91-92) to be dreamt into being and enacted.[20] The project around the legacy of Bloke Modisane for today's youth is an example of this. To defend imagination and dreaming as a useful technique of what other realities featuring "good things" could be like, against the pragmatic acceptance sought by youth, is an act of self-determination in itself, both synchronizing and imaginative (further reading see Fink 2015b).

Example III: Collective curating as inherently inclusive practice

In 2010, I worked in cooperation with colleagues from the University of Johannesburg and Johannesburg citizens on a project devoted to challenging master representations of the suburb of Sophiatown, an iconically charged and symbolically important space throughout the pre-Apartheid and Apartheid regimes as well as the democratic Republic of post-1994 (Fink 2015a, 2015b). The collective curatorial endeavor was the outcome of a "Photo-Voice"-project, designed to uncover and make visible alternative perspectives on an overdetermined suburb and mythologically charged place. After a months-long process of taking and discussing photographs, the group decided it would be a good idea to show selected photography from the various sets. The curatorial process, facilitated by art activist Jennifer van den Bussche[21] and me, was a slow and intense, at times tedious one. In a long series of meetings, criteria for the selection of images were defined. One of them was that no image should harm the feelings of members of the community. For example, a picture that dealt

20 From 2019 onwards, a project curated by the same group of people stands emblematically for this: The Sophiatown Arts Festival, an act of "community curating", as the project description reads. See: www.sophiatownartsfestival.co.za. (last access 05.04.2020).

21 See Jennifer van den Bussche's work in Diepslot and other places: www.stickysituations.org (01.05.2017).

with a controversial bus accident in a then "white" suburb during Apartheid days was considered "too harmful" to be put in a public space.

To showcase the multiple shapes and the synchronicity of life beyond the normalized narrative of *diversity* was very important for the participants: showing alternative and lesser-known images of spaces which served as shared spaces. Discussion after discussion led the group of people to a selection of images, the writing of explanatory notes and invitations. In this project, differences were discussed in terms of particular histories, the recent past of separation and the effects of these policies on the present. The guiding questions of the project – part of a larger project on community life in the suburb – were: How do we want to live together in the future; how can we find images and words for shared experiences and spaces; and how does the "we" that we are operating with constitute itself? The discussions in the process of curation mirrored what Sternfeld following Clifford proposed:

> [By condensing Clifford and Mouffe], it becomes possible to describe our processes with the idea of an 'agonistic conflict zone' as one that is open and decidedly partisan at the same time. In the agonistic contact zone it is not a matter of 'socially acceptable speaking', but rather of the possibility for all those involved to take a position. Our position here is therefore not exclusionary, but also not at all neutral, but rather dissentual and convincing. (Sternfeld 2011, no page)

Regarding the location of the show, people were outspoken about a "no-go area" for their exhibition: the museum. It was obvious to everyone involved that nobody would go to a museum if they did not have to. The selected images were blown up to A3-size and stuck to boards, which had been painted in a light blue in the garden of one of the participants. After the color had dried, they were, also as a collective task, positioned in a public space, at a shopping mall's parking lot, being the most inclusive space in terms of accessibility at that time. In contrast to the local museum, the place was even wheelchair accessible and public in the sense that it is normal for people to go there, not burdened with elitist expectations.

On the day of the opening, visitors indeed poured into the square – not to see the show in the first place, but rather to do their Saturday morning shopping. Yet, when finding themselves confronted with images and text from their everyday surroundings while doing their weekend shopping, people embraced the situation. They stopped, looked, chatted, exchanged stories and identified sites of shared experiences within their suburb. These exchanges drastically differed from their experiences with museums. Here, the multiplicity of possible stories and the accessibility of the techniques of display achieved what no indoors-museum practice would have achieved on this morning. The photos on display transformed "(the)given into a question", which is how Foucault defined "problematizing", as the conversations on the very day showed. The project challenged the notion of a finite display of a diverse life. On the contrary, it stressed the unrepresentability (Sternfeld 2010) of a singular story and the need for an ongoing discussion and development of tools for dismantling *diversity*.

In order to stress that the need for connectivity is a global request made to museums, allow for a discursive change of scene. I jump to Germany. In 2016, I worked with friends and the Jewish community in a small Bavarian town on the life of a largely forgotten poet from Bayreuth, Germany: Hilde Marx (1911-1986). As the only child of a family of upper middle-class entrepreneurs, Marx was a successful writer already at a young age. Having completed her A-levels, she left for Berlin to study journalism and literature from winter term 1931 onwards. This rush of freedom, her life as a single woman in the exhilarating city of Berlin, promising more excitement and grander opportunities than her beloved Bayreuth[22], turned out to be a short-lived affair. In 1933, studying at university became more and more difficult for Jewish students and Hilde Marx was forced to quit her studies. Now limited to publishing and speaking in formats marked "Jewish", the young woman created a remarkable career for herself out of a dire situation. She briefly migrated to Prague from where she managed to emigrate to the United States of America. Arriving in 1938 in New York City, she faced the fate of many people arriving from all walks of life in Europe right now: Alone, not knowing the language, and no networks in comparison to the ones at home. Still, she made a decent career as a female writer and public speaker. Only once did she return to the city of her childhood. When she left Bayreuth for the last time, she knew that the term home/*Heimat* did not hold any meaning for her anymore.

In order to make this life's journey, hidden in the archives, visible and open to links with the present, we designed an exhibition which deliberately focused on the connectivity of the story we were telling: A young woman, who has lost the security of a home and has to start again from scratch. Also, a woman with an outspoken life that holds complicated decisions and political positions — one that caused dissensus in the curatorial team. Like her praise-poetry for the founding of the state of Israel, which she referred to a "birth" – which today has to be discussed in its historical context, yet still considering its implications. We deliberately invited people who are currently living through similar situations of seeking

22 See her poem "Brief an eine Stadt", Marx (1934/2016).

refuge to take part in the exhibition-as-process – contemporary neighbours in Bayreuth, with experiences of having lost their homes in Afghanistan and Syria.

This was a great experience for all sides involved – a humbling journey, not always joyful, at times ripe with conflicts, at times failing to live up to the complexity of the situation and biographies, one time, as I have to admit when re-assessing the project in writing this, shying away from a severe confrontation – for the Israelitische Kultusgemeinde, the family of Hilde Marx, and the organizers in particular[23] – to work together on making the story an inclusive and inviting one, in which everyone was invited to participate. The exhibition focused on telling the single historic experience of the Shoah in an accessible way. It told the story of a survivor, a self-conscious, independent woman who looked beyond her own experiences of exclusion and suffering in order to create an inclusive tale against all violations of human rights. This translated especially into the educational and arts programs of the exhibition. Manape Shogole, spoken word poet from Johannesburg, worked on[24] the themes of Hilde Marx from the point of view of a young woman writing from an African perspective. Together with people from all over the world, we interpreted the persecutions of the 1930s and 1940s from a contemporary perspective. Speaking of Aleppo and Damascus with a similar fondness and nostalgia as Hilde Marx had expressed for her hometown Bayreuth and her life in Germany, the participants who had been forced to leave their hometowns showed the resilience of young people on the move today. It was crucial to invite people to talk about their very experiences and thereby create the exhibition's content, its storyline, which is a fluid one with a core narrative. This act is a piece of poetry in itself, created by a – fragile, temporary, perhaps unstable – community of shared interest. Only by this, an at times disputatious process of argument, of to and fro, listening and speaking to each other in spaces which are marked as "representational", can we regain the museum as a powerful space for the difficulties of today's society. It is only possible together. By the establishment of a space for the exchange of thoughts, questions, and experiences we can create an entry point for an intensified dealing with racism and anti-Semitism, which is extremely important in the current political landscape. Racism cannot be grasped as a

23 More details on the project available at: www.hilde-marx.de (01.12.2016).

24 At the invitation of the Bayreuth Academy of Advanced African Studies, University of Bayreuth.

non-structural phenomenon, as Ahmed's argument on the "non-performativity" of institutional work demonstrates. Neither can anti-Semitism be allowed to be treated as a "historical" issue. Projects like the dealing with the life of Hilde Marx help to update stories from the past, from (proto-) National Socialist Germany of the 1920s to the 1940s into the present and make them impossible options for the future.

I cited these three brief examples from South Africa and Germany to emphasize the following point: Inclusive museum work, using participatory tools, advocates the relational aspects of making single stories part of a larger narrative of potentiality. As such, it is a helpful utopian tool not only in enriching the discussion around whose stories are being told in spaces considered "non-public" or still as inaccessible because of invisible rigid barriers. The process of critically curating diverse perspectives should not be understood as placing side-by-side "different" perspectives. In the Sophiatown-related Photo Voice project, the images and their stories challenge the notion of a single narrative by making plausible its "danger" (Chimamanda Ngozi Adichie 2009). The process of taking pictures, discussing, and arranging them revealed the powerful dispositive of trademarking a rich and complex, enmeshed history into the black-and-white singularity of a happy, marketable poster version of a very complicated society with many "unpacified ghosts" (Murphy 2011). *Inclusivity*, understood in an intersectional way and much more than mere than a flat understanding of *diversity*, provides the tool for dissecting why it is that some stories are seen to matter, and why some are ignored when they raise a voice of their own – an angry, "unpacified", demanding voice.

Sharpening the tools: Practicing aesthetics of relation

Though it might read as a bit of an abrupt change, I want to turn to a discursive moment about aesthetic theory to deepen the discussion. Nicolas Bourriaud, art theoretician, in the 2000s claimed a "relational aesthetic" that stepped aside from art as a holistic, societally disconnected regime. Relational aesthetics, meaning "[a] set of artistic practices which take as their theoretical and practical point of departure the whole of human relations and their social context, rather than an independent and private space" (Bourriaud 2002: 113), is ranked high in the discursive charts, though often considered airy, imprecise and a characteristic expression of insubstantial art hipsterism. Definitely, these critiques have a point. Indeed, reading the work, the by now retro-hipster tone is at times hard to bear. Yet, still, I believe that the undisciplined translation to a different field might support the re-entangling of experience, preparation, and execution of creative action. Departing from this art-world-based discussion, the discussion around inclusive art and museum practice gains substance from this. As the examples cited above show, putting "relations" into the focus of curatorial practice and dismantling *diversity* manifests as qualitative, intellectual and artistic gain. It allows to see what Garland-Thomson stressed as the analytic capacity of problematizing diversity much clearer, and thereby unmasks the notorious notion of the "norm" because "[t]he disability system excludes the kinds of bodily forms, functions, impairments, changes, or ambiguities that call into question our cultural fantasy of the body as a neutral, compliant instrument of some transcendent will" (Garland-Thomson 2004: 77).

So, I suggest conceptualizing and implementing inclusion in an open understanding as a tool to analyze intersectional power relations. In the exhibition context, this works towards a practice which does not only begin to matter when the exhibition is up and running, and the visitors are pouring in, but as a technique, an ethos, and an aesthetics of relation which works on many layers, such as understanding the pattern of "socially disabling" people not meeting the "cultural fantasy" (Garland-Thomson 2004: 77) of the norm. This requires an inward look at our own profession as well: Though proclaiming otherwise, the chasm between professional and nonprofessional museum activities runs deep.

Concluding: The radical power of all that jazz

As the hushed voices in a museum setup, conversations on a parking lot, as well as an excursion into art speech showed: *An inclusive approach to curating and discussing*, rather than one celebrating *diversity*, requires moving beyond attesting the *status quo*, often operating along lines of difference set by regimes which form the recent past. In fact, it requires claiming the *beyond*, with all its postcolonial, queer, utopian and collective connotations. In the case of South Africa, the discourse around "diversity" and multiculturalism, in its uncritical form, re-works the trenches of race, often in an affirming manner. Going beyond this requires imagining what an equal and just society could look like with "inclusion" as a tool directed to many sides: Analytical of the current situation, projecting into a future, acknowledging situations of grown dispossession and disabling structures. What we can achieve with a multilayered approach –

above, I sketched out three of the manifold layers of connecting narrative and surroundings, opening space for contradiction, clash and wonder, and addressing privilege – is to professionally support people, visitors, friends and collaborators in the tackling of assumed fixed meanings not only to "excel in admiration"[25] but also to "excel in questioning and disagreement". Thinking and enacting inclusive institutions as a "gain" for all of us requires an understanding of a shared preciousness of life. Inclusive institutions are the goal and the imperfect solutions and informal approaches on the way there are pit stops for the soul on the journey to "become common". The examples discussed as *synchronizing* and *collective* curating showed that leaving a major narrative in place and not challenging the sole power position of curators, directors and people in the same peer group does not help. *Diversity limited* needs to be dismantled. An open understanding of an inclusive practice has to take its place; one that celebrates the glitter and political sparkle that difference can mean while busy dissecting politics of inequality. With that, there's more justice, more joy; and a deeper experience for everyone involved. Or, as the optimistic headline we departed from suggested: When performing is inclusive, good things might indeed happen.

List of Abbreviations

ANC	African National Congress
BMBF	Bundesministerium für Bildung und Forschung (Federal Ministry of Education and Research in Germany)

References

Allemann-Ghionda, Cristina (2006): Klasse, Gender oder Ethnie? Zum Bildungserfolg von Schüler/innen mit Migrationshintergrund. Von der Defizitperspektive zur Ressourcenorientierung, in: Zeitschrift für Pädagogik 52:3, 350-362.

Bal, Mieke/Crewe, Jonathan V./Spitzer, Leo (1999): Acts of Memory: Cultural Recall in the Present. Hanover.

Bloch, Ernst (1988): The Utopian Function of Art and Literature. Cambridge.

25 As David Rieff writes about his mother Susan Sontag's devotion to aesthetic experiences in his introduction to his edition of Susan Sontag's essay under the title "At the same time" (2013: 15): "She excelled in admiration".

Bourriaud, Nicolas (2002): Relational Aesthetics. Dijon.

Butler, Judith (2006): Hass spricht. Zur Politik des Performativen. Frankfurt am Main.

Ciardha, Éammon Ó/Vojvoda, Gabriela (2015): Politics of Identity in Post-Conflict States: The Bosnian and Irish Experience. London.

Dougherty, Dale (2016): "When Making Is Inclusive, Good Things Happen." Available at: www.makezine.com/2016/03/11/fab-dream-making-inclusive-good-things-happen/ (12.01.2016).

Fink, Katharina (2015a): Un-doing Sophiatown. Contemporary Reverberations of a myth and in a suburb. Bayreuth.

Fink, Katharina (2015b): Close-up Sophiatown: Transnational Perspectives on Past, Present and Future of an Iconic Suburb, in: African Studies 74:1, 10-25.

Foucault, Michel (1977): The Confession of the Flesh. Gordon, Colin (1980). Power/Knowledge Selected Interviews and Other Writings. New York, 194-228.

Foucault, Michel (1984): Polemics, Politics and Problematizations: An interview conducted by Paul Rabinow in May 1984. Available at: https://foucault.info/doc/foucault/interview-html (12.12.2016).

Gandhi, Leela (2014): The Common Cause. Postcolonial Ethics and the Practice of Democracy, 1900-1955. Chicago.

Garland-Thomson, Rosemarie (2004): Integrating Disability, Transforming Feminist Theory, in: Smith/Bonnie G./Hutchinson, Beth. Gendering Disability, New Brunswick, 73-106.

Ha, Kien Nghi (2005): Hype um Hybridität. Kultureller Differenzkonsum und postmoderne Verwertungstechniken im Spätkapitalismus. Bielefeld.

James, Marlon (2016): "Why I'm done talking about diversity. Or, why we should try an all-White diversity panel". Available at: http://lithub.com/marlon-james-why-im-done-talking-about-diversity/# (12.01.2016).

Kazeem, Belinda/ Lauré al-Samarai, Nicola/ Piesche, Peggy (2009): Museum, Raum, Geschichte: Neue Orte politischer Tektonik. Kazeem, Belinda/ Martinz-Turek, Charlotte/Sternfeld, Nora. Das Unbehagen im Museum. Postkoloniale Museologien. Vienna, 167-184.

Kros, Cynthia (2005): Secularity in a world 'torn by difference': A consideration of the French headscarf affair from South Africa, in: Politikon South African Journal of Political Studies 32: 1, 1-16.

Latour, Bruno (2005) From Realpolitik to Dingpolitik: or how to make things public. Latour, Bruno/Weibel, Peter. Making things public: atmospheres of democracy. Cambridge, 14-41.

Lorde, Audre (1984): Sister Outsider. New York.

Marx, Hilde (1934/2016): Brief an eine Stadt. Fink, Katharina. Dreiklang/Im Vers Gefangen. Bayreuth, 50.

Muñoz, José E. (2009): Cruising Utopia: The Then and There of Queer Futurity. New York.

Murphy, Fiona (2011): Archives of Sorrow: An Exploration of Australia's Stolen Generations and their Journey into the Past, in: History and Anthropology, 22: 4, 481-495.

Sontag, Susan (2013): At the Same Time. London and New York.

Steyn, Melissa (2010): Critical Diversity Literacy: Diversity Awareness in twelve South African Organisations, in: Innovative Issues and Approaches in Social Sciences, 3:3, 50-83.

Sternfeld, Nora (2010): "Unglamorous Tasks: What Can Education Learn from its Political Traditions?". Available at: www.e-flux.com/journal/14/61302/unglamorous-tasks-what-can-education-learn-from-its-political-traditions/ (01.05.2017)

Sternfeld, Nora (2011): "Memorial Sites as Contact Zones. Cultures of Memory in a Shared/Divided Present". Available at: http://eipcp.net/policies/sternfeld/en (12.12.2016).

Vertovec, Sven (2007): Super-diversity and its implications, in: Ethnic and Racial Studies, 30: 6, 1024-1054.

Witz, Leslie (2010): Museums, Histories and the Dilemmas of Change in Post-Apartheid South Africa, in: University of Michigan Working Papers in Museum Studies 3.

Witz, Leslie/Rassool, Ciraj/Minkley, Gary (2000) The Boer War, museums and Ratanga Junction, the wildest place in Africa: public history in South Africa in the 1990s, in: BAB Working Paper (2), 1-34.

Intermezzo towards Experience

In the Dead of Night

Kevin Mwachiro

As she sleeps,
I dream of you, lying next to me
Your stillness my security
Your warmth my cloak
Your gentle breaths, lull
Unbeknown to you, my kisses butterfly
Tingles.
But, she sleeps besides me.
Not you.

His eyes wide shut again
These sleepless nights
The only constant
Our sheets barren
For love doesn't live here anymore
Now strangers we endure the night
Society enslaves
Be you!

As she sleeps,
I let myself dream
Our dawns and dusks united
Where we are fearless, full and free
Our passion blazes
Your touch lights a fire
I am phoenix
Loved by you.

The stars offer no rest
For we bed with our facade
And yet this our truth
Our bodies are wanderers
We sheet our nakedness
My touch now my lover
Souls parched
Duped into a lie
I pity you.

As she sleeps
I long for your arms
To drape my night
Spooned.
This must be eternity
Our forbidden now normal
We dream.
I am you.

Words have fled this prison
We fret
Fighting in silence
Scared that truth will free us of us
Wasted nights
I am too petrified to sleep
For I will dream of lovers
Who aren't you.

Diversity Within

Some Thoughts on Deaf Diversity in Uganda

Carsten Mildner

This contribution explores the diversity of what it means to be deaf in Uganda. I will argue that global concepts of Deaf Culture are as insufficient to understand the complexity of deaf lives in Uganda as are generalized perspectives of medical and social models of disability. Instead I wish to highlight the variations of deaf experience and suggest that being deaf varies from individual to individual. I will reference interviews, conversations and participant observation I conducted during two exploratory research trips to Kampala in winter 2014/2015 (three weeks) and summer 2015 (six weeks). Given the short research period, my insights have no claim of completion or broader validity. With this contribution, however, I wish to shed some light on the complexity of deaf experience in Uganda and raise some questions for future inquiry (see also Mugeere et al. 2015). Three short empirical accounts emphasize the social embeddedness of phenomena and experiences associated with deafness: What being deaf means for the individual is not only highly dependent on the broader and immediate social contexts but also on the individual physiological experience. I will close with a reflection of the possibility of a d/Deaf community and deaf sociality in Uganda.

Conceptualizing being deaf

Some people do not hear, or only barely do. It is a perceptional dysfunction that is easily labeled as a classic disability: A dimension of the human sensory system is not working as expected. The social model of disability, developed in the disability rights movement in the United Kingdom (Barnes/Mercer/Shakespeare 1999, for a critical reflection, see Shakespeare 2010, see also Windisch, Sackey, and Hughes in this volume), sees disability as a social experience and a reaction to impairment. The main disability resulting from not being able to hear is the social exclusion based on communication barriers: "Deafness as such is not the affliction; affliction enters with the breakdown of communication" (Sacks 1989: 117). Oliver Sacks emphasizes that the possibility of abstract communication is a prerequisite for how deaf people communicate with hearing people, but mostly with other deaf people. Contact and socialization with people around – for the time being notwithstanding whether deaf or hearing – are the prerequisites for any feeling of community or belonging of the deaf individual (Sacks 1989: 8-9). Identity and a sense of self, developed by means of identification and distinction, can only be established through contact and exchange with others (Jenkins 1996; McIlory/Storbeck 2011: 494).

Being deaf may thus be understood in sociocultural terms by arguing that being Deaf is rather a cultural experience and in combination with a sign language forms a linguistic minority. Many authors and activists spell Deaf with a capital *D* (cf. Woodward/Horejes 2016, Ginsberg/Rapp 2013, McIlroy/Storbeck 2011) when talking about those who identify as members of a linguistic and cultural minority. The establishment and maintaining of the Deaf community is of major importance to the Deaf (cf. Lane 1999). Boarding schools are crucial spaces for the acquisition of sign language, creation of communities and the development of Deaf Culture (Padden 1980, Evans/Falk 1986, van Cleve/Crouch 1989). Anthropological inquiry found a fruitful domain in deaf experience that drifts between bodily, social and cultural realms. By exploring hereditary deafness on Martha's Vineyard, Massachusetts, where a significantly high share of the population was deaf, Nora Ellen Groce (1988) scrutinized the disability focus in many hearing views of deafness. Whereas her retrospective study – Groce did not meet deaf Vineyarders in person anymore – described the island as a kind of deaf paradise (Groce 1988: 108), Annelies Kusters' work challenges the idea of shared signing communities as *inclusive utopia* by examining the conflicts and tensions that emerge (Kusters 2009). Kusters undertook the first anthropological in-depth study of deafness in Africa in her work on the shared signing community in Adamorobe in southern Ghana (Kusters 2015). She also shows that in a space where being deaf is considered normal, deafness per se is not positively valued. Even though shared deaf experience is appreciated and celebrated (Kusters 2015: 202), the deafness as impairment is still seen as mischief (Kusters 2015: 108). In a meticulous analysis of how sociality and belonging are practiced and produced in deaf spaces (Kuster/Friedner 2015) in Adamorobe, Kusters shows how deafness as difference matters; even when sign language is shared among the deaf and the hearing (Kusters 2015: 130). To deal with this complexity, McIlroy and Storbeck developed the concept of "DeaF identity" based on ethnographic interviews in South Africa (2011; see also McIlroy 2010). Whereas the capital *D* implies a belonging to Deaf culture, the capitalized *F* refers to the conviction that cultural belongings and identities are always *fluid*. They argue that although in some contexts, deaf individuals feel part of a Deaf culture and do not consider themselves disabled, they might also move in contexts where they experience disability based on their hearing impairment (McIlroy/Storbeck 2011: 507). This approach might be an interesting perspective to extent to other experiences of disability, and the limitation to "*bi*-cultural identity" (McIlroy/Storbeck 2011: 508, my italics) may also be expanded in order to analyze disabled and Deaf identities as fluid, context-dependent and *multiple*.

Recent works question the epistemological value of Deaf Studies' founding concepts of Deaf culture/community/world (Kusters 2015: 20, Kusters/de Meulder/O'Brien 2017). Deaf anthropologists scrutinize the concepts, which are rooted in American identity politics, as being exclusionary and therefore of limited use to understanding deaf experience. Instead, the more inclusive "deaf sociality" (Friedner 2014, 2015) refers to local moral worlds where values and norms of deaf mutuality are learned and practiced. Both Culture and sociality often base the widespread trope of "DEAF-SAME" or deaf similitude (Friedner/Kusters 2014) that refers to both sociocultural similitude and the shared experience of not being able to hear. Through these immediate negotiations, various, sometimes interconnected local ways of being deaf evolve that are less monolithic than the notion of a capital *D* Deaf community (Monaghan et al. 2003).

Deaf culture/community/world is, however, a traveling model that finds support and supporters in places in the global South where the range of its political implications might not make sense (Myers/Fernandes 2010) – for example among some deaf in Uganda. I will use a small *d* when referring to the deaf in Uganda because I intend to include all deaf people whether they identify with an idea of d/Deaf culture or not. Even though notions of similitude, international belonging and community were present, a capital *D* was not argued for by my interlocutors. However, Ahmad[1], one of the three deaf people portrayed below, did take part in deaf sociality and might also identify with d/Deaf culture and community. I will pick up the question of his identification in the conclusion. For the two other people, however, being deaf seems to mean experiencing disability and social exclusion.

1 All names are pseudonyms.

Ugandan particularities

A feature that makes Kampala a particularly interesting setting to study deafness is Uganda's diversity which crystallizes in its capital. The 2014 census lists nine major ethnic groups and languages, leaving the 'others' with an overwhelming 32.1 percent[2], and a broad variety of Christian denominations, Islam and 'others' (UBOS 2016). Ugandan society is structured along those linguistic, ethnic and religious lines since its formation as a colonial territory, its establishment as a state, and the decades of reconfiguration (Karugire 1988, Mugeere et al. 2015); a process that is still going on. As Karugire shows, these boundaries were used time and again to nurture the animosities within the Ugandan population and thereby keeping the country in a state of unrest from independence to the reformation of the state in the mid-1990s. In the early 1990s, when an assembly carved out a new constitution for the divided and war-torn country, a founding member of NUDIPU (National Union of Disabled Persons in Uganda) managed to enter the negotiations and successfully attached some basic rights for disabled Ugandans. For example, they are represented in all parliamentary bodies from the national through the regional to the district level, every parliament has two disabled Ugandans, one male and one female, to serve as representatives and counsel the political bodies (see also Whyte 2019). Laws against discrimination against disabled people have been installed and international agendas like the United Nations Convention on the Rights of Persons with Disabilities (UN 2006) are being turned into national disability action plans. Uganda was the first country in Africa to recognize a signed language as a national language (Lutalo-Kiingi/de Clerck 2015b: 4, Wallin et al. 2006: 6); which underlines the political commitment towards disability issues in Uganda – at least in theory. Interviewing a legal advisor working for NUDIPU, I learned about the challenges and obstacles the realization of these laws meets in practice.[3] Most political tools are not effective, she said, and both public and private employers fail to fulfill their legal obligations. The fact that Uganda is at the forefront of implementing the legal requirements by the United Nations convention does create, however, a rights-based atmosphere that many of my interview partners referred to.

2 In another listing, the census mentions more than 60 Ugandan ethnic groups (UBOS 2016: 71f), without foreign ethnic groups.

3 Interview on the NUDIPU premises, 31.07.2015.

The actual initiative comes from nongovernmental organizations and associations: At some point, NUDIPU was even facilitating accessible elections for disabled people – a task that would usually be the responsibility of the state[4]. The NGO Signhealth Uganda offers sign language classes for teachers and medical professionals[5]. Small local and international NGOs attempt to include disabled children into their programs for vulnerable children and youth[6]. All these actions are enabled by local activists and are mostly funded by international donors. Many NGOs focusing on deafness have been or are being funded by the Norwegian Association of the Deaf or the Danish Deaf Association. This exchange introduces the concepts of Deaf culture/community/identity to deaf and hearing Ugandans (see also Mugeere et al. 2015).

Deafness in Uganda is an intersection where the consequences of medical standards, exchange through international advocacy and development cooperation, academic discourse and local practices of distinction and belonging meet and mingle. Major differences between Ugandan and European settings are quite likely to be due to differences in access to and quality of medical treatment. Most cases of deafness in Uganda are acquired in earliest and early childhood years due to complications at birth, infant illness or wrong medication (Nassozi 2009, UNAD 2010: 12, several interviews in August 2015). The (medically explained) causes of deafness have major influence on the social lives of deaf people. In Europe/US and Adamorobe/Martha's Vineyard, deaf people have a higher chance to be born into families that have experience with deafness – either siblings or parents, or in their family history. In Uganda, I did not meet and was not told about any family with hereditary deafness. This is of course not to say that it does not exist, but among the deaf and activists, it is not a common experience or a topic that came up in my interviews. Ugandan families whose children acquire deafness at an early age have little experience or knowledge about the condition. The family networks that play a major role in Ugandan society, especially regarding impairment and social support (Whyte 2005), are thus of limited use to deaf people because they

4 Interview with a representative of NUDIPU on their premises, 06.01.2015. A critical discussion of deaf people organizing to provide their own services in the wake of neoliberal forms of government can be found in Friedner 2010.

5 Interview with a representative of Signhealth Uganda on their premises, 12.08.2015.

6 Interview with Kezrine, a local NGO agent, Bwaise, 06.08.2015; interview with Noah, a teacher in a Christian school, Nakasongola, 27.08.2015.

usually are the only deaf ones in their close family. The community that some Deaf activists claim to be universal and the first point of reference regarding their belonging and identity is therefore beyond their reach. This reality is also reflected in the fact that only five percent of deaf Ugandans know Ugandan Sign Language (Lutalo-Kiingi/de Clerck 2015a: 811); nonstandardized sign language communication is pejoratively referred to as "village sign" or "local sign"[7].

In the following section, I am going to introduce three deaf Ugandans living in Kampala to illustrate how these discourses are experienced on an individual level.

Three ways of being deaf in Kampala

As mentioned above, deaf and disability rights movements estimate the number of deaf Ugandans at 528,000 (Lutalo-Kiingi/de Clerck 2015a: 811); this number includes people who are very hard of hearing, though the authors do not specify what this means exactly. I had an interview with Kezryne, talking about deafness in the slum that his NGO was working in. Our discussion made him think of Paul, who is hard of hearing and did not identify as deaf himself. Yet, Kezryne thought of him as a deaf person, so I will start my accounts of three ways of being deaf with Paul.

Paul – hard of hearing[8]

Kezryne had told me that Paul was almost deaf but could read lips fairly well. When we met, we could talk in English quite easily as soon as I got used to facing him straight and pronouncing a bit more clearly than I might have usually. Paul has been hard of hearing for a long time. In school, he made it through the first years with the help of friends who would jot down some information for him or repeat what had been said in-

7 Interview with George, my Ugandan Sign Language teacher, 12.08.2015, Ntinda. I learned Ugandan Sign Language in an adult course in the school for the deaf in Ntinda, Kampala, and with research participants during conversations and participant observation. Often when I was using a sign somebody else taught me, the present signers or my teacher would comment "NO NO NO, VILLAGE SIGN", meaning that they were just made up, they were not *real* sign language.

8 Interview on the premises of an NGO in Bwaise, 10.08.2015.

to his one better ear. However, he was the object of his classmates' derision as well as a nuisance to his teachers who grew tired of him repeatedly demanding them to speak up or repeat themselves. Apparently, he once had an opportunity to have a surgery that would increase his hearing. There was also some funding by "white doctors" available. The hospital, however, still wanted to charge his parents more than they could ever afford – so the surgery never took place.

When his friends left school, he did not have much of a choice but to drop out as well, he said, because he could not follow the classes without their support. He moved in with his brother who taught him to be a plumber and who towed him along to jobs in the neighborhood where many people knew him. This reduced the risk of conflict, as they knew well enough not to get angry with him when he did not react sometimes. They learned to explain their demands clearly into his better ear. He makes his living on working for his brother and from some small jobs he gets hired for alone. It seems, though, that these jobs are mostly offered by those who know him and his situation.

Being hard of hearing is a burden for Paul. He feels insecure and ashamed around people, possibly because he has experienced so much discrimination in his childhood and youth. The people in his immediate environment, however, know his situation and try to cater for him. His brother takes care of him, the community pays attention to him and he gets jobs every once in a while. What lets him conduct his life by his own terms are the people that surround him. But that can also become a problem. He lives in one of Kampala's biggest slums. Its everyday is a lively and young space where people try to make a living. But Kezryne, who spent his entire life in that part of town, also told me that it is a space of crime, of prostitution, of poverty, of gangsters and other adversities. It is not a place to go; it is a place to go *through*. Many inhabitants are new arrivals in the capital, and almost everybody who is there wants to leave. The slum is just an entry, a passage. People long to move to the safer parts of the city, the nicer parts[9]. But Paul is stuck. Once he tried to leave – but he came back when he found he could not settle and work in an environment that does not adjust to him to some degree. He needs people who

9 Interview with Kezryne on his NGO's premises, 06.08.2015. The term *slum* and its connotations happen to be discussed critically in urban anthropology and social geography. This description, though, bases not on my impression but on account of a Ugandan NGO worker in his late twenties who spent his entire life in the slum.

know him, who know how to deal with him, and those who *want* to deal with him.

When we were talking, he was shaking. I asked him if talking to me made him nervous; if he would rather not have the interview. He said it was all fine, and we agreed to meet again. When I told Kezryne about it, he said: "Well, he's an alcoholic, he drinks too much. And he has fewer jobs than he probably told you."

Sheila – without language?[10]

Kezryne also got me in touch with Sheila, a teenaged deaf girl. We met on the premises of the local NGO. I was signing to her as much as my limited competence in Ugandan Sign Language allowed me to. She did not react at all, apart from smiling shyly and politely. I wrote down who I was, that I was interested in talking to deaf Ugandans, and that it was totally fine if she did not feel like talking to me. The reaction – after looking at the paper for a minute or two – was another polite smile. It took some time until her mother came over, together with a neighbor who might or might not have been her uncle. The interview situation became increasingly weird as her mother was talking Lango, which Mahmoud, another friend from the NGO, did not understand. So the neighbor was translating from Lango to Luganda, which Mahmoud translated into English for me. Through this chain of interpretations, I learned why Sheila would not sign to me. She knows neither how to sign nor how to read or write. She deafened as a baby due to wrong medication, the neighbor told us. At home, she is told what to do with mimicked gestures – like sweep the floor, do the laundry, or wash the dishes. There seems to be no communication beyond expressions of orders, demands, and needs. Once they took her to Ntinda to the school for the deaf. Apparently, she "reacted very positively" – as Mahmoud translated – to the signing children. Sheila's mother could not afford the money for the regular commute, much less the school fees. The experience of Ugandan disability activists shows that families tend to send their (disabled) sons to school rather than their (disabled) daughters; for education is expensive and the girls leave the family when being married

10 Interview with Sheila's mother, her neighbor and some friends from a local NGO, on the NGO's premises, 10.08.2015.

off anyway[11] (see also Kiyaga/Moores 2003). Investing in a daughter's, and especially in a disabled daughter's future, apparently makes little sense.

So, Sheila stayed at home and helped in the household while some of her hearing siblings enjoyed at least limited primary school education. Sometimes she worked in neighbors' households, earning a little money that she spent on shoes and clothes. Both at home and at the neighbors', she did get angry a lot, mostly when people mocked her, or when people did not understand her. She had a reputation of being very short-tempered and aggressive. As a matter of fact, the idea that the deaf are more aggressive and irascible is a notion that often in occurs in Uganda[12] and beyond (Kara/Harvey 2016: 80, Kiyaga/Moores 2003: 22, Kusters 2015: 98). Towards the end of the quite exhausting multicornered interview, I expressed how I was sorry I could not speak their languages and that I could not talk to Sheila directly. The neighbor, as a means of courtesy I suppose, ordered Sheila to greet me "the way the Baganda girls greet men", which resulted in her kneeling down in the dust in front of my plastic chair, her face on the ground. This was the only time she interacted with anyone during the few hours we spent together. Apparently, she did acquire some competence in the customs and *proper behavior* of her environment. That custom, though, seemed like an expression of submission.

On another occasion, Rachel, an old woman using a wheelchair, told me what is usually done with girls "like that". By "like that" she meant disabled girls who cannot talk – either because they were deaf or mentally disabled. Rachel said those girls were usually married off at a very young age. The families get a small bride wealth, the girls are taken care of, and the families "get rid of them"[13].

Ahmad – entering deaf community[14]

One Sunday, I had an appointment with a bunch of young deaf women who invited me to go to deaf church with them. When I arrived at their compound in a rather poor part of Kampala, there was a group of deaf people around that I had not met before. One of them was Ahmad, the

11 Interview with a representative of SU on their premises, 12.08.2015.
12 Conversation with a fellow sign language learner in Ntinda, 12.08.2016.
13 Conversation 22.08.2015, Kansanga, see also Zoanni 2018.
14 Conversations on 16.08.2015 and 23.08.2015.

deaf husband of one of the women. We chatted in Ugandan Sign Language and he complimented me for my horrible signing. The oldest of his hearing children, a girl of maybe seven years of age, helped us with the few English words she knew. After introducing me to more people than I could remember the names[15] of, we walked towards the deaf church. On the way, we kept meeting both deaf and hearing people who had short sign language conversations with Ahmad. Following my inquiry, he told me that they were of various ethnic and religious backgrounds; it was the sign language that connected them. We had enough time to converse; he would repeat phrases many times and teach me what I did not understand. He worked for Riham, a huge Indian beverage company, as did some of his deaf friends. As a bricklayer, he formed part of a team that repaired what there was to repair around the factories. Other deaf friends worked in sorting and labeling bottles. He said that, though the pay was bad, it was better than what he did before, which was road building at northern by-pass, hard work in the sun.

Arriving at the church, I met more and more deaf people who were sitting around and chatting. The sermon was held in Ugandan Sign Language by a deaf priest and translated into English for those incapable of understanding sign language. When the church service was over, we sat down in the shade to chat with a bunch of young deaf women and men. After hanging out, Ahmad, some women and I walked back towards town. We kept on talking. The careful reader of this article might have realized already by Ahmad's name, but somehow I only realized when he told me: The guy I just went to church with was a Muslim. As a reaction to my surprise, he signed "WHY? GOD ONE. CHRISTIAN GOD, MUSLIM GOD, SAME." Furthermore, he explained that the mosques do not offer any prayer or exchange in Ugandan Sign Language. Thus, he and other deaf Muslims go to the Protestant church for the deaf. While they obviously do so in order to meet other deaf people to practice deaf sociality (Friedner 2014), he also said that he likes going to church and praying with the Christians. He remains,

15 Sign Language names are given to people as soon as they start to learn Sign Language. In Uganda (as in Germany), these names usually have nothing to do with their written names but pick up a special feature in the appearance or character of the named individual. My sign language name, for example, given to me by my German Sign Language teacher, refers to a prominent birth mark on my forehead. This made immediate sense to those deaf Ugandans I met, while my sign name caused confusion among signers in the United States of America or in Benin where names usually base on the person's initials.

however, a Muslim and the Christians also do not try to convert him. Thinking back, I did not remember any word on Islam in the sermons I went to in the deaf church. Shared deafness here apparently trumps religious differences. Ahmad would, though, not express this as the trope of "DEAF-SAME" or deaf similitude. Instead, he emphasized that they had the same language, refraining from referring to their deafness as such. After inviting me to a tournament of deaf football teams, Ahmad left me at the matatu stage and walked home to his wife and kids.

Those stories show three (of many) shades of what it means to be deaf in Kampala. Paul was "the least deaf", as one might say in a medical sense, but he suffered from his impairment a lot more than Ahmad. The profoundly deaf Muslim knew sign language and moved around confidently in the street life on Kampala, proudly teaching me his language. Moving from one deaf space to another, he encountered several people of various backgrounds he knew through church, sports, or just by recognizing each other by both knowing sign language. Profoundly deaf, he was integrated into a broader society of signing deaf and hearing people. His impairment turned out to be less disabling than Paul's. Sheila, however, could neither hear nor sign, she also did not have a sign language name. Her mother said she had no friends, could not share her feelings nor thoughts, fears nor joys, with anybody[16]. Understandably, this drove her mad at times. Her family felt bad about it but didn't see a way to deal with her better than involving her in the daily chores of household life.

The three stories, though only roughly sketched, demonstrate how important *the social* is in the experience of deafness. Due to the social network he was part of, Ahmad was a proud deaf Muslim among his signing peers. Paul, on the other hand, was part of the hearing society. He did not sign. His way of communicating was meager communication based on his ability to read lips. He experienced being incomplete, a defective participant in communication, in interaction, in society. To him, his daily life demonstrated his insufficiency, over and over again. Due to the lack of access to society, he was disabled by structure, while on the other hand, the close community around him enabled him to work, mingle, and participate

16 In his book *Being and Hearing*, Peter Graif (2018) discusses the complex ways that hearing people's understanding of deafness shapes deaf people's lives in Nepal. I am aware that Sheila's life and experience have many more shades and dimensions than can be discussed here or accessed in the short encounter I had with her and her family.

in society on a small scale. Sheila appears to not really be part of any community or sociality; assuming that sociality consists of shared values, stories, and practices, as not even Sheila's mother could say much about what her daughter felt, what she liked. Without language, she has only very limited access to beliefs, custom, knowledge, and to what always seems to be a basic community-building activity: gossip (Kusters 2015: 62, Groce 1988: 60, 66f, Mildner 2019: 19).

These three stories raise certain questions: Is Ahmad living in a deaf utopia? Is he spending his time, sharing his life with people of his choice, or is his choice limited by the fact that he needs deaf peers? Is Sheila's life as isolated as her family and neighbors suggest? And how about Paul: does he experience himself as being between the categories of "hearing" or "deaf"? If all three of them met, not just in this paper, but in reality; would they feel connected? Would it make sense for them to be listed side by side?

Conclusion: Ugandan Deaf culture/community/world?

Being part of a community is a question of belonging, of *feeling* and *being considered* part of a certain social group (following Max Weber, see Griese 2004: 140). This notion splits in half here, the internal and the external classification (see also Jenkins 1996). In choosing the three examples, I followed the external and somewhat medical perspective: All three have a hearing impairment and need to organize their lives around it. The decision of feeling part of a deaf community, of participating in deaf sociality or not is a completely different one than the external classification based on assumptions about the physical ability.

Deaf sociality means learning and practicing deaf values and norms (Friedner 2014: 39) and sharing a way of being (Kusters 2015: 20). Most of all, however, it is about a shared language – not only in order to get in touch with each other, but also in order to agree or disagree about those values, stories, shared experience and ways of being. In this sense, Sheila and Paul are excluded from taking part in deaf sociality or community life. Ahmad, on the other hand, considers the shared language and deaf experience to be above the (potential) social divisions of ethnic or religious belonging, as his flexible approach towards church and religion suggests.

What, though, does this feeling of community mean if only less than five percent of deaf Ugandans know Ugandan Sign Language? Are the others, the 500,000 others, part of the Ugandan deaf community? Do Ahmad and Sheila have a feeling of commonness? It might be that Ahmad would think so, but would Sheila? And would it not be paternalistic if the signing minority of deaf Ugandans claimed to speak for the huge majority that cannot participate in deaf sociality? Is it appropriate when the proud signers praise Ugandan Sign Language while looking down at what they disparagingly call "local sign", that is, the not formalized communication that develops in small deaf communities or families? Deaf culture/community/world is exclusive as it establishes clear lines demarcating who belongs and who does not (Nakamura 2006: 22, Myers/Fernandes 2010, McIlroy/Storbeck 2011: 496). Given the small group of deaf Ugandans who know Ugandan Sign Language, how can they define where those lines are? But then again, who should, and why?

Despite the emphasis that the deaf associations and organizations in Kampala put on Deaf culture/community/world, they do not impose such a strict distinction between Deaf and disabled as some movements in the US or in Europe do. The ideas of Deaf culture and Deaf gain (Bauman/Murray 2014) are in line with ideas of Disability Pride – the notion to re-value disability, to claim rights without redefining the category. This is in line with the fact that UNAD is a member of NUDIPU. Associations and organizations of the deaf as of the disabled go side by side in advocacy, lobbying and awareness campaigns[17]. Regarding deafness, the main demand remains the improvement of deaf education and increase of the use of Ugandan Sign Language in medical and public services. The more deaf people can get involved in forming the community as a political body, the stronger their voices will be. So far it seems to me that the idea of a Deaf culture among Ugandan Deaf activists was inspired by the exchange with actors from other countries. Many projects were funded by Scandinavian deaf associations, some scholars I met studied Deaf Studies in renowned universities in Europe. Ideas of Deaf culture/community/world cannot, however, be easily imported to Uganda. As Ginsburg and Rapp have stated (2013: 59), Deaf cultures vary nationally and internationally. If Ugandan Deaf activists wish to articulate their Deaf culture, they will need to appropriate ideas and melt them with their own experience into their own Ugandan deaf or Deaf culture/community/world. This only seems legitimate, though, if more deaf Ugandans learn sign language and participate

17 Interviews with representatives of the Ugandan National Association of the Deaf (UNAD, 13.08.2015), the National Union of Disabled Persons in Uganda (NUDIPU, 31.07.2015; 06.01.2015), and Signhealth Uganda (29.07.2015; 12.08.2015; 19.08.2015).

in deaf sociality – wherever that may lead. It seems that associations and organizations are heading that way, and time will show what a Ugandan Deaf culture or deaf values may or may not be. Merely importing the idea of Deaf culture runs the risk of being paternalistic (see Moriarty Harrelson 2015, Friedner/Kusters 2014) – as happened before with well-intended discourses of development, human rights, or good governance (Easterly 2006).

Until then, coming back to the models of disability, it appears that deafness is often a disability in the social sense. Regarding Paul and Sheila, their hearing impairments turned into strong constraints in their lives. Their environments were not able or willing to adapt to their impairments and were thus creating experiences of disability. In Sheila's case, the lack of mutual understanding and communication led to conflicts and frustration, even if all people involved had the best intentions. For Paul, his constant experience of being insufficiently abled, of feeling rejection and lacking a prospect of improving his life apparently – following his friend's opinion – led him to alcoholism. If education and the spread of sign language improve, there is a chance that more deaf Ugandans can take part in deaf sociality. That is not to say that as soon as sign language is accessible for more deaf Ugandans their lives will be hunky dory. But through communication and exchange, through sociality and community, they may stand a chance to make, master or goof their lives as anybody else, whether hearing or deaf.

Furthermore, research on being deaf requires a higher awareness of the diversity of deaf experiences. Focusing on individual experience can contribute to understanding the complexities that are easily covered with a global Deaf culture/community/world perspective. While more and more deaf people around the world claim their own ways of being deaf – framed in terms of Deaf culture or not – a large proportions of the world's deaf people do not have access to sign language education, deaf sociality or even deaf peers. Yet, their lives, like Sheila's and Paul's, also constitute what deaf being in the world is.

List of Abbreviations

NGO	nongovernmental organization
NUDIPU	National Union of Disabled Persons in Uganda
UNAD	Ugandan National Association of the Deaf

References

Barnes, Colin/Mercer, Geoffrey/Shakespeare, Tom (1999): Exploring Disability. A Sociological Introduction. Malden, Mass.

Bauman, H-Dirksen/Murray, Joseph (eds.) (2014): Deaf Gain. Raising the Stakes for Human Diversity. Minneapolis.

Easterly, William (2006): The White Man's Burden: Why the West's Efforts to Aid the Rest Have Done So Much Ill and So Little Good. New York.

Evans, A. Donald/Falk, William W. (1986): Learning to be Deaf. Contributions to the Sociology of Language, Berlin, New York, Amsterdam.

Friedner, Michele (2010): Biopower, Biosociality, and Community Formation: How Biopower is Constitutive of the Deaf Community, in: Sign Language Studies 10: 3, 336-347.

Friedner, Michele (2014): The Church of Deaf Sociality. Deaf Churchgoing Practices and 'Sign Bread and Butter' in Bangalore, India, in: Anthropology & Education Quarterly, 45: 1, 39-53.

Friedner, Michele (2015): Valuing Deaf Worlds in Urban India. New Brunswick, NJ.

Friedner, Michele/Kusters, Annelies (2014): On the possibilities and limits of 'deaf-deaf-same': Tourism and empowerment camps in Adamorobe (Ghana), Bangalore and Mumbai (India), in: Disability Studies Quarterly, 34: 3, 1-22.

Griese, Hartmut (2004): Kritik der "Interkulturellen Pädagogik": Essays gegen Kulturalismus, Ethnisierung, Entpolitisierung und einen latenten Rassismus, Münster.

Graif, Peter (2018): Being and Hearing: Making Intelligible Worlds in Deaf Kathmandu. Chicago.

Groce, Nora E. (1988): Everyone Here Spoke Sign Language: Hereditary Deafness on Martha's Vineyard. Boston.

Jenkins, Richard (1996): Social Identity. London.

Kara, Nazira/Harvey, Clare (2016): The social construction of 'deafness'. Explored through the experiences of Black South African mothers raising a deaf child, in: South African Journal of Psychology, 47: 1, 72-83.

Karugire, Samwiri R. (1988): Roots of Instability in Uganda. Kampala.

Kiyaga, Nassozi B./Moores, Donald F. (2003): Deafness in sub-Saharan Africa, in: American Annals of the Deaf, 148: 1, 18-24.

Kusters, Annelies (2009): Deaf Utopias? Reviewing the Sociocultural Literature on the World's "Martha's Vineyard Situations, in: Journal of Deaf Studies and Deaf Education, 15 (1), 3-16.

Kusters, Annelies (2015): Deaf Space in Adamorobe: An Ethnographic Study in a Village in Ghana, Washington, DC.

Kusters, Annelies/Friedner, Michele (2015): Introduction: deaf-same and Difference in International Deaf Spaces and Encounters. Friedner, Michele/ Kusters, Annelies. It's a Small World. International Deaf Spaces and Encounters. Washington, DC, ix-xxix.

Kusters, Annelies/ Meulder, Maartje de/ O'Brien, Dai (2017): Innovations in Deaf Studies: Critically Mapping the Field. Kusters, Annelies/ Meulder, Maartje de/ O'Brien, Dai. Innovations in Deaf Studies. The Role of Deaf Scholars, New York, 1-53.

Lane, Harlan (1999): The Mask of Benevolence: Disabling the Deaf Community, San Diego: DawnSignPress.

Lutalo-Kiingi, Sam/ Clerck, Goedele A. M. de (2015a): Ugandan Sign Language. Jepsen, Julie Bakken et al.. Sign Languages of the World. A Comparative Handbook. Berlin, 811-840.

Lutalo-Kiingi, Sam and Goedele A. M. de Clerck (2015b): Introduction: Sub-Saharan African Signed Languages and Deaf Communities. Cooper, Audrey C./Rashid, Khadijat K.. Citizenship, politics, difference. Perspectives from Sub-Saharan signed languages. Washington, DC, 3-8.

McIlroy, Guy (2010): Discovering Deaf Identities: A Narrative Exploration of School Experiences on Deaf Identities. Saarbrücken.

McIlroy, Guy and Claudine Storbeck (2011): Development of Deaf Identity: An Ethnographic Study, in: Journal of Deaf Studies and Deaf Education, 16: 4, 494-511.

Mildner, Carsten (2019): Soziale Geografien der Gehörlosigkeit in Benin, in: Das Zeichen 111, 10-22.

Monaghan, Leila/ Schmaling, Constanze/ Nakamura, Karen/ Turner, Graham H. (eds.) (2003): Many ways to be Deaf: International Variation in Deaf Communities, London/New York.

Moriarty Harrelson, Erin (2015): SAME-SAME but Different. Tourism and the Deaf Global Circuit in Cambodia. Friedner, Michele/ Kusters, Annelies. It's a Small World. International Deaf Spaces and Encounters. Washington, DC, 199-211.

Mugeere, Anthony/ Atekyereza, Peter/ Kirumira, Edward K./ Hojer, Staffan (2015): Deaf identities in a multicultural setting: The Ugandan context, in: African Journal of Disability, 4: 1, 1-9.

Myers, Shirly Shultz/ Jane K. Fernandes (2010): Deaf Studies: A Critique of the Predominant U.S. Theoretical Direction, in: Journal of Deaf Studies and Deaf Education, 15: 1, 30-49.

Nakamura, Karen (2006): Deaf in Japan. Signing and the Politics of Identity. Ithaca, NY.

Padden, Carol (1980): The Deaf Community and the Culture of Deaf People. Baker, Charlotte/Battison, Robbin. Sign Language and the Deaf Community. Essays in Honor of William C. Stokoe. Washington D.C., 89-103.

Sacks, Oliver (1989): Seeing Voices: A Journey into the World of the Deaf. Berkeley and Los Angeles.

Shakespeare, Tom (2010): The Social Model of Disability. Davis, Lennard. The Disability Studies Reader. New York, 266-273.

UBOS (Ugandan Bureau of Statistics) (2016): "The National Population and Housing Census 2014: Main Report". Available at: www.ubos.org/wp-content/uploads/publications/03_20182014_National_Census_Main_Report.pdf (10.04.2020).

UN (United Nations) (2006): „Convention on the Rights of Persons with Disabilities“. Available at: www.un.org/development/desa/disabilities/convention-on-the-rights-of-persons-with-disabilities.html (10.04.2020).

UNAD (Ugandan National Association of the Deaf) (2010): Information Handbook. Mukono.

van Cleve/ Vickrey, John/Crouch, Barry A. (1989): A Place of Their Own. Creating the Deaf Community in America. Washington, DC.

Wallin, Lars/Lule, Dorothy/Lutalo-Kiingi, Sam/Busingye, Bonny (eds.) (2006): Uganda Sign Language Dictionary. Kampala.

Woodward, James/ Horejes, Thomas (2016): deaf/Deaf: Origins and Usage. Gertz, Genie/ Boudreault, Patrick. The SAGE Deaf Studies Encyclopedia. Volume 1. Los Angeles.

Whyte, Susan (1998): Slow Cookers and Madmen: Competence of heart and head in Rural Uganda. Jenkins, Richard: Questions of Competence: Culture, Classification and Intellectual Disability. Cambridge, 153-175.

Whyte, Susan (2019): In the Long Run, in: Current Anthropology, 61, supplement 21.

Zoanni, Tyler (2018): The Possibilities of Failure. Personhood and Cognitive Disability in Urban Uganda, in: The Cambridge Journal of Anthropology, 36: 1, 61-79.

Diversity as Sociocultural Difference – Middle Class Milieus in Urban Kenya

Dieter Neubert and Florian Stoll

Introduction[1]

The ongoing discourse on *diversity* discusses this topic either as an opportunity for society or as a challenge. According to the first meaning, diversity is usually understood as a resource that enriches the social sphere, for instance, by introducing new perspectives on everyday life. The second meaning of diversity is also normative, but it considers more the marginalization of those who differ from the mainstream and thus claims respect instead of social exclusion. Both meanings of diversity can be found in a wide range of fields covering, in particular, questions of class, gender, race, disability, employment and many more. The normative claim of diversity focuses in this discourse on the interactions with persons that differ from the assumed mainstream. In this chapter, however, we do not treat diversity as a normative claim in the sense of an opportunity or challenge. Instead, we ask whether diversity permeates all parts of society as a central feature of the sociocultural composition. Diversity is here an analytical perspective for differentiation and not only a difference of the assumed mainstream. This view offers new insights into a field where the question of diversity has hardly been in focus up to now, namely, the debate about *middle classes* in Africa. The new discussion follows a general debate on *middle classes* in growing economies in Asia and South America.

The term *middle class* is used to refer to a middle-income group, whose income is above the poverty threshold. There is an extensive debate concerning what threshold values to use in defining the middle class. On the

---

1 This text is a slightly revised and extended reprint of the Working Paper "Socio-Cultural Diversity of the African Middle Class. The Case of Urban Kenya." Academy Reflects 1. Bayreuth African Studies Working Papers 14. The working paper is a slightly revised and expanded version of a paper presented at the Congress of the German Sociological Association in Trier on 6.-10.10.2014. It was translated by Ruth Schubert. Many thanks to Eberhard Rothfuß for his constructive comments.

one hand, it is defined from a comparative global perspective, including the OECD countries; on the other hand, it is defined in respect to specific regions or countries in the Global South, which leads to lower threshold values. The middle class is usually defined as people with a daily per capita income of between two and ten US dollars at the lower end, and between ten and one hundred US dollars at the upper end (based on purchasing power parity).[2] This debate will not be carried on here (for an overview, see Neubert 2014: 24f). For a discussion of sociocultural differentiation, the categories proposed by the African Development Bank (AfDB 2011) are helpful as a rough guide and can be applied to the case of Kenya, which is presented in this chapter. The African Development Bank uses the following categories: 2-4 US dollars as *floating class*, which lives above the poverty line but is threatened by poverty; 4-10 US dollars as lower middle class and 10-20 US dollars as upper middle class.

While the existence of a middle class has long been acknowledged in Asia, North Africa and Latin America, the development of a large middle class in African countries south of the Sahara is a relatively new phenomenon which has attracted special attention. In a number of studies, the growing middle class is seen as representing an important economic potential for the development of Africa, since it also stands paradigmatically for a more positive economic image of Africa (AfDB 2011; McKinsey Global Institute 2010; Ncube/Lufumpa 2015). In all studies of the middle class in the Global South, it is remarkable that everyone talks of *the* middle class (Easterly 2001; Kharas 2010; Milanovic/Yitzhaki 2002). Apart from the difficulties of agreeing on a socioeconomic definition, the implication is that this middle class has many common features. This also applies to Africa. At first glance, there are good reasons to speak of *the African middle class*. From an economic perspective, this is a group with greater consumption opportunities. The studies also underline the importance of education and careers. However, especially in Africa, regional and ethnic identities continue to be important, even for the middle class.[3] Moreover, this is often bound up with a marked rural orientation. At least since the wave of democratization at the beginning of the 1990s, wide-

---

2 The threshold values range from 2-10 US dollars (Banerjee/Duflo 2008); 2-13 US dollars (Ravallion 2010: 446); 2-20 US dollars (AfDB 2011: 2); or even 10-100 US dollars (Kharas 2010: 9).

3 Despite many differences between the countries of sub-Saharan Africa, the aspects described here also apply in differing degrees to many of these countries. It is therefore justified to speak here of "Africa" without further distinction.

spread pro-democratic views can be observed in parts of the middle class. Our own research shows that great importance is still attached to family and wider kin groups, as well as religion. In addition, the middle class has intensive international contacts. The money sent home by family members is important for financing education and other investments. A remarkable number of members of the middle class have migration or diaspora experience. Taken together these features seem to reflect the sociocultural homogeneity of the African middle class as the socioeconomic definition implies. But on a closer look, this is not so clear.

The normative assumptions we have mentioned are not restricted to the middle class, but also apply to large parts of the lower class. The desire for education and social advancement, family values, religion, regional identities, democratic views and the importance of having contact with family members who live abroad are not limited to a specific socioeconomic class. Features which at first might appear to be typical of the African middle class are in fact typical of large parts of African societies. The main difference between the middle class and the other groups is a socioeconomic one based on the better position of the middle class regarding consumption opportunities. The members of the middle class are financially better off than members of the lower class and this is their most distinctive attribute in comparison to the lower class. An important consequence of their higher income is that they are in a better position to buy consumer goods. But this is only a very broad way of describing the special realities of the middle class, which is defined by this socioeconomic position.

There is plenty to suggest that it would be a gross simplification to regard Africa's middle class as a uniform, socioculturally homogeneous group with largely similar or identical attitudes and orientations. Thus, the question is not whether the desire for education and social advancement, family, ethnicity, religion, diaspora relations and other characteristics are positive values for members of the middle class, but how these elements influence their everyday practices and their hopes and plans for the future. Very different orientations can be seen in connection with Africa's political development, as an example will show. In Africa there is a significant group which cultivates liberal, cosmopolitan and democratic values and forms the core of the civil society. But there is another significant group which has a neotraditional orientation. These groups have different views regarding "traditional authorities", the political role of ethnicity, ethnic micronationalism and the issue of abortion (see also Daniel/Neubert 2014).

From the existence of a middle class in the socioeconomic sense we cannot conclude that this class is socioculturally homogeneous as is implied by classical concepts of class. On the contrary, we observe in Kenya a remarkable sociocultural differentiation. With this chapter we want to show how sociocultural differentiation within the African middle class can be grasped conceptually and empirically. This analysis of sociocultural difference adds a further dimension to the analysis of social structure beyond socioeconomic stratification and/or class. There is no existing analysis of sociocultural differentiation in Africa and large parts of the Global South. To date, social structure analyses relating to the Global South have been limited to the analysis of socioeconomic strata, or class in the (neo-) Marxist or Weberian sense, or they use class in an unspecified way. In most cases, sociocultural differentiation has been perceived and studied only in terms of ethnic or religious identities. For the purpose of analyzing sociocultural differences, we refer to approaches that have been used for the analysis of sociocultural differentiation in European societies, especially for Germany: *sociocultural milieus* and *small lifeworlds*. These approaches are hardly known in the Anglophone scholarly debate. One reason for this is that these approaches to the study of sociocultural differentiation were developed in Germany and these texts have only recently been published in English (for example Zifonun 2015). The main idea behind these concepts is that the differentiation of social groups cannot be described only in terms of socioeconomic differences, although these are still important. Moreover, we have to consider that people in the same socioeconomic position do not share necessarily the same values and lifestyles. Subgroups that do share the same values and lifestyles are categorized as sociocultural *milieus*. The social settings where people meet in a particular sphere of their everyday life are conceptualized as *small lifeworlds*.

In the first part of this chapter we will present and discuss these approaches (Conceptualization of sociocultural diversity: social macro-milieus and small lifeworlds). In the second part of the chapter we will adapt the milieu approach to urban Kenya with an empirical focus on Nairobi, the capital of Kenya, supplemented by information from Mombasa, Kisumu and Eldoret (Milieu analysis for Kenya). In a further step we present two examples of (urban) Kenyan milieus (Two examples: neo-traditional and religious Christian milieus). In the final part we discuss the scope and the limits of this analysis (Conceptual conclusions and further challenges). To be clear, we do not ignore the existence of socioeconomic differences, nor do we claim that this inequality is not important. In this chapter we simply want to show that for the understanding of social differentiation we have to consider sociocultural differentiation too.

The discussion is based on the first results of a current research project entitled "Middle Classes on the Rise – Concepts of the future between freedom, consumption, tradition, and morality", which is part of a broader project entitled "Future Africa – Visions in Time", conducted at the Bayreuth Academy for Advanced African Studies and funded by the German Federal Ministry of Education and Research. The authors of this chapter are responsible for the sociological part of the project, and Erdmute Alber, Lena Kroeker and Maike Voigt for the anthropological aspects. The empirical dataset of this chapter is based mainly on participant observation and 82 biographical interviews carried out by Florian Stoll in Mombasa and Nairobi in 2013 and 2014, in the course of three periods of fieldwork totaling six months. Other important sources of information are observations and interviews conducted by Lena Kroeker, Erdmute Alber, Maike Voigt and Dieter Neubert. Furthermore, insights were gained from supervising the theses of eight MA-students who each spent at least six weeks in 2014 doing field research in Nairobi, Eldoret and Kisumu on the topic *middle classes*.

Conceptualization of sociocultural diversity: social macromilieus and small lifeworlds

At least since the 1980s, sociocultural differentiation – in addition to class and class differences – has been an important topic in German social structure analysis. Social differentiation is described not only in terms of socioeconomic positioning, but also in terms of (sub-) cultural differences.[4] One point of reference is the internationally acknowledged theory developed by Pierre Bourdieu (1982) which links sociocultural differentiation to specific class positions. In Germany this idea was extended and developed by Vester et al. (2001). Vester's approach combines the analysis of milieus with a class analysis by examining the connections between position in the division of work and cultural features. The debate in Germany rejected the analysis of classes in favor of a more descriptive approach.

4 For a good overview of classic and new approaches to social structure analysis and the analysis of social differentiation, see the edited volume by Solga et al. (2009).

The study of sociocultural differentiation was based either on the concept of *milieus*, without Bourdieu's reference to classes, or on what were called different *lifestyles*. The concept developed by the Sinus Institute, which will be discussed below, links socioeconomic positionings, on the basis of a descriptive model, with different sociocultural orientations or "milieus" (see Sinus Sociovision 2009; on the background to this conception, see Flaig et al. 1993).

Hradil (1987) goes a step further and conceptualizes not classes but social positions, where in addition to the typical criteria for distinguishing different social strata, such as occupation, income and education, other criteria are also considered, such as job security, place of residence or access to infrastructure and social services. The milieu construction basically corresponds to the Sinus model. In his attempt to distinguish different lifestyles, Schulze (1992) attaches more importance to identifying sociocultural differences. In addition to contrasting value preferences, he places leisure behavior in the foreground and links this up with theoretical considerations in respect of the *thrill-seeking society* (*Erlebnisgesellschaft*). This discussion was mainly restricted to German-speaking countries. For an overview, see Isenböck et al. (2014) on milieus and Rössel and Otte (2012) on lifestyles.[5] These approaches all concentrate on the analysis of milieus in Germany and are applicable to the African context only to a certain extent and with adaptations (Neubert 2005). There are, however, a few studies which offer some reference points for milieus, on the basis of Bourdieu's approach, in non-European countries such as Brazil (Stoll 2012) or Laos (Rehbein 2004 and 2007).

The Sinus concept of milieus (Sinus Sociovision 2009; Flaig et al. 1993), which was developed in Germany but is now used in a number of OECD and emerging countries, has gained importance as a descriptive model in applied (market) research. The special feature of this approach is the way it is able to take into account sociocultural orientations that transcend class boundaries, as well as different sociocultural orientations within the same socioeconomic class. This descriptive concept of class as a socioeconomic stratum is easier to operationalize and apply empirically than the more complex concept of "social positions". Due to its flexible approach to the positioning of milieus and its more simple concept of class, the basic idea of the Sinus model can be adapted to African societies south

5 In the US there were only scattered echoes, such as Mitchell (1983), who suggested an implicit hierarchy of different lifestyles.

of the Sahara (or the whole of the Global South). This model does not presuppose a more or less fixed class structure, the existence of which may be doubtful or disputed. The descriptive division into strata is usually possible on the basis of the available data, and the milieu definition of this concept is open enough to be able to apply it to non-European contexts with appropriate adaptations.[6]

The Sinus concept reconstructs "[…] subcultural units within a society which group together *people with a similar view of life and way of life*" (Flaig et al. 1993: 55; italics in original). These units are called *milieus*. This is clearly a social structure analysis which considers more than just limited social units. Rather, it claims that society as a whole can be described in the form of distinct (macro-) milieus.[7] This macromilieu concept works with two dimensions. In addition to the socioeconomic division into lower class, lower middle class, middle middle class, upper middle class and upper class, a second dimension is created on the basis of differing cultural orientations. These range from preservation of tradition to modernization, individualization and re-orientation. This structure is visualized by means of *fields*, which may overlap, located within a coordinate system. A milieu is defined in terms of a particular combination of so-called "milieu building blocks" (Flaig et al. 1993: 71). These relate to social position, aims in life, work/performance, image of society, family/partnership, leisure, ideals or role models, and lifestyle. Depending on an individual's values and orientation in relation to these building blocks, he or she will be assigned to a milieu, in the sense of social macromilieus.[8] The Sinus Institute now offers milieus for emerging markets in countries of the Global South (see Fig. 1).

Assignment to a milieu thus depends on people's values, normative orientations and everyday practices. This way of analysing social differentiation is closely connected with people's visions of the future and shows

---

6 The question whether *class* is an appropriate concept to describe social inequality precisely, especially in Africa, is not the topic of this paper. Nor will we discuss the term *elites* that has been used especially in the 1960s and 1970s (for the discussion see Lentz 2015; Neubert 2005: 181ff and 2014: 23) Therefore, we follow – despite our doubts – the general practice and use the term class.

7 We speak here of *macro*milieus because this term can be used to refer to large social macrogroups which should not be confused with scenes, small subcultures or socioculturally homogeneous face-to-face groups.

8 A chart showing the Sinus milieus can be seen on the website of the Sinus Institute, available at: www.sinus-institut.de/en/sinus-solutions/sinus-meta-milieus/ (09.11.2018)

that such visions can vary greatly within a society. They are reflected in ideals and role models, people's image of society, and, more concretely, their aims in life. Milieus thus not only show existing sociocultural orientations and practices but are also linked to aspirations which mean that actions are directed towards attaining future goals.

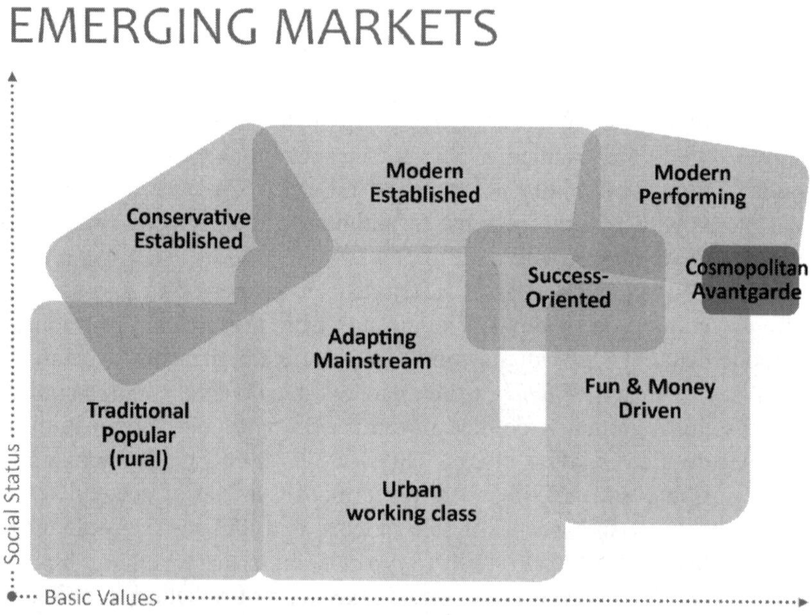

Fig. 1: Sinus-Meta-Milieus in emerging markets (Sinus Institute 2018)

The milieu concept, and the whole Sinus approach, like the lifestyle approach, has been subject to various criticisms (see for example Otte 2005; Geißler 2006: 116-119; Hitzler/Honer 1984). It is said that the concept lacks a theoretical framework and consists only of a descriptive division into milieus based on the distribution of orientations in relation to the milieu building blocks. Moreover, milieu and lifestyle studies that follow this approach tend to use different definitions and delimitations of the various milieus. This means that their results in respect of one and the same society are not necessarily comparable. They are also sometimes accused of being arbitrary. It is not always clear how the values named by respondents relate to concrete practice. It is claimed that there is no great difference between values and practice within milieus, meaning it can be assumed that the milieus are relatively homogeneous. Milieu approaches and empirical studies both give the impression that families or households belong as a rule to the same milieu. With its concentration on the macro level, the milieu approach ignores individual deviations, and phases in which individuals are unsettled. In addition, there is no place for individualized realities, so that single individuals may fit into the pattern only to a limited degree. This is bound up with a fundamental critique of the macro orientation of milieu approaches, similar to the critique of class concepts, since the description of general features cannot explain the logic of social practices on the micro level.

Different approaches to the study of sociocultural differentiation include, for instance, the analysis of specific subcultures as *scenes* (Hitzler et al. 2001), or the use of concepts such as *small lifeworlds* or *micromilieus*. These are based on the work of Anne Honer and Ronald Hitzler in the 1980s (Honer 1985; Hitzler/Honer 1988), who began by using the term lifeworlds with reference to Berger and Luckmann (1966). In order to distinguish these more clearly from macromilieus, we use the term *small lifeworld* (Rebstein/Schnettler 2014). Small lifeworlds are voluntarily chosen part-time lifeworlds or communal spheres that share common interests, meanings and behaviors such as sports clubs, fitness studios, rabbit breeders' associations, migrant organizations and political groups (Soeffner/Zifonun 2008; Zifonun/Cindark 2004; Zifonun 2010). In contrast to macromilieus, membership in a small lifeworld is limited to a specific time and space. Thus, people may belong to different small lifeworlds at the same time. A member of a fitness studio can also be a member of a migrant organization or a political group. The other members of the same fitness studio may belong to other small lifeworlds, such as a sports club or a particular subcultural scene.

The special feature of this approach is that the different sociocultural orientations of individuals can be observed and analyzed together. The fact that a person belongs to one small lifeworld says nothing about his or her other small lifeworlds. Different combinations of small lifeworlds are an expression of individuality, of people's independence from bigger group structures in which all spheres of life are shared. The small lifeworlds approach thus differs from those milieu concepts which assume that all spheres of life are similar for the members of a particular milieu – or which do not consider this issue at all. Defenders of the small lifeworlds approach doubt whether it is useful or reasonable to divide a society into distinct and homogeneous milieus. In contrast to the macromilieu method, this approach adopts the perspective of the subjects (subject-oriented approach).

These small lifeworlds can be studied empirically using qualitative ethnographic methods, with a relatively high level of ethnographic *accuracy*. Subjective views of the self can also play a role here. But this approach is not suitable for social structure analysis. Those researchers who use the concept of small lifeworlds sometimes also doubt whether social structure analysis along sociocultural differentiations is possible at all in view of the great variety of subjective orientations (e.g. Hitzler/Honer 1984; Rebstein/Schnettler 2014: 55).

Despite all criticism, the description of social macromilieus continues to be used as a method in market research. Its strength lies in its relatively high statistical accuracy and it offers a rough estimation of sociocultural differentiation on a macrolevel. In addition, the milieu categories are similar to everyday categories of sociocultural differentiation, since they often clearly bring out typical features of lifestyles, even without a sociological analysis. A particular advantage of this macromilieu approach is the avoidance of predetermined normative assumptions. It allows an open and unprejudiced, empirically based analysis of the sociocultural differentiation of societies and it can add new milieus to do justice to changes that take place within societies. With all due caution, we will now ask to what extent the concept of macromilieus can be used to examine sociocultural differentiation in middle the strata in the Global South. We will do this using the example of the middle class in urban Kenya, especially in Nairobi.

Milieu analysis for Kenya

The question whether specific small lifeworlds exist in Kenya, or whether it is possible to analyse macromilieus, can only be answered by empirical studies. During our fieldwork in Nairobi and other towns, we discovered a large number of small lifeworlds. These include, for example, sports studios (fitness or bodybuilding studios), nightclubs, and human rights and women's rights groups, but also religious groups – mainly involving women – and various self-help groups for income-generating activities or rotating savings and credit groups. All these small lifeworlds are tied to concrete times and places. Within each small lifeworld, certain values and activities relating to the common purpose are shared.

Based on the available data it is also possible to identify potential macromilieus. These include a specific "young professionals" milieu, which has already been described in an impressive ethnography by Rachel Spronk (2012). In addition, we have found a group of conservative and religious milieus with various Christian backgrounds, and possibly also with Muslim or Hindu backgrounds, although this cannot be clearly decided on the basis of our research so far. We have also identified a neo-traditional milieu that is equally conservative but with different orientations. Other milieus are liberal cosmopolitans, to which the abovementioned human rights groups and other nongovernmental organizations belong, an apolitical stability oriented pragmatic milieu, and a milieu of apolitical social climbers without any particular religious or neo-traditional affiliation.

This tentative list of milieus was created by using the milieu *building blocks* discussed in Flaig et al. (1993: 71). The criteria for the building blocks were adapted on the basis of our empirical findings to make them applicable to Kenya, and specific points were added that were relevant to Kenya or to other African countries south of the Sahara, including the category "spaces and places". This resulted in the following criteria for the milieu building blocks[9]:

- Demography/social position: age, marital status, socialization (rural/urban), place of residence (rural/urban), education, occupation, languages used, social networks (ethnic, socioeconomically homogeneous/heterogeneous)
- Space and places: important places and meeting places, current mobility profile (more in the home/more outside the home), spatial dimension of social networks including long-distance contacts (internet, telephone), urban-rural contacts, diaspora contacts, personal experience of migration and travel
- Aims in life: basic values, identity, home (rural/urban), savings, investments, consumption, what is a *good life*, perspectives for old age, burial place
- Work/performance: role of occupation (just a job or constitutive of identity), career orientation, work ethos, socioeconomic mobility, attitude to education
- Image of society: basic social principles, political and civil society engagement, satisfaction with political and social system, perception of social problems, bases/sources of trust.

9 These milieu building blocks are the first result of our research. They are very broad and not yet clearly distinguished. The creation of significant categories is possible only on the basis of extensive empirical data. However, these building blocks serve to indicate the features of milieus that can be labeled empirically, and they offer a first empirical approach to a description of differentiations.

- Family/partnership, gender roles: family values, gender roles, partnership, sexual morality
- Leisure and communication: Leisure activities: family, nightclubs/dancing, events, reading, DVDs, sports (active/passive), general hedonism

  Communication: role of the internet, IT social networks, newspapers, TV, radio
- Everyday aesthetics: clothing, home, furnishings, equipment, hairstyle, body image, art, demonstrative consumption, status symbols
- Ideals and role models: elements of a "good life", wishes, dreams, role models, visions or plans for the future, fundamental value orientations, consumption and savings behavior

The additions made can be illustrated by a few examples. For Kenya and other African countries, which as a rule are multilingual, the languages used by people in their everyday lives are important, as well as the question of ethnically homogeneous or heterogeneous networks. The degree of a person's attachment to their home village, together with the desire to grow old and be buried there, also proved to be important criteria for differentiating between milieus. This also applies to the question of the sources of trust, which may be anchored in the family, the ethnic group, a region or an institution. There are clear differences in people's conceptions of gender roles and sexual morality. In the area of leisure and communication, the important activities and forms of communication are often not the same as in Europe. For instance, an important marker is the consumption or rejection of alcohol, while typical European markers such as going to the theatre or choosing particular television programs are not important.

Two examples: neo-traditional and religious Christian milieus

The way milieus may be distinguished from each other can be shown by taking the example of two conservative milieus. Although these two milieus overlap with regard to certain basic orientations, in this case certain conservative values, it is also possible to identify distinct differences between them. They can be described by means of the abovenamed milieu building blocks. These two conservative macromilieus agree especially on the importance of the family and share the same conservative ideas about gender roles or the rejection of homosexuality. However, there is also a whole range of prominent differences between them.

In neo-traditional milieus, social networks are mainly based on a shared ethnic identity such as Kikuyu, Luo, Luhya or Kalenjin[10]. In these networks a person's place of origin and the local language are important. There is a collective orientation focused on ethnic belonging, which can potentially be bound up with a political micronationalism focused on a particular region of Kenya. This may also involve claiming specific ethnically legitimized land rights on the basis of ethnic settlement patterns in the region. This ethnopolitical orientation is an important component of visions of the future. Referring to tradition is a way of legitimizing conservative values. This includes a special reference to extended families and rules and rituals associated with marriage (such as payment of a bride price), which can be combined with Christian or Western practices (a *white wedding*). Members of the same ethnic group have, at least nominally, a right to mutual aid, for instance with the financing of burials, including conveyance of the corpse to the hometown or village. Leisure activities often take place within ethnically homogeneous networks, and by no means exclude things like dancing and alcohol.

Importance is attached to the maintenance of traditional customs or dances, and tendencies toward folklorization can be observed. This includes an affinity for *neo-African clothing*[11] and corresponding objects and symbols. Respected elders are important role models for men, and for both sexes marital status and age determines the assignment of gender roles. Economic success in the rural environment and investment in the farm or in cattle are particularly important. As in Kenya generally, a high value is attached to education and getting a good job, but these are not core elements of the value system and are not pursued with the same degree of seriousness by all members of this milieu.

Information from interviews illustrates the complex relationship between members of the neo-traditional milieu in Nairobi and their rural home area. Joseph (interview, 14.04.2014),[12] a 52-year-old man from the ethnic group of Luhya in the Western part of Kenya, works as a taxi driver in Nairobi. He lives with three of his children on the outskirts of Nairobi

10 Due to the multiethnic population of Nairobi we find specific ethnic networks for nearly all Kenyan ethnic groups.

11 This is a term used to refer to garments made of batik cloth or kanga (a swathe of light cotton printed with *typically African* designs). These are fashions borrowed from West Africa or from the East African coast and have very little to do with what people wore in precolonial times.

12 All names in this chapter have been anonymized.

but also has close ties to his rural home. His job as a driver in Nairobi provides him with a stable income and he just finished building a house in his home area and plans to build another one in the next months. With his brother he grows back home tea, bananas, beans and maize, and they have also three cows. However, the financial gains are rather modest for Joseph because his brother uses most of the food and the money from sales to provide for relatives in their village. Joseph also helps occasionally relatives in Nairobi on their shamba (farm) and in return receives sometimes fruits and vegetables from them. The significance of family to him can also be seen in his answer to the question what is important in his life: "[I]mportant for me is just to put up my family strongly, support them [...]." Joseph is the head of his extended family which puts him in a respected position but brings also responsibility for relatives, including the families of his uncles. He inherited this position from his father because he was the first grandson and proved that he was reliable. The members of his extended family inform Joseph about their plans and discuss them with him.

Joseph is as well a respected elder in his home village, which includes several social duties such as solving arguments about demarcations of land, questions of marriage and disputed fatherhoods. Joseph spends most of his time in Nairobi and so he often gives advice by phone. He emphasizes that people in his village often ask him for money as they think he earns a lot in Nairobi and so they ask him for support. In spite of being an elder now, he has not always been physically present in his rural home. Joseph left his home village in 2003 after his wife had died there and and moved to Nairobi. He did not visit the village for seven years, but he also lacked the financial means to do so as he did not at first succeed to find work in the city. Like other members of the neo-traditional milieu, Joseph has two centers of life, one in the city and one in the countryside. In spite of living in the city, the community in the rural home area remains a very important point of reference in his life.

For members of the religious Christian milieu, the church community constitutes the main social network and is the chief point of reference in everyday life, in addition to the family. Contact with the extended family and with one's place of origin is an individual matter and not part of the joint canon of values. Particularly in towns, there are also ethnically heterogeneous church communities. Even in ethnically homogeneous congregations, ethnic ties do not play an important role in everyday life apart from sharing a common language. Conservative values are legitimized by referring to the Bible and not to tradition. This includes, at least nominally, the acknowledged duty to help socially disadvantaged people regardless of their ethnic or religious affiliation. While such help is often given to members of the congregation, the degree of willingness to help other socially disadvantaged people varies from group to group, despite general claims that this is an obligation. The ideal to live up to is a life that is pleasing to God, which means distancing oneself from leisure activities that are regarded as immoral and refusing to drink alcohol. Clothing must be modest and dignified in conformity with these moral ideas. Especially in protestant and fundamentalist groups, importance is attached to economic success, which brings to mind Max Weber's reading of Protestantism (2001 [1920]) as the expression of a godly life. Many Kenyan Christians regard worldly success as a sign of God's favor. Visions of the future are shaped by these religious ideas, together with religiously based career ambitions. Apart from having conservative values, Christian milieus do not represent any particular political orientation.

Betty (interview, 14.08.2014) is a 48-year-old woman who lives in Nairobi and says that she spends her life running a small business and preaching the gospel. She travels regularly to Mombasa and to Uganda where she buys clothes and other goods such as kikoys (a rectangular piece of woven fabric with many uses), shoes and tea that she sells in Nairobi. However, the most important part of her life is her Christian faith. After working from 1986 to 1995 in a company, she gave up her regular job and started selling things because she received the call to preach. Betty is not the head of a church, but she preaches regularly in Baptist and other parishes. She is on Thursdays, Saturdays and Sundays in church and has a fellowship meeting in her apartment with members of her church. In spite of her unstable financial situation, she was studying at the time of the interview at a Christian University.

According to Betty, she knows most of her friends from church or from her studies. These friends from religious contexts are from different ethnic groups and live in Nairobi, Mombasa, Eldoret and other Kenyan cities where she visits them regularly. She emphasizes that gospel-centered friendships are more important to her than the ones from business and she speaks with her Christian friends several times a week on the phone. While her religious beliefs are very important to Betty, she somewhat regrets that she will likely be buried in the Langata cemetery in Nairobi and not in the family plot in her rural home region in the Western part of Kenya where her parents are from. She says she misses having a rural home, but the current focus of her life is her religious activities. Before the death of her husband religion played a less central role in her life and they were married according to the customs of her own ethnic group, the Luhya. In contrast to Joseph, she does not have the same intense contact to her extended family. Also, her security networks are rather from religious circles and it was these friends who have supported her financially, for instance paying the university fees of her son.

The two milieus described here show that despite common conservative values, there are distinct differences with regard to values and orientations and that a different emphasis is laid on particular values and attitudes. The other milieus which were identified in the course of the fieldwork can be described in a similar way. These are: young professionals, social climbers, other conservative and religious milieus (Muslim, Hindu), liberal cosmopolitans and an apolitical stability oriented pragmatic milieu. The basic patterns of the two milieus outlined here that Joseph and Betty represent are shown in the table below with some added elements.

	Neo-traditional milieu	Christian milieu
Demography/ social position	All age groups; great importance of local language; often ethnically homogeneous networks; extended family important	All age groups; mostly grew up in rural areas; church as social network; group includes low and high incomes; differing degrees of contact to extended family
Space and places	Socialization in a rural area to at least some degree; place of origin is an important reference point; regular contact with place of origin, even when living elsewhere	Church as an important spatial point of reference; frequent meetings with church members (including activities such as Bible study or help for the poor); differing degrees of contact with place of origin
Aims in life	Maintenance of (ethnic) traditions and of ethnic customs; support of ethnic and local identity and belonging; family, village home; burial in home village; financial transfers and investments in village house/farm/cattle	A life conducted according to Christian values; economic success; preservation of Christian identity; respect and appreciation of the con-gregation; salvation in the afterlife

Work/ performance	Career is not of first importance; contact to local and ethnic group is preserved (for instance when studying abroad, or through activities to promote development in the home region)	Career is important and (if possible) high sums are invested in education and work; long working hours; desire for social advancement
Image of society	Solidarity/collective orientation (micronationalism); social and political engagement and trust along ethnic bonds; public observation of moral standards	Christian values very important; critique of immorality; help for socially disadvantaged people; importance of success
Family/ partnership/ gender roles	Importance of local family values and gender roles; importance of lineage or clan and the local community	Importance of Christian family values and gender roles; often a demonstrative rejection of sex before marriage
Leisure/ communication	Visits to family and relatives in home region; leisure time often spent with members of the same ethnic group	Leisure time often spent at church and in church groups (apart from time spent with family); many friends are church members
Everyday aesthetics	Clothing with strong 'African' elements (especially on festive occasions); importance of 'traditional' objects and symbols	Classic clothing; (if possible) manifestation of success through cars, clothing or type of home; (generous) donations to the church as sign of status
Ideals and role models	Respect elder; respected mother or father, grandmother or grandfather, successful farmer or herder	Economic success in agreement with Christian principles; success as expression of godly life; respect for religious authorities

Table 1: Comparison of neo-traditional and Christian milieus (Neubert/Stoll)

Conceptual conclusions and further challenges

The milieu building blocks and typology presented here represent a first attempt to describe sociocultural differentiation within the Kenyan middle class. Our identification of the milieus is based on an ongoing qualitative field study. Without systematically collected quantitative data, it is not possible to determine the size of these milieus, nor to say for certain whether they constitute a complete picture of all social milieus in urban Kenya. Highly visible and distinctive milieus can be identified and described using the qualitative data. Visibility is created by common institutions (such as churches), common organizations (such as so-called councils of elders as keepers of ethnic traditions) or sociopolitically active groups (such as women's rights organizations). Public self-representation is also helpful for identifying and describing specific milieus. For example, the "young professionals" milieu is easy to identify because its members demonstratively spend high sums on specific leisure activities. By contrast, for a long time we failed to register the milieu we have called *apolitical stability-oriented pragmatic*, since, apart from paid employment, the main activities take place inside the home.

Although this is still an ongoing study, our results confirm the existence of different milieus. The analysis of sociocultural differences adds a new dimension to any purely socioeconomic division into classes. The Christian milieu, for example, spans different socioeconomic classes. Each church community may be relatively homogeneous in socioeconomic terms, but the different communities share the same basic ideas and everyday practices that transcend socioeconomic boundaries. With improved data, the picture can be completed and sharpened. An important general finding is that milieu membership can be determined in the first place only for individuals, not for families. This can be seen for instance in the case of the Christian milieu, in which women predominate. The church is often not the middle point of their husbands' lives, even if the men are practicing Christians and regular churchgoers. Moreover, it is not uncommon for husband and wife to belong to two different churches.

However, against the backdrop of the milieu structure outlined here we need to ask whether the macromilieus capture all members of the Kenyan society. In the course of our fieldwork we began to doubt whether the whole of the Kenyan population can be allocated to macromilieus. According to our findings there are a number of individuals who cannot be unequivocally assigned to a particular macromilieu because they combine features of several milieus or switch between milieus according to the social setting. Nonetheless, the milieus identified here and the two examples discussed show that there really are subcultural units in Kenya consisting of people who share similar ideas and lifestyles. In these cases, where most social contacts outside the workplace happen in a uniform social space, the concept of macromilieus serves very well. These individuals share much more than just the specific behavior and norms of a part-time setting in a particular place (such as a fitness studio, a discotheque or a women's group). The common social reality of the members of such a milieu is comprehensive and consists of many overlapping small lifeworlds. Furthermore, their commonalities are based on shared basic norms and values and go far beyond a social network with a specific purpose or a loosely connected small lifeworld. We are therefore inclined to conclude that the macromilieu concept (as in the Sinus model) and the small lifeworld concept are not mutually exclusive. Rather, there is plenty of evidence to suggest that in Kenya there are macromilieus which can be described in social structural terms, and a considerable number of Kenyan citizens who cannot clearly be assigned to any of these milieus. This latter group is involved in several different small lifeworlds with differing, and in some cases contradictory, values.[13] We therefore plead for a comprehensive analysis which distinguishes certain milieu cores, around the borders of which are people who only partly share or live the basic values and practices of the milieu in question. This results in clear overlapping areas between milieus and a large group of people who belong simultaneously to very different milieus or small lifeworlds.

This leads to the question whether this open milieu approach could also be used to describe societies in the Global North. The continuing statistical accuracy of the macro-milieu method suggests that in Germany and Europe there might also be milieus which could accurately be described as milieu cores. This also suggests that further conceptual work on group structures is necessary, using the available data. It is important to note here that in Germany and Europe, too, families and households do not necessarily belong to the same milieu, as many studies seem to suggest. At the same time, the small lifeworld approach makes it possible to include those people who do not fit into the fixed pattern of macromilieus in an analysis of sociocultural differentiation on a lower level of social aggregation. This takes into account the fact that these small lifeworlds are too diverse to be considered as macromilieus. Additionally, this concept allows us to analyze how these small lifeworlds are connected.

For the analysis of African societies it is necessary to continue developing the criteria for distinguishing different milieus (milieu building

13 One example is a young woman who is an active member of a Christian women's group which strictly refuses alcohol and promotes sexual abstinence. At the same time, she has a sexual liaison with a married man and goes dancing, enjoying alcoholic drinks in the clubs.

blocks), making them as specific and meaningful as possible. Only then will it be possible to produce empirical evidence of the existence of sociocultural milieu cores by means of quantitative studies. This sociocultural analysis of the African middle class (taking Kenya as an example) is only a first step. In a subsequent step, the analysis must be extended to include the upper class and especially the quantitatively dominant lower class. Our study of the middle class may serve as a beginning. Due to their better socioeconomic position, members of the middle class have more freedom of choice with regard to planning their future and consumption preferences. They are able to put different values into practice which makes sociocultural differences clearer. At the same time the middle class is more easily accessible for research of this kind than the upper class, which is often isolated and aloof. An analysis of sociocultural differentiation in the middle class can close an important gap in the analysis of the structure of African societies.

As we said in the beginning, focusing on sociocultural differentiation should not lead to leaving out the existence and consequences of social inequality. Employment insecurity, the uncertain success of small and medium-sized businesses and dependence on sociopolitical power structures that go beyond milieu boundaries are common conditions affecting peoples' lives which cannot be ignored. This has been described and analyzed for people living in poverty (Freeman et al. 2004; Githinji 2000; Ouma 2006), but also applies – with less severe consequences – to the middle class. The next step towards a comprehensive analysis of social structure would be the combination of socioeconomic inequalities with all its consequences with the analysis of sociocultural differentiation. Our contribution to this much larger project is to underline that the analysis of social structure needs to include the sociocultural diversity. We contribute with the analysis of macromilieus despite its limits an approach that reaches beyond ethnic or religious differences and might pave the way for the conceptualization of sociocultural differences against the backdrop of socioeconomic inequality.

This analysis of sociocultural differences extends the concept of diversity to the dimension of social differentiation. Most authors in the diversity debate point to individuals and their right to be respected and accepted with their particularities. In contrast, the study of socialcultural differentiation and the concepts of *milieu* and *small lifeworlds* focus on differences between groups, which are marked by similar sociocultural orientations or shared practices. In this case study on Nairobi, diversity is an empirical fact that contradicts simplified notions of *the* middle class. The diversity debate points to claims and rights of individuals who should be recognized as equal persons and citizens despite differences in race, color, sexual orientation or body performance. This highlights the fact that two discourses of difference, sociocultural differences and diversity, represent different perspectives. First, the normative claim of diversity asks for acceptance of marked difference as different and at the same time claims to ignore the difference as a minor fact that does not have to interfere with social interactions and social positions. Sociocultural difference highlights sociocultural diversity as an empirical fact and states that certain practices, beliefs and norms are the reason why groups (milieus) live in different ways. Difference is an element of their particular ways of life, which distinguish them from other milieus. This difference overarches all parts of society as a whole. Apart from the claim to be part of the society the difference is considered as an element of their particular identities that is important too. The diversity debate claims equality despite diversity and stresses the legitimacy of social inclusion. Sociocultural difference marked by ways of life (milieus) underline difference as expression of separate identities and of being different. When we refer to diversity, we need to consider these contradicting perspectives as social inclusion on the one hand and analytical perspective on sociocultural difference on the other hand.

List of Abbreviations

AfDB	African Development Bank
OECD	Organization for Economic Cooperation and Development

List of Figures

List of Tables

References

AfDB (African Development Bank) (2011): "The middle of the pyramid: dynamics of the middle class in Africa. Market Brief. April 20, 2011". Available at: www.afdb.org/fileadmin/uploads/afdb/Documents/Publications/The%20Middle%20of%20the%20Pyramid_The%20Middle%20of%20the%20Pyramid.pdf (02.04.2017).

Banerjee, Abhijit V./Duflo, Esther (2008): What is Middle Class about the Middle Classes around the World?, in: Journal of Economic Perspectives, 22: 2, 3-28.

Berger, Peter L./Luckmann, Thomas (1966): The social construction of reality. A treatise in the sociology of knowledge- Garden City.

Bourdieu, Pierre (1982): Die feinen Unterschiede. Frankfurt am Main.

Daniel, Antje/Neubert, Dieter (2014): Middle classes and political instability in Kenya: Civil society organizations during the post-election violence of 2007/2008. Dominique Darbon/ Toulabor, Comi. L'invention des classes moyennes africaines. Enjeu politique d'un catégorie incertaine. Paris, 155-184.

Easterly, William (2001): The Middle Class Consensus and Economic Development, in: Journal of Economic Growth, 6: 4, 317-335.

Flaig, Berthold B./Meyer, Thomas/Ueltzhöffer, Jörg (1993): Alltagsästhetik und politische Kultur: Zur ästhetischen Dimension politischer Bildung und politischer Kommunikation. Bonn.

Freeman, Ade H./Ellis, Frank/Allison, Eddie (2004): Livelihoods and rural poverty reduction in Kenya, in: Development Policy Review, 22: 2, 147-171.

Geißler, Rainer (2006): Soziale Klassen und Schichten – Soziale Lagen – Soziale Milieus: Modelle und Kontroversen. Geißler, Rainer. Die Sozialstruktur Deutschlands. Zur gesellschaftlichen Entwicklung mit einer Bilanz zur Vereinigung. Wiesbaden, 93-120.

Githinji, Mwangi W. (2000): Ten millionaires and ten million beggars. A study of income distribution and development in Kenya. Aldershot.

Hitzler, Ronald/ Honer, Anne (1984): Lebenswelt – Milieu – Situation: terminologische Vorschläge zur theoretischen Verständigung, in: Kölner Zeitschrift für Soziologie und Sozialpsychologie, 36: 1, 56-74.

Hitzler, Ronald and Honer, Anne (1988): Der lebensweltliche Forschungsansatz, in: Neue Praxis, 18: 6, 496-501.

Honer, Anne (1985): Beschreibung einer Lebens-Welt. Zur Empirie des Bodybuilding, in: Zeitschrift für Soziologie 14: 2, 131-139.

Hradil, Stefan (1987): Sozialstrukturanalyse in einer fortgeschrittenen Gesellschaft. Von Klassen und Schichten zu Lagen und Milieus. Opladen.

Isenböck, Peter (2014): Die Form des Milieus. Zum Verhältnis von gesellschaftlicher Differenzierung und Formen der Vergemeinschaftung, in: Zeitschrift für theoretische Soziologie/Sonderband 1, Weinheim.

Kharas, Homi (2010): The Emerging Middle Class in Developing Countries, OECD Development Centre Working Paper 285.

Lentz, Carola (2015): Elites or middle classes? Lessons from transnational research for the study of social stratification in Africa, in: Working Paper of the Department of Anthropology and African Studies, 161, Mainz.

McKinsey Global Institute (2010): "Lions on the move: The progress and potential of African economies". Available at: www.mckinsey.com/insights/africa/lions_on_the_move (04.04.2015).

Milanovic, Branko/Yitzhaki, Shlomo (2002): Decomposing World Income Distribution: Does the World have a Middle Class?, in: Review of Income and Wealth, 48: 2, 155-178.

Mitchell, Arnold (1983): The nine American lifestyles: Who we are and where we're going. Basingstoke.

Ncube, Mthuli/Lufumpa, Charles L. (eds.) (2015): The Emerging Middle Class in Africa. London and New York.

Neubert, Dieter (2005): Kulturelle Differenz und soziale Strukturierung in Afrika. Kößler, Reinhart/Kumitz, Daniel/Schultz, (Ulrike eds.): Gesellschaftstheorie und Provokationen der Moderne. Peripherie-Sonderband 1, Münster, 178-192.

Neubert, Dieter (2014): What is "Middle Class"?. In Search for an Appropriate Concept, in: Middle East: Topics & Arguments, 2, 23-35.

Ouma, Owuor Samuel (2006): Bridging the urban-rural divide. Multi-spatial livelihoods in Nakuru town, Kenya. Research Report, 81, Leiden.

Otte, Gunnar (2005): Hat die Lebensstilforschung eine Zukunft? Eine Auseinandersetzung mit aktuellen Bilanzierungsversuchen, in: Kölner Zeitschrift für Soziologie und Sozialpsychologie, 57: 1, 1-31.

Ravallion, Martin (2010): The developing world's bulging (but vulnerable) "Middle Class", World Development 38 (4), 445-454.

Rebstein, Bernd/Schnettler, Bernt (2014): Sozialstrukturanalyse ‚feiner Körnung' oder subjektzentrierte Lebensweltanalyse? Ungleichheitsbezogene und wissenssoziologische Ansätze der Milieuanalyse. Isenböck, Peter/Nell, Linda/ Renn Joachim. Die Form des Milieus: Zum Verhältnis von gesellschaftlicher Differenzierung und Formen der Vergemeinschaftung, 1. Sonderband der Zeitschrift für Theoretische Soziologie. Weinheim and Basel, 46-68.

Rehbein, Boike (2004): Globalisierung in Laos: Transformation des ökonomischen Feldes. Münster.

Rehbein, Boike (2007): Globalisierung, Sozialkulturen und Sozialstruktur. Einige Konsequenzen aus der Anwendung von Bourdieus Sozialtheorie in Südostasien, in: Soziale Welt, 58: 2, 187-202.

Rössel, Jörg/Otte, Gunnar (2012): Lebensstilforschung, in: Kölner Zeitschrift für Soziologie und Sozialpsychologie, Sonderheft 51.

Schulze, Gerhard (1992): Die Erlebnisgesellschaft. Kultursoziologie der Gegenwart, Frankfurt am Main and New York.

Sinus Sociovision (2009): "Informationen zu den Sinus-Milieus 2009". Available at: www.sinus-institut.de/uploads/tx_mpdownloadcenter/informationen_2009_01.pdf (04.04.2015).

Soeffner, Hans-Georg/Zifonun, Dariuš (2008): Integration und soziale Welten. Soeffner, Hans-Georg/Neckel, Sighard. Mittendrin im Abseits. Ethnische Gruppenbeziehungen im lokalen Kontext. Wiesbaden, 115-132.

Solga, Heike/Powell, Justin/Berger, Peter A. (eds.) (2009): Soziale Ungleichheit. Klassische Texte zur Sozialstrukturanalyse. Frankfurt am Main and New York.

Spronk, Rachel (2012): Ambiguous Pleasures: Sexuality and Middle Class Self-Perceptions in Nairobi. New York and Oxford.

Stoll, Florian (2012): Leben im Moment. Soziale Milieus und ihr Umgang mit Zeit in Recife, Brasilien. Frankfurt am Main.

Vester, Michael/Geiling, Heiko/Hermann, Thomas/Müller, Dagmar/von Oertzen, Peter (eds.) (2001): Soziale Milieus im gesellschaftlichen Strukturwandel. Zwischen Integration und Ausgrenzung. Frankfurt am Main.

Weber, Max (2001 [1920]): The Protestant Ethic and the Spirit of Capitalism, New York.

Zifonun, Dariuš (2010): Ein ‚gallisches Dorf'? Integration, Stadtteilbildung und Prestigeordnung in einem ‚Armenviertel'. Zifonun, Dariuš/Marion Müller (eds.): Ethnowissen. Soziologische Beiträge zu ethnischer Differenzierung und Migration. Wiesbaden, 311-328.

Zifonun, Dariuš (2015): Milieu as Structures of Interaction. Vertovec, Steven. Routledge International Handbook of Diversity Studies. New York, 102-105.

Zifonun, Dariuš/Cindark, Ibrahim (2004): Segregation oder Integration? Die soziale Welt eines ‚türkischen' Fußballvereins in Mannheim, in: Deutsche Sprache, 2: 3, 270-298.

Individual Pluralities

Hypermarginal Strategies: Refugees with Disability in the Danish Welfare State

Thomas Hughes

Introduction

This article seeks to contribute anthropological knowledge on strategies, issues of belonging and identity of refugees with disability in their engagement with systems of social and health support from the Danish welfare state as well as Danish society more generally[1]. While faithful to this area of investigation, the project proceeds with caution so as to not simply reproduce or loop (Hacking 1995) the categories, problems and dichotomies presumed by this research task. The lives of refugees with disability and their families have been investigated before in Denmark, but there is little in the way of anthropological work. Much of the research has been from a public health or policy research perspective, often with a focus on *barriers*. According to one report "barriers cause many families with ethnic minority backgrounds to be marginalized" in their engagement with state services (Lyhne 2007: 19). The processes of *marginalization* have a bodily aspect, as ethnic minority groups in Denmark rate their overall health lower than *ethnic Danes* with more health problems including disability related illnesses (Vinther-Jensen 2010; Andersen et al. 2011: 1; Singhammer 2008). While this focus on *barriers* can be helpful in some ways, the concept of a barrier assumes a rather simplistic pathway. From an *experience-near* approach we see a more complex image of pressing social dilemmas and strategies, as well as subjective implications emerge.

1 I am critically aware of the common pitfall of presuming immigrants and refugees to be a problem (Hervik 1999) or "burden" for the welfare state (Olwig/Pærregaard 2011: 10).

Methodology

I employed the anthropological techniques of participant observation, ethnographic interviews, focus groups (Macun/Posel 1998) and audio/visual tools. This anthropological approach specifically allows for an ethnographic exploration of "everyday life and the dimensions of individual's experiences and agency – the processes by means of which identity and belonging are *lived* and negotiated, created and transformed by migrants as agents" (Tošić 2012: 114). This article is based on a multisited (Marcus 1995: 95) and multisided fieldwork across various relevant Danish treatment centers, social fora, governmental social initiatives, and civil organizations. My methodological vantage point was to let my informants be the experts (Spradley 1980: 465), while remaining critical and analytical. In order to counteract the effect of potentially being understood as "part of the system" when talking to informants at government institutions, I also found informants through more informal ways, i.e. my connections with various ethnic minority civil organizations and my existing network from previous fieldwork in Denmark. In this process I was able to collect and compare a multiplicity of coexisting, and sometimes directly competing, points of views present in this field (Bourdieu 1991: 3) and look for the incongruences and gaps in the culturally inflected logics at play.

This yearlong fieldwork was based in Copenhagen, but included many trips to other regions of Denmark. As an anthropologist, participant observation was my *core methodology*, allowing me to come closer to an experience and understanding of my informants' worlds from their point of view (Hume/Mulcock 2005: xi). Using my social self as a research tool (Powdermaker 1966: 19) allowed me to attain a general understanding of the dynamics present in this field and helped me to formulate relevant questions for my interviews (Bernard 2006: 355). In this fieldwork, my position as a fellow foreigner (Hughes 2013) was generally advantageous. My status as an American citizen who has lived in Copenhagen for seven years at the time allowed me an interesting third position in a political climate of *us and them* (see Larsen 2013). I seemed to fit in neither and this was often of benefit. When speaking with people with recent immigrant backgrounds, I was able to at least partially meet them on some level of the *immigrant experience*. This held true surprisingly even when dealing with Iraqi informants. In these interactions, not being *Danish* proved more important than any negative associations with the United States. My status as a foreigner also often made it easier for informants to open up to me by providing an automatic topic of discussion as well as a mutual understanding.

This fieldwork was institutionally based at the Copenhagen Disability Center, but also included data collected during a collaboration with a Copenhagen Municipality on a initiative to improve support for youth with disabilities and non-Danish backgrounds, and from a collaboration[2] with the patient organization conglomerate Danish Handicap Organizations on the project *Double Minorities*, which aimed at greater inclusion of ethnic minorities with disabilities in Danish civil society (*civilsamfundet*). I was also in close contact with the Danish Islamic Center and the Disabled Student Center. I documented my observations in the form of field notes, photography and video, including collaborating with a former humanitarian refugee and social activist on a short film about life in a wheelchair.

In this fieldwork, I carried out 25 semi-structured interviews with eight families with physically disabled members of refugee background, as well as with other individuals with disability (including a further five non-refugee families with non-western immigrant backgrounds), disabled *ethnic Danes*, municipal case workers, Copenhagen Disability Center personnel, and various local experts and researchers. I approached these interviews as an integrated part of my participant observation (Rubow 2003). Rather than solely focusing on the exchange of words, I included my observations of the social context and circumstance of these encounters as empirical material. The context of the interviews was also a source of data and these meetings often took place at the informant's home, giving great insight into their lives. The circumstances that led to an interview and the atmosphere created by this process were also considered in my data collection (O'Reilly 2005: 115). The use of categories was of key importance in this field and I relied on an *auto driven* interview style (Clark 1999) in order to allow my informants to navigate me through the complex (re-)production of emic categories in the field.

---

2 Each of these collaborations consisted of the municipality and the patient connecting me with relevant informants (e.g. community organizers, experts, people with disability), while I provided feedback on their initiatives based on the existing research in the area. I also presented early findings for the municipality in workshop for caseworkers.

Fig. 1: Informant showing me around Aalborg (Photo by Thomas Hughes, 2015)

Working with(in) Categories

A careful look at the vague and politically charged (Kasnitz/Shuttleworth 2001: 2) categories of *ethnic minority*, *refugee* and *disability* already points to a more complex social landscape. These categories are in themselves variant, complex, and to some degree *fractured* entities. An aim of this article is to provide some nuance to the dilemmas surrounding these categories in this social arena and their negotiation's impact on social identity and experience.

The focus of this chapter is on so-called *physical* disability, although other forms of disability were also included in the study. *Disability* is in itself a quite complex and complicated category. Research by Western scholars is often informed by the British social model, in which there is differentiation between biological anomaly, i.e. *impairment* (Barnes/Mercer/Shakespeare 1999: 28), and its social consequences, i.e. *disability* (see Barnes et al. 1999; Oliver 1990). This sharp analytical distinction has been rightfully criticized for its clean divide between the *bodily* and the social (Shakespeare 2006; Shuttleworth/Kasnitz 2004; Thomas/Corker 2002; Tremain 2002; see also Staples 2011). Disability should rather be viewed as consisting of a complex composite of interrelated social and bodily aspects, much as Arthur Kleinman argues mental illness to be conceptually located "where culture and biology reciprocally interact" (Kleinman 1988: 187). While medical sociologist Tom Shakespeare argues concisely that "people are disabled by society and by their bodies and minds" (Shakespeare 2014: 5), it is important to emphasize and examine the nebulous interconnections between these defining elements of what constitutes *disabled* personhood.

Now to approach the complexity of the category *refugee*, we must briefly look at how it is intertwined with a larger discussion on immigration in Demark. Despite popular conception, Denmark has had a long history of immigration and international flux (Olwig/Pærregaard 2011; see also Kristensen 2002; Nelleman 1981; Willerslev 1983). In light of this we may assume that neither the category of *ethnic minority* nor the category of *refugee*, though more specific, represent homogenous (Bektovic 2004: 31) internally integrated social groups. Ethnic minorities and the Muslim *community* are not cohesive groups with harmonious relations among themselves and to others. As one informant observed, "the Arab kids fight with the Somalis. Honestly it is shocking how much racism there is in the mosques and my backyard." Immigrants and asylum seekers come to Denmark with widely differing educational, sociocultural, political, and demographic profiles (Galal 2002: 113; Petersen et al. 2012; Lyhne 2007: 19). My informants are primarily people who came to Denmark as refugees, often *humanitarian* refugees, in the 1980s and 1990s, which is to say not in the current highly politicized *influx* of refugees regularly shown in the media. Despite their origin, many of my informants would not readily self-identify as *refugees* or even *former refugees*. This reflects a certain social stigma associated with the category, especially in the current Danish political discourse around immigration and asylum seekers.

In *Mistrusting Refugees* (1995) anthropologists Errol Daniel explores the importance of the category refugee to conclude that "in a very profound sense, one becomes a refugee before ever fleeing the society in which one lives, and one continues to be a refugee even after receiving asylum in the new place one is received" (Daniel 1995: 10). Refugee status, beyond its political meaning, is in this sense a *permanent* condition, however also a potentially impermanent or conditional aspect of personal identity that is contextually negotiated. That is to say, this category is in no way a monolithic identity marker, but rather a particular aspect of a multidimensional, perhaps fractured, personhood, which provides a theoretically significant and methodological useful index. From the start of this project, I thus decided not to apply the category of *disability*, nor *ethnic minority*, nor *refugee* to the individuals and families in the field, rather I followed how the categories were self-applied (or not) and how categories were (re)produced in the mechanics of the Danish welfare state.

Analytical Approach and Theoretical Frame

The analytical approach of this project seeks to effectively conceptualize, analyze, and situate the subject's experience of health, illness and sociality. The dilemmas of individuals and families were approached from a phenomenological standpoint inspired by the work of medical anthropologists Arthur and Joan Kleinman and Byron J. Good. This was done in an effort to provide an "experience near" analysis in contrast to more quantitative and top down perspectives prevalent in this field of interest. The overall arch of this analytical project followed in step with ideas developed by Byron J. Good while working in Indonesia. I began by working *inward* through a cultural phenomenology of the voices of my informants in order to investigate how my informants' experience and meaning-making are woven into their ethnicity, disability, and health and social support strategies (Good et al. 2007: 18). These emerging subjectivities are then interpreted outward in analysis of linkages to larger processes that shape this discourse. This look at the macrostructural is imperative in any fieldwork (Wacquant 2008: 9) and it provides critical balance to the phenomenological interests in this study. This theoretical framing considers the conflicts many of my informants negotiate between multiple spheres of identity, belonging and support. Although the focus of this paper centers on issues of disability and ethnicity, larger discussions of marginalization, and overlapping stigma or intersections of spoiled identities (Goffman 1963) are also relevant in an effort to conceptualize the dilemmas negotiated by outsiders among outsiders.

In a phenomenological exploration of these subjectivities, dilemmas of identity demand theoretical engagement. The continual reflection on constraints and tensions with and between categories and identity led naturally to an interest in Crenshaw's *intersectionality* concept in attempts to *map the margins* of a social context. The focus of *intersectionality* was originally on the overlap of categories of race and gender, but it was later expanded to encompass other categories such as class, sexual orientation, and age. This concept seeks to "account for the multiple grounds of identity when considering how the social world is constructed" (Crenshaw 1995: 358) and is useful for thinking about *multi minorities* in Denmark. However, we must also account for how this intersection is negotiated and its subjective impact. Furthermore, I wish to emphasize that this subject position involves facing more than just a doubled form of oppression (Stuart 1993), but rather these forms of oppression are exponential and *compounding*. The particular *compounding* (Spencer 2014) effect here is a reference to an intensification from intertwinement of acts of victimization and subsequent social conditions. The point here is that there can be multiple and overlapping social dynamics of marginalization at play, which can produce a "compounding effect". Rather than being socially marginalized on two planes – ethnicity and disability – they are rather at the margins of already marginalized communities. To emphasize the exponential and compounding aspect of this intersectional position, I use the term *hypermarginality*.[3] This could apply to any subject with a marginal position in an already marginalized community.

Looking through these subjectivities to more macrostructural processes, it then becomes useful to think with perspectives from Wacquant's work on marginality in a contemporary and urban European context. What Loïc Wacquant terms *advanced marginality*, with *advanced* referring to the fact that these forms of marginality "stand ahead of us" (Wacquant 1996: 123), are perspectives on the social and geopolitical context of this phenomenological pursuit. The trends he identifies are increasingly visible in Denmark and generally in the Scandinavian welfare states. Wacquant's extensive work on the dynamics of marginality in Europe and North America points to emerging processes of precarity and novel forms of urban mar-

3 The term is also partly inspired by Mary-Jo Good's concept of "hyperdiversity" in *Shattering Culture* (2011).

ginality in Western Europe. Wacquant notes a "symbolic fragmentation of marginalized populations" (Wacquant 1996: 121). He describes an "absence of a common idiom by which to unify themselves symbolically accentuates the objective social dispersion and fragmentation" (Wacquant 1996: 128) that marginalizes people in this context.

Fig. 2: A fractured political landscape: "Stop Facismen" on Danish People's Party Poster (Photo by Thomas Hughes, 2015)

Inspired by this idea of *fragmentation*, and theories of intersectionality, this article aims to address some of the practical elements and subjective impacts of *compounding* social dilemmas of category and identity encountered at the meeting of disability and ethnicity in Denmark. The term *hypermarginality* is not meant to indicate a more severe life condition or *victimhood* as such, but rather suggests a conceptual focus on understanding the negotiation and impact of multiple and compounding levels of social exclusion. In fact, many of my informants felt that they were the *lucky ones*, in that they made it to a country with a comparatively well-developed infrastructure to *support* citizens with disability and furthermore *lucky* that they arrived in a different political climate of refugee placement in Europe. A focus on hypermarginality allows us to highlight some of the social dilemmas that nevertheless present themselves in this seemingly *supportive* Danish environment. The issue of common idioms or categories is clearly relevant; however, in the subjectivity explored below in the case story, we will see a more complex picture of various forms of strategic social engagement and disengagement.

Abuukar

The following excerpts are from the first conversation I had in Spring 2015 with Abuukar[4], a middle-aged man born in Somalia who came to Denmark via Kenya as a humanitarian refugee in the 1990s. Abuukar's story shares many of the elements of other informants' experience. Although this narrative is set in the past, the material can also provide some perspective on the present dilemmas of inclusion/exclusion negotiated by many of my informants. As he says, there are many who feel like him and this interview set me on a path of exploring the field in terms of a negotiation of multiple layers of social inclusion/exclusion. We had only briefly spoken on the telephone before I went to visit him for the first time, where he told me his story. A testament to Abuukar's assertive personality and agency, he contacted me in response to a flyer with my information circulating on social media. His email was short and to the point, as was our conversation on the phone. He said he had something to say about 'minorities with disability' because he was one. I traveled from Copenhagen to meet him in his home, a quiet and modern looking assisted living community in the suburbs of Aarhus, Denmark's second largest city. Throughout our first interview he was very forthcoming; in fact, it was more of a monologue than a dialogue. He was eager to share his story. These ethnographic excerpts are an attempt to *let him speak*, following the flow of his narrative as he laid it out. His "history" starts with the day of his car accident:

> I start first with myself, with my history. I became disabled in 1998, no 1988 in Somalia. At that time I was very young, 19, 20 years, and at that time I got my first job at the United Nations office, you know in the capital of Somalia. I worked with the United Nations, but I got in this car accident and I got the spinal cord injury that left me without legs. I lost all my young ability.[5]

Abuukar seems to emphasize his job at the United Nations in order illustrate his agency and capability. This push-pull of agency and victimhood is a running theme in our encounters. It was important to him to present himself as an *able* and empowered person, perhaps to counter prejudices, while he was also keen to point out forms of exclusion he has encountered. There is, however, more to the story of how he *became disabled*, the day he *lost* his youth. In order to understand his injury, it is important to

4 This is a pseudonym.

5 This interview was conducted in English.

understand the historical and social context, namely that this car accident occurred during the start of the ongoing Somali Civil War in the mid-1980s.

> I was 14 or 15 months in the hospital, you know the doctors… well the Somali Civil War just started and you know most of the doctors and United Nation workers, they flew out of the country. And you know everything was collapsing, hospitals, schools, everything you know. And I was just lying in the bed with my family, you know my father, my brother, my sister were there. I don't get any treatment what so ever. In a way, I was very lucky because you know it was my spinal cord, I don't have any pain. It was a fracture of the L1, *so if I had got to see a doctor like here in Denmark maybe I would not have become disabled.* It is a very, very small fracture, but I didn't have any doctor or any treatment there.

Abuukar was in this way partially "disabled" by the structural violence of a civil war. He received social support from his family but was unable to access the necessary treatment. When telling me this, he does not seem bitter, sad, or angry. In fact, he emphasizes how he felt "lucky" at the time because at least he was not in pain. He mentions Denmark in reference to the biomedical possibilities and another thematic tension appears: Denmark as a place of alienation and social exclusion versus Denmark as a place of support and infrastructure, especially for disabled people. These two dynamics can be difficult to square, as was made clear when he went on to talk about struggles of subsequently arriving and living in rural Denmark as a refugee. He mentioned the bewildering and frustrating experience of social and practical difficulties that, despite his efforts, seemed to plague him more than his impairment.

> At the end of 1994 I got the [placement] in Denmark with my family. I come here with my sister, my two sons and my wife. We come to Ålborg[6]. So I start to learn this language, I start school (vocational training) and we got a home there, so we are very happy. This first year was very hard, because we come here in February, in the wintertime. It was very hard. It was very cold, we don't know how to speak the language, we don't even know how to use the washing machine [laughs]. You have to accept it though. We didn't have another choice [laughs]! We didn't have anywhere to go back to. Our country was collapsing...

Though he laughs here, it is clear that this was a very difficult and painful time for him and his family. His wife and children are noticeably absent from his life now. This feeling of being trapped and confused, the uncertainty of life in Denmark, and, above all, the feeling of social exclusion from the Danes seems to shake him in the interview more deeply than the

6 A mid-sized city in the north of Jutland.

tragedy of his *disablement* in Somalia. There he knew what to expect, however poor the conditions, and he had a sense of belonging. Living in Denmark was difficult on many levels: language barriers, sense of social and geographic alienation, and disability – all these challenges had a compounding effect. In facing multiple social and practical dilemmas, it is difficult to see a starting point, to find a handhold. Abuukar went on to describe a very practical instance of compounding difficulties in his early life in Denmark:

> I was in the bathroom by myself and because of my injury I have no feeling in my legs you know. My leg was touching what was the heater and I didn't know what it was. I didn't know it. Suddenly I was badly burned, but I didn't know how to call the doctor or the ambulance and most of the Danish people then didn't speak English, so it was a very hard first. Also, I couldn't even use my bank account in the first month. I couldn't access the money I had [laughs] because the bank was very far and, as I said, I was afraid to go outside. I was not so active then. I didn't understand the culture. You know in Africa at the refugee camp, you don't have any access. There is dirt, there is stone, you can't drive this wheelchair, it is very hard. You can't move 100 meters, very hard [in] Africa. You need every time someone to help you. Here there were roads, but no one to help you…

Here we see further dilemmas of support and belonging, but on a very practical level. What matters more: Social or structural inclusion/exclusion? Abuukar expresses feeling in a way torn facing these compounding dilemmas and in turn his sense of self as a Somali, an African, and a disabled person problematically coexist. He was, however, determined to overcome these challenges in his life. He eventually embraced more avenues of infrastructural support for disabled people in Denmark. He later tells of the wonder of learning to drive a car, something he never thought possible before. Nevertheless, despite infrastructural support from the Danish welfare state, his feelings of social alienation and exclusion persisted.

Fig. 3: Abuukar showing me around Bazar Vest (Photo by Thomas Hughes, 2015)

So I got the training. You know the Danish call it "genoptræning" (rehabilitation) for disability. Eventually, I got a better wheelchair, I got a disabled bathroom, I got a disabled apartment.

I remember when a driving teacher come to me and say Abuukar you have to learn to drive a car. But how? "By hand." And I say I can't, you can't! But I got a car for the first time in my life. After a while I thought everything will be ok. It took a really long time, but things were becoming normal, but we were still living a really hard life. I know this country. They are some very racist people. That is my

> own research, I did my own research. You know the people near Zealand[7] are more open. In the North people are very strict. They didn't like the foreigners, they didn't like refugees, they didn't like asylum seekers. You know they even don't like the small kids of these people in the schools. So it is very hard and the Ålborg city, at that time, you know the Danish government was tasked to resettle people there, but you know "integration", it was a new theory.

He went on to discuss his experience of general skepticism from local Ålborg society. He and other Somalis felt blamed for the terrorist attacks and piracy ever present in the western media. These pressures took a toll on his family, as his socially alienated sons eventually moved away.

> When they saw Muslim women with the hijab, they stood there and stared, their faces looking very [disapproving and hostile], and say what are these people and where do they come from? Who are they and what are they doing here? We don't need these kinds of people. Every day you see some bad article in the newspaper, so we say "ooohh we don't like to live here", but you know you have to accept it. We don't have another choice, haha. We don't have anywhere to go back to. Our country was collapsing, we don't have any government. So we don't have any other choice and so we have to accept it, but it is hard. You know my kids were having problems in the school with the teacher. You know the … it is very hard.

> They told him [my older son] "we don't need black people; we don't need you" and sometimes they would hit him. And so he came to me and said father, "I don't want to live here." So I sent him back to Africa. He went there for three months over the holiday. When he come back, he was more aggressive. Over there he felt freedom, he made friends. He told me over the phone "father I don't want to be in Denmark anymore". I told him, you have a future here and Kenya is not your country either.

The paradigm shift after 9/11 towards paranoia surrounding Muslims in general in Denmark has been well documented (See Rytter/Pedersen 2011). Islam and a Muslim identity are being, and have been, used in the contemporary Danish integration debate to increase the perception of a rift between the values of *us* and *them* (Larsen 2013: 11; see also Henkel 2011; Hervik 2004; Jensen 2007; Rytter/Pedersen 2011; Schmidt 2007). For Abuukar, this skepticism seems socially unavoidable amongst *the Danes* and what pains him most is how it affects his children.

> They are automatically blamed (for violence committed by other Muslims) by the teacher, school friends and their families, out in public, the shop, on TV, everywhere. So you become very angry, you think why?![8]

---

7 Zealand is one of the islands that the capital city Copenhagen is located on.

8 The 2016 suicide bomber attack on a Daallo Airlines flight by a Somali man who allegedly used his wheelchair status to evade security likely does not help in this

This sense of *undeserved* social stigma leads to anger and frustration in him and his family. However, Abuukar also has to deal with other layers of social stigma. As a Somali refugee he felt like an outsider in Denmark, but as a disabled person he also felt like an outsider in his own community's *culture*:

> I read something once about Somalia, disability, and culture. We have a disability stigma as our culture. Myself when I became disabled, I was very shy to go outside because my friends [would see me and call me] "nin dheer". "Nin Dheer" means the tall man. I am two meters. They would say "nin dheer" is sitting and can't get up. So in our culture, disability is something bad… I felt bad. You know the disabled Somali people are mostly hiding inside. That is our culture.
>
> The problem is when a person who is already shy of their disability enters another culture and looks for support and there is nobody. In Denmark, no one is asking me to be a part of disability organizations and in my own culture disability is bad. No one is asking me to be a part of the society…

He felt like he was on the outskirts of his *own community* and the Danish community. He neither feels included in Danish social circles of disability nor in Danish society at large. He feels excluded from Danish society as an ethnic other, yet he is also ostracized from his own ethnic community for being disabled and from this point of social exclusion he is also disconnected from a Danish community of disabled people. He felt tribeless, no one was inviting him in to *their society*. As opposed to many disabled ethnic Danes, he was not involved in a political or social organization related to disability. There is a widespread and stark underrepresentation of ethnic minorities in Danish civil society, including disability organizations. His feelings of exclusion do not necessarily mean that there have been no efforts to include him. It is crucial to note that a civil organization had reached out to him and he found my contact information on their Facebook page. Eventually Abuukar finds his "own way to live in this Danish government." After feeling excluded from the labor market and frustrated by attempts to seek further education, he resolved to start his own business, a charity to support people with disabilities in Africa.

> I have an outside wheelchair, and this is my inside wheelchair, but my friends back home don't even have one and they can't move one step. So I made the decision and I said, I need to help these people. I have sent from Denmark maybe 45 containers to East Africa, Kenya, Somalia, Djibouti to help support disabled people.

---

regard. The al-Shabaab fundamentalist group declared that it was behind the terrorist attack.

He cofounded a civil organization on his own terms to help the less fortunate. This was possible by utilizing the very Danish infrastructure (for creating civil organizations) that he felt so alienated from.

Hypermarginal strategies

If we follow a phenomenological line of inquiry that emerges through Abuukar's story and the lives of my other informants, we see a kind of fragmentation of categories and identities. This fragmentation occurs through compounding tensions around dilemmas of belonging and access to resources and problematic and partial group memberships. Abuukar navigates these complex intersectional dilemmas of identity often from a marginal position. He is socially located not at the intersection of a Venn diagram of social spheres, but rather on the outside of several. He is subjectively divided at these intersections, with partial, marginal membership in each. If we look through these subjective intersectional categorical dilemmas at the greater structural context, questions of social, spatial, and economic processes of marginalization appear. In terms of the structural and even spatial setting, it is helpful to think further with Wacquant's work on 'advanced marginality', where Wacquant describes "territorial fixation and stigmatization; spatial alienation and the dissolution of place; the loss of a viable hinterland; and the symbolic fragmentation of marginalized populations" (Wacquant 1996: 121). Wacquant mentions this phenomenon reaching the Nordic states. The Disability Center was in such a marginalized area, as well as the homes of many of my informants. There are interesting implications of Abuukar's conflicts of identity and belonging. In terms of sociospatial formations, while Abuukar lives in an assisted living center due to his disability, he claims the city's "immigrant ghetto" (his words) as his home, when taking me on a tour of "his Århus". His sense of self is often in conflict with the social possibilities of his environment.

Intersectional perspectives are useful to a degree, however this more *experience-near* perspective reveals deeper nuances. Here we see a contrast to conceptualizations of intersection or a doubling of minority statuses, a doubled form of marginality. Rather than double minorities, my informants were minorities within minorities. Such social exclusion has a compounding and socially fracturing impact. While intersectionality emerged in a North American context, my focus is on the Danish welfare state. Crenshaw's concept of intersectionality is a product of North American *identity politics*, whereas the Danish context presents new dynamics and dilemmas. For one, the ideal of *multiculturalism*, or the myth thereof, is not a given in the Danish context. On the other hand, there is greater state infrastructure of health provision and social services. Despite his engagement with several sources of support in the Danish welfare state, Abuukar describes feeling largely disconnected from the broader Danish disabled community and political organizations. He is fighting battles on several fronts, the sum of which is greater than the parts, as one social struggle bleeds into another. We must account for the compounding aspect of this position and experience of being a minority within a minority. His bewilderment with the language and Danish "culture", his feelings and experiences of racism and other forms of social exclusion, and his feelings of stigma in his own community intertwine and result in an existential rending for Abuukar. The *barriers* he faces as a refugee, as an ethnic minority, as a disabled citizen, and as a disabled Somali are overlapping and occasionally overwhelming. This is what is implied by *hypermarginality* in this case: Rather than being a social minority due to his ethnic background (and feeling inclusion in his *own community*) in addition to being a social minority due to his disability (and feeling inclusion in a Danish community of people with disability), these two categories intersect to create a form and experience of social exclusion that is of a greater magnitude than simply being additive.

While my informants are generally at the margins (people with disability) of marginal groups (ethnic minorities), it is important to note drive and agency as key components of their experience. With the term *hypermarginality* I do not seek to place my informants in the confines of a narrative of victimhood, nor imply passivity, rather I seek to characterize some of the subjective dilemmas that they face as active and strategic agents. As seen in the story of Abuukar, he has been and is still actively searching for his "*own way to live*" and belong in this constellation of hypermarginality. For example, despite his alienation from Danish patient organizations, he has cofounded his own *forening* (civil organization) for charity work in his home country of Somalia. In this way he operates on the outskirts of Denmark's social infrastructure to find his "*own way in this Danish government*" and social status in his own community. It should be noted that such tenacity is not a rule of thumb, but rather that actors in this social situation (refugees with disability) are not necessarily hopeless social pariahs and victims, but rather must navigate strategically at certain social junctures. Such is the case in many of my informants' lives. I adhere to Rønsbo and Jensen's (2014) caution:

> Human suffering presents the social sciences with a fundamental dilemma. As social scientists, we often withdraw from suffering or reduce the suffering bodies to the status of hapless victims – or we look for agency and force of individuals who can beat the system they suffer or remake their own experiences of suffering in transcendental form. (Rønsbo/Jensen 2014: 1)

We must account for the complexity of agency in the life story of Abuukar and others.

Abuukar eventually found a greater sense of belonging and community in Denmark. His narrative reflects a reality that is also present for other informants in my research. Hypermarginality does not necessarily denote a social or economic position of absolute and permanent hopeless destitution and isolation, but rather provides a starting point for examining the particular excluded social position and corresponding experiential state, i.e. conflicts and possibilities around belonging and identity that Abuukar and others like him must reckon with. It offers a theoretical frame for the frustration, fear and anger that Abuukar described, but also for his emancipation. He became involved in charity work and this pursuit has been very rewarding for him personally and socially, allowing him to gain greater social status and self-esteem. His assertive personality and confidence shine through these layers of social stigma. He has accumulated prestige in spite of these compounding barriers through charity involvement and social engagement. He no longer feels the same *shyness* in his own community but does not deny the existence of this stigma either, as I could see when he took me on a tour of Aarhus and exchanged many kind greetings with other Somalis. I would also like to note that the potential social stigma around disability is hardly culturally bound or specific to ethnic minorities and refugees, but prevalent in Denmark and the Western world in general as well.

Conclusion

This article analyzed complex categories of identity, belonging and experience by theoretically placing the subject in a social space characterized by a compounded set of conditions of social dilemmas of inclusion/exclusion, correlating to an existential state. This frame allowed for an investigation into the interplay of multiple layers, "spoiled identities" (Goffman 1963), including the subject's potential disenfranchisement and frustration. In this space we see the lattice of acts, practices, and interactions producing processes of exclusion with a crucial multidimensional quality, not just a matter of conflicting identity practices in the greater context of late capitalism in Europe. Rather than simply a case of intersectionality, this article goes beyond unidirectional processes of social exclusion to account for a more complex negotiation and navigation of resources, identity, and belonging. Through this phenomenological investigation of social dilemmas, fragmented selves in a fragmented social landscape emerge. Abuukar and my informants more generally negotiate belonging, identity and support on multiple social planes, and this was observable from my multisited methodological approach.

Hypermarginality provides a frame for the specific conditions and dilemmas, both practical and internal, in which *multiminorities* navigate, including the possible experience of being torn between multiple senses of identity. In the above we saw how Abuukar was conflicted on the axis of agency and victimhood, belonging and access to resources (i.e. *Somali self* vs. *disabled self*), and the dissolution of place. These are conflicts and challenges that can occur from this hypermarginal position, however life at this position does not resign one to a life of passive victimhood. We see rather an active agent negotiating a problematic social landscape of resources, identity and belonging. What I am addressing are broader forms of *disablement*, to use the language of the British social model, but these obstacles can be overcome in emancipatory processes. Eventually, Abuukar was able to partially overcome multiple forms of *disablement* by founding a civil organization that supports other people with disabilities in Somalia. The literal fracture to his L1 vertebra is permanent, but through his indomitable spirit he is able to at least partially mend the *fractured* social landscape he is living in.

List of Figures

References

Andersen, Pernille T./Bak, Carsten K./Vangsgaard, Susanne/Dokkedal, Unni/Larsen, Pia V. (2011): Self-rated health, ethnicity and social position in a deprived neighborhood in Denmark, in: International Journal for Equity in Health, 10: 5, 5-11.

Barnes, Colin/Mercer, Geof (2003): Disability. Cambridge.

Barnes, Colin/Mercer, Geof/Shakespeare, Tom (1999): Exploring disability: a sociological introduction. Cambridge.

Bektovic, Safet (2004): Kulturmøder og Religion: Identitetsdannelse blandt kristne og muslimske unge. Copenhagen.

Bernard, Russell (2006): Research Methods in Anthropology: Qualitative and Quantitative Approaches. Oxford.

Butler, Judith (2004): Precarious life: The power of mourning and violence. London.

Bourdieu, Pierre (1991): Language and Symbolic Power. Cambridge Mass.

Clark, Cindy Dell (1999): The autodriven interview: A photographic viewfinder into children's experiences, in: Visual Sociology, 14, 39-50.

Crenshaw, Kimberlé (1989): Demarginalizing the Intersection of Race and Sex: A Black Feminist Critique of Antidiscrimination Doctrine, Feminist Theory and Antiracist Politics, in: The University of Chicago Legal Forum, 140, 139-167.

Crenshaw, Kimberlé (1995): Mapping the margins: Intersectionality, identity politics and violence against women. Crenshaw, Kimberlé/Gotanda, Neil/Peller, Gary/Thomas, Kendall. Critical Race Theory: The Key Writings that Formed the Movement. New York, 357-383.

Daniel, E. Valentine (1995): Mistrusting Refugees. Berkeley.

Galal, Lise Paulsen (2002): Nye danskere. At leve sin biografi som muslim. Alberdi, Francisco. Transkulturel Psykiatri. Copenhagen, 112-137.

Goffman, Erving (1963): Stigma: Notes on the management of spoiled identity. New York.

Good, Mary-Jo DelVecchio/Willen, Sarah S./Hannah, Seth Donal/Vickery, Ken/Park, Lawrence Taeseng (eds.) (2011): Shattering Culture: American Medicine Responds to Cultural Diversity. New York.

Good, Byron J./Good, Mary-Jo Del Vecchio/Subandi, Subandi (2007): The subject of mental illness: Psychosis, mad violence and subjectivity in Indonesia. Biehl, Joao/Good, Byron/Kleinman, Arthur. Subjectivity: Ethnographic Investigations. Berkeley, 243-272.

Gullestad, Marianne (1991): The transformation of the Norwegian notion of everyday life, in: American Ethnologist, 18, 480-499.

Hacking, Ian (1995): The looping effects of human kinds. Sperber, Dan/ Premack, David/Premack, Ann J.. Causal cognition: A multidisciplinary debate. Oxford, 351-383.

Henkel, Heiko (2011): Contesting Danish Civility: The Cartoon Crisis as Transnational Drama. Olwig, Karen F./Paerregaard, Karsten. The Question of Integration: Immigration, Exclusion and the Danish Welfare State. Newcastle upon Tyne.

Hervik, Peter (1999): Den generende forskellighed: danske svar på den stigende multikulturalisme. Copenhagen.

Hervik, Peter (2004): The Danish cultural world of unbridgeable differences, in: Ethnos, 69: 2, 247-267.

Hughes, Thomas (2013): Struggling towards recovery. An ethnographic investigation of mental illness, treatment, and belonging among non-western immigrants in Copenhagen. Unpublished master's thesis. Copenhagen.

Hume, Lynne/Mulcock, Jane (2005): Introduction: Awkward Spaces, productive places. Hume, Lynne/Mulcock Jane. Anthropologists in the Field: Cases in Participant Observation. New York, xi-xxvii.

Jensen, Tina G. (2007): Hvor går man hen, når man 'går ud'? Forestillede og praktiserede fælleskaber blandt omvendte danske muslimer. Olwig, Karen F./Paerregaard, Karsten. Integration. Antropologiske perspektiver. Copenhagen, 37-62.

Kleinman, Arthur (1988): Rethinking Psychiatry: From Cultural Category to Personal Experience. New York.

Kleinman, Arthur/Kleinman, Joan (1991): Suffering and its Professional Transformation. Toward an Ethnography of Interpersonal Experience, in: Culture Medicine and Psychiatry, 15: 3, 275-301.

Kristensen, Majken (2002): Indvandring i Danmark. Alberdi, Francisco. Transkulturel Psykiatri. Copenhagen, 263-272.

Larsen, Birgitte R. (2013): Tid og Forbrug i etniske minoritersfamilier: En kvalitativ undersøgelse af hverdagslivet blandt familier i Danmark med pakistansk, tyrkisk, palæstinensisk og irakisk baggrund. Copenhagen.

Lyhne, Jette (2007): Etnicitet og handicap: bidrag til et overblik. Copenhagen.

Macun, Ina/ Posel, Deborah (1998): Focus Groups: A South African experience and a methodological reflection, in: African Sociological Review, 2: 1, 114-135.

Marcus, George E. (1995): Ethnography in/of the World System: The Emergence of Multi-sided Ethnography, in: Annual Review of Anthropology, 24, 95-111.

Nelleman, George (1981): Polske landarbejder i Danmark og deres efterkommere: Et studie af landarbejderindvandringen 1893- 1929 og indvandringens integration i det danske samfund i to generationer. Copenhagen.

Oliver, Michael (1990): The politics of disablement. London.

Olwig, Karen F. and Paerregaard, Karsten (2011): The Question of Integration: Immigration, Exclusion and the Danish Welfare State. Newcastle upon Tyne.

O'Reilly, Karen (2005): Ethnographic Methods. London.

Petersen, Maria et al. (2012): Sundhedsfremme for udsatte borgere med anden etnisk baggrund end dansk: Erfaringer fra ti gode virkerum i København. Copenhagen:.

Pedersen, Marianne H./Rytter, Mikkel (2011): Islam og muslimer i Danmark. Religion, identitet og sikkerhed efter 11. september. Copenhagen.

Poulsen, Charlotte (2005): Taler vi om det samme? Når etniske minoriteter med sjældne handicap møder social- og sundhedsvæsenet. Copenhagen.

Powdermaker, Hortense (1966): Stranger and Friend: the way of the anthropologist. New York.

Ronsbo, Henrik/Jensen, Steffen (2014): Histories of Victimhood. Philadelphia.

Rubow, Cecilie (2003): Samtalen: Interviewet som Deltagerobservation. Hastrup, Kirsten. Ind I Verden. Copenhagen.

Sachs, Lisbeth (1995): Disability and migration: A case story. Ingstad, Benedict/Whyte, Susan R.. Disability and culture. Berkeley.

Schmidt, Garbi (2007): Muslim i Danmark – muslim i verden: En analyse af muslimske ungdomsforeninger og muslimsk identitet I årene op til Muhammedkrisen. Copenhagen.

Shakespeare, Tom (2006): Disability rights and wrongs. London.

Shakespeare, Tom (2014): Disability Rights and Wrongs Revisited. New York.

Shuttleworth, Russel P./Kasnitz, Devva (2001): Introduction: Anthropology in Disability Studies, in: Disability Studies Quarterly, 21: 3, 2-17.

Shuttleworth, Russel P./Kasnitz, Devva (2004): Stigma, community, ethnography: Joan Ablon's contribution to the anthropology of impairment-disability, in: Medical Anthropology Quarterly, 18, 139-161.

Singhammer, John (2008): Etniske minoriteters sundhed. Copenhagen.

Spencer, Dale (2014): Exposing the conditions of precarity: compounding victimization and marginalized young people, in: Contemporary Justice Review, 17:1, 87-103.

Spradley, James (1980): Participant Observation. New York.

Staples, James (2011): At the intersection of disability and masculinity: exploring gender and bodily difference in India, in: Journal of the Royal Anthropological Institute (N.S.), 17, 545-562.

Stuart, Ossie (1993): Double oppression: an appropriate starting point?. Swain, John et al.. Disabling Barriers- Enabling Environments. London, 93-101.

Tošić, Jelena (2012): Migration, Identity, and Belonging: Anthropological Perspectives on a Multidisciplinary Field of Research. Messer M./Schroeder R./Wodak R.. Migrations: Interdisciplinary Perspectives. Vienna.

Thomas, Carol/Corker, Mairian (2002): A journey around the social model. Corker, Mairian/ Shakespeare, Tom. Disability/postmodernity: embodying disability theory. London, 18-31.

Tremain, Shelley (2002): On the subject of impairment. Corker, Mairian/ Shakespeare, Tom. Disability/postmodernity: embodying disability theory. London, 32-45.

Vinther-Jensen, Kirsten (ed.) (2010): Etniske minoriteter i det danske sundhedsvæsen: en antologi. Copenhagen.

Wacquant, Loïc (1996): Revisiting territories of relegation: Class, ethnicity and state in the making of advanced marginality, in: Urban Studies, 53: 6, 1077-1088.

Wacquant, Loïc (2008): Ghetto, Banlieue, Favela, et caetera: Tools for Rethinking Urban Marginality. Wacquant, Loïc. Urban Outcasts: A comparative sociology of Advanced Marginality. Cambridge, 1-12.

Willerslev, Richard (1983): Den glemte indvandring: Den svenske indvandring til Danmark 1850- 1913. Copenhagen.

Antidiscrimination Policies, (Disability) Mainstreaming, and Intersectionality

Monika Windisch

Introduction

Focusing on diversity, considered to be one of the most urgent challenges nowadays, social and political approaches usually assume that mutual respect and recognition of cultural patterns, identity models and life plans are indispensable for social development. At the same time, the European Social Protection Committee (SPC) points out that, even if a favorable evolution on the labor market can be observed, there is a "general continued deterioration in the relative poverty situation, its depth and persistence" (SPC 2016: 6). Given the high risk of poverty or social exclusion in all European member states the Committee underlines "that the inclusiveness and fairness of social protection systems is a key challenge across the EU" (SPC 2016: 7). The SPC report additionally highlights that privileged treatment, social discrimination, disempowerment and social inequality are increasing factors in European member states and Europe is thus asked to develop overarching conceptions of social justice which could provide a basis for policy development, social investment and the distribution of valued resources, goods and services.

Diversity and antidiscrimination policy approaches assume that societies are structured by various dimensions of difference like race, class and gender that influence to a high degree cultural value systems, social attributions, personal identity conceptions and associated senses of belonging. Following Fracer (1998: 2) most of the categories above are two-sided incorporating culture as well as power relations and economy. In this context, race, class and gender are frequently valued as the most important "axes of difference" (Klinger/Knapp 2007: 20). Seen as determining, interdependent factors of social inequality these social categories constitute the foundation of interlocking social patterns, social hierarchies and systems of domination. Associated with biographical experience, in various cultural contexts and social institutions, all of us are subjected to a "matrix of dominance" (Collins 2000), defined by structural, disciplinary, hegemonic and interpersonal domains. Within this framework, ideas that describe what a "good" life and social equality might be are well established in society. Law, politics, religion and economy define social structures and contribute to power relations, legitimated by personal capacities, efficient work and social rationality. Indeed, differences between social groups are associated with specific, virtually stable power relations, which manifest themselves in specific organizational, intersubjective and representational forms (Yuval-Davis 2006: 198). The resulting consequences are institutionalized within mechanisms of social regulation and distribution with the effect that marginalized social groups are frequently confronted with unequal opportunities of living, with limited possibilities to represent their concerns and with restricted participation in social and political life. Especially given the current economic and demographic trends it is very important to recognize that not only race, class and gender but also other inequality dimensions are comparably important. Knapp (2008) underlines that social locations, power resources and life opportunities are determined by other distinguishing structural categories like age and health. Besides that, religion, sexual identity and dis/ability are the most often mentioned social categories that affect access to power and privileges, influence social relationships and shape people's everyday experiences (Andersen 1996).

Even if all forms of oppression should be recognized as equally important, the degree of institutionalized representation and the ranking of political relevance vary widely between different social groups (Verloo 2006). Parallel to demographic change the political mainstream has also changed, which could be a reason why disability just now starts to achieve more policy attention and social relevance. Aiming to minimize personal and social risks related to disability, it is increasingly important to develop a set of political strategies that ensure equal rights, environmental accessibility, social protection and participation in society. The Convention on the Rights of Persons with Disabilities (United Nations 2006) sets out these concerns as central targets and has motivated governments worldwide to take the related requirements more seriously. European antidiscrimination laws show a raising awareness to reduce social inequalities grounded on disability and – to a limited extent – enable equal access to valued resources, goods and services. Critical voices, however, complain that there is a wide gap between political statements, legal requirements and the realization of social justice, protection, corporate responsibility and solidarity. Therefore, it might be time to go beyond rhetoric and reflect deeply rooted social power relationships like Ableism as well as antidiscrimination policies, mainstreaming and intersectional approaches, which promise concrete strategies, capable of providing equal rights to everyone.

Ableism

Self-actualization and personal development are central concerns in neoliberal discourses and practices – crucial for success, social progress and justice. It seems to be part of modern identity conceptions and social expectations to be efficient, flexible, mobile and self-determined. Even in everyday life, most of us imagine ourselves frequently as nearly invulnerable, well-appointed with abilities, without serious physical and mental burdens and largely free from impairments. Starting from such imaginations, Ableism points out that idealizations of human ability, invulnerability and perfection is an integral part of social power relations which clearly privilege people without disabilities. Realizing that we all live with bodies and minds that sometimes cause problems should remind us that we probably all face significant limitations of personal opportunities during our lifetime and "[…] need understandings of disability and handicap that do not support a paradigm of humanity as young and healthy" (Wendell 1996: 18). With that in mind, dis/ability concerns cannot be interpreted as special interests of a fringe group. Quite the contrary, they represent general social issues and should be recognized in their fundamental political relevance.

In many cases, medical approaches assume "that disabled people's problems stem mainly or exclusively from their impairment" (Thomas in Waldschmidt 2005: 16). Therefore, minimizing the effects of an impairment, living "as normal as possible" and getting equal access to health and social services are often interpreted as the most important goals. In addition, disability is frequently associated with limited possibilities of personal development, defined as the unavoidable consequence of biology. Related impairment-effects might be interpreted as personal risk factors, but

> […] most of those problems can be traced to the social arrangements, to the human created structures and practices in which people live and their arrangements that are created with the majority of people without impairments in mind; they could be re-created, they should be re-created to make the world a more possible place for all its citizens. (Asch in Makkonen 2002: 5)

Perceptions of disability as a tragic stroke of fate and the following assumptions of individual *deficits* often are used to justify social inequalities, which have their roots in society rather than in biology. Therefore, questioning social norms, performance expectations and *normality* is necessary to realize that they represent often invisible aspects of social power (Link 1998). As the social model of disability (Shakespeare/Watson 2002) points out, values, norms and even social structures are based essentially on the needs, skills and opportunities of nondisabled persons. In this view, systematical limitations of social organization hinder all disabled persons to lead their life and shape society in a well-considered and self-determined way. Primarily (man-made) barriers and unequal power relations constitute the severe social restrictions that prevent persons with disabilities from enjoying full social, cultural, economic and political participation in society. Deeply embedded within culture and secured by knowledge systems, Ableism extends this perspective by considering networks of beliefs, processes and social practices which – corresponding to an existing presumption of compulsory ableness in society – establish a particular kind of Self and corporeal standards (Campbell 2008: 153). Moving the focus from individual experiences of discrimination, an Ableism perspective takes a critical look to structurally anchored social and institutionalized power relations based of personal skills and dis/abilities. Social power-dynamics resulting from ableist mechanisms contribute to an essentialized and negatively rated ontology of disability, which – more or less – has remained substantially unchallenged, even in societies that see themselves as pluralistic and rate diversity as a gain.

One of the biggest challenges today is the current confrontation with a world of growing ableist performance. As Fiona Campbell points out,

> one must constantly participate in processes of disability disavowal, aspiring towards normativity, a state of near able-bodiedness, or at very least to effect a state of "passing." (2008: 156)

At first sight it seems to be obvious that the orientation towards personal achievement can be useful to ensure social participation and growing possibilities for living. Assuming that we all have – at least to a certain extent – internalized associated social values, however, raises the question if ableist concepts have a deep impact on processes of subjectivation. Social constructions of abled subjects become the standard of the normal. These unconscious, pre-discursive but fundamental bases of positive self-images devaluate people with disabilities and frequently justify their social position as an inferior, marginalized social group.

Even if subjectivation never follows a unitary way, determined by social norms, attributions and expectations, internalization of ableist values cannot be interpreted as a neutral gesture. Devaluation and recognition of personal skills, capabilities and potentiality shape and inspire personal development. They influence the way we perceive social issues and interactions and frequently inform knowledge systems, social regulations and institutionalized practices. Considering that people with disabilities experience and create a specific way of subjectivation, we have to broaden the perspective that places primarily impairment-effects and social barriers in the center of the debate. Looking through a lens, influenced by Ableism, one reason for this could be that disabled people are – on the one hand – repeatedly reminded of negative attributions and ontologies related to them, on the other confronted frequently with social advantages granted to those who are "ready" for abled bodied performances. This area of personal as well as social tension suggests disabling personal experiences of vulnerability and oppression day after day. Furthermore, it is very likely that social power relations and negatively rated attributes affect people internally and could lead to some incorporation of internalized ableism, either on a conscious or unconscious level.

> Once oppression has been internalized, little force is needed to keep us submissive. We harbour inside ourselves the pain and the memories, the fears and the confusions, the negative self-images and the low expectations, turning them into weapons with which to re-injure ourselves, every day of our lives. (Mason in Campbell 2005: 157)

Even if one can observe social developments through which disability acceptance and self-determined design options are increasingly available, a significant number of disabled people still miss positive images of disability, experiences of self-efficacy and possibilities to reject social expectations. Nevertheless, more and more people are telling stories of success *in spite of impairment*, reclaiming disability identities characterized by dignity and pride (see Fox in this volume). Still, political interventions worldwide are necessary to make social inequalities and challenging live situations visible, to strengthen people with disabilities in their (legal) rights.

Politics of identity

Taking account of social experiences of minority groups, social movements and civil society organizations frequently interpret identity politics as a valuable tool for political work and resistance. Associated approaches suggest frequently that the living conditions of social groups are largely similar, so that there might be good reasons to assume common social interests and political demands. Within the social movement of persons with disabilities it has been important to consider disability as a starting point of political, educational and social frameworks. Public representations as a homogeneous group with common concerns have been essential for developing political demands because this strategy contributed to political debates, strengthened political argumentations and ensured group cohesion and solidarity. As Makkonen highlights:

> For all practical and political purposes, groups are always presented […] as more homogenous than they really are. Simplification and generalization makes the speaking of a group more pragmatic, as it would be burdensome to keep the true diversity of the group in mind all the time. An agenda, which would represent the true interests of the whole group in all its diversity, would simply be too diverse, unclear and perhaps self-contradictory, and would hence not be viable and would have little chance of political success. (Makkonen 2002: 23)

Even if it is neither possible nor meaningful to represent the actual degree of difference in a political framework, claiming common interests and political demands also implies that some requests remain unmentioned and visible only to a limited extent. One result of these dynamics could be to establish narrow and essentialist concepts of political group interests. This necessarily involves denying power relations, levelling different political positions and silencing dissident voices. Patterns of interpretation, contents and opinions within the disability movement are developed in the light of different personal experiences, with different senses of identity and in diverse political contexts. There is one special group within the disability movement, however, that dominates key issues and political demands: physically disabled, white men, situated particularly in the middle class (Waldschmidt 1997: 50):

> The staff and leadership of the disability movement in the United States [is] almost completely white, middle class, and until recently, male. In each of the early historical shifts of the disability movement, however, women, people of color, gays and lesbians, and others who did not fit the proffered stereotype were active members. Evident in anecdotal accounts and early writings on the lived disability experience were representatives of all these groups who were important players doing important work for the community without public acknowledgment or equal rewards for their contributions (O'Tool Corbett 2004: 295).

From this perspective, it is highly debatable which discourses, which sense of identities, which political positions and which goals become visible in the public. Even if we cannot assume a certain tendency to prefer a special segment of interests within the disability movement, this kind of representational politics could be problematic. One of the effects might be that the specific social localization of the representatives leads to limited perspectives. Since unequal readiness and the lack of opportunities to get involved prevent full participation for many disabled persons, a minority within the social group takes on the responsibility to defend the social interests and political requirements of persons who are less embedded in political contexts and who stay marginalized. This is succinctly put by Uccellari (2008: 29):

> Any measure aimed at addressing the disadvantage of the group as a whole, without distinction, will be inappropriate to improve the situation of the whole group, because the causes of the disadvantage will not be the same for all within its parameters. Further: such efforts may only be of assistance to the 'dominant' members of a disadvantaged group and so not target those who are the most disadvantaged within the disadvantaged.

Even if the political language has changed and the life opportunities of persons with disabilities seemingly opened in the last decades, one must assume that the extent and structure of social inequalities within "the disabled" are different. Representation politics, however, remains purely symbolic if the requirements do not reflect the interests of marginalized persons within this social group. Focusing on disability as a homogeneous master category contributes to specific power relations and increases social risks within the social group. Another possible effect might be that political actors and decision-makers frequently refer to oversimplified analysis that takes account of just one cause of disadvantage, which risks misunderstanding multiple discrimination. It can be assumed that the social localization and status of persons with disabilities affects – and is affected by – structural issues and the specific intersection of personal, economic, legal and political aspects.

Convention

While governments usually avoid measures that have negative impacts on people with disabilities, it is necessary to point out that disability policies are usually concerned with health, impairment prevention and social care rather than social participation and equal rights (Degener 2009). Nevertheless, important steps to improve the living conditions of persons with disabilities have been taken – even in the context of neoliberal development and far-reaching welfare state reforms. The *Convention on the Rights of Persons with Disabilities* (United Nations 2006), seen as crucial for ensuring equal citizenship, is used as a starting point for social development. Dignity, equality, accessibility of the environment and social participation are recognized as central guidelines of this UN framework, which changed the status and legal rights of persons with disability in a significant way. Following a rights-based approach, universal access to equal political, economic, cultural and social opportunities is the central political demand of the convention. Within the framework of this contract, 167 states worldwide undertake various efforts to realize corresponding requirements and objectives. The removal of physical and social barriers, the development of universal design and accessible technology and the expansion of inclusive public programs and services are valued as the most important political interventions to improve living conditions and make social change possible.

These key issues within the Convention on the Rights of Persons with Disabilities (CRPD) set an antidiscriminatory international standard, which has influenced many governments to take disability rights more seriously. Following one of the major concerns of the convention, international disability organizations, more than 400 nongovernmental organizations and disabled experts participated in the development processes, implementation, monitoring and evaluation (Degener 2009). Their experience, knowledge and interests have been used as an indispensable starting point for research, political analysis and decision-making. Aiming to make disability concerns an integral dimension of social protection and inclusion, mainstreaming strategies are emphasized as important instruments to implement equality policies. Considering the political demands of people with disabilities in all policies, social routines and political innovations would set a positive precedent in public international law. Mainstreaming a disability perspective is:

> …the process of assessing the implications for women and men with disabilities of any planned action, including legislation, policies and programmes in all areas and at all levels. It is a strategy for making people with disabilities' concerns and experiences an integral dimension of the design, implementation, monitoring and evaluation of policies and progammes in all political, economic and societal spheres so that women and men with disabilities benefit equally and inequality is not perpetuated. The ultimate goal is to achieve disability equality. (Handicap International 2012)

Disability mainstreaming is interpreted as one of the most important political tools to reach full social participation for people who face – permanent or for a significant period of time – social restrictions caused by impairments or other medical conditions. Starting from a rights-based perspective and taking specific needs of disabled people into account, mainstreaming strategies should lead to political, economic and social transformations. Associated strategies, however, require fundamental changes in perspective and political commitment because they are moving "away from charity-based or medical-based approaches to disability to a new perspective stemming from and firmly grounded in human rights" (Pillay in Degener 2009: 201).

Based on the political framework of the CRPD, the European Union focuses on antidiscrimination law and equality norms, tailored to the various ways how persons with disability live their daily lives. With equality goals in mind, targets cover both civil and political rights in and outside the field of employment. Associated policies center primarily on efforts to reduce the risks of social exclusion and poverty and to ensure equal access to healthcare and other valued goods and social services.

As the *European Network of Legal Experts in Gender Equality and Non-Discrimination* points out, in the last decade social development and some progress in addressing disability concerns can be observed. However, the network highlights that "in many EU member states there have been no significant changes introduced in law and policy following ratification of the CRPD" (Waddington/Broderick/Poulos 2016: 150). Given that European states are constituted by very different economic, sociopolitical and legal systems, which might be a cause for nationally specific policy processes, this is hardly surprising. Nevertheless, "there remain significant problems on the ground in terms of achieving equality, equal opportunity and equal access for people with disabilities across many fields, not least of all education" (Waddington/Broderick/Poulos 2016: 17). These results validate a report of the *United Nations Committee on the Rights of Persons with Disabilities* (2015), which provided a first overview on how disability policies and requirements have been realized since the CRPD came into force. Related to European Union policies the committee observed that awareness-raising strategies on the rights of persons with disabilities are not continuous, do not include all institutions and exclude certain groups of persons with disabilities. Even if Europe failed to conduct a cross-cutting, comprehensive review of its legislation, important progress and positive trends in some social sectors can be seen. Critical voices, however, underline that lasting success is not possible if little effort is made to develop harmonized policies and strategies.

Additionally, there is a lack of a systematic and institutionalized approach to mainstream the rights of persons with disabilities across all of Europe. Developing disability mainstreaming policies requires an emancipatory research framework and data collection as well as the continuous participation of persons with disabilities. Others go further and insist on structural changes in all spheres of society and a sufficient distribution of financial resources (Verloo 2006). The subsequent efforts to social change might help to develop a growing knowledge about supportive factors, contributing to improved standards of living, access and full participation in society.

Mainstreaming

Gender mainstreaming, considered as a set of innovative and transformative political concepts and equality strategies, is usually valued as a guiding principle in European Anti-Discrimination Law. Introduced at the *Fourth World Conference on Women*, which took place in Beijing in 1995, gender mainstreaming strategies entail "[t]he systematic integration of the respective situations, priorities and needs of women and men into all policies" (Commission of the European Communities 1996: 67) and should help to strengthen gender equality worldwide. The Council of Europe offers the following definition of gender equality:

> Gender equality means an equal visibility, empowerment and participation of both sexes in all spheres of public and private life [...] Gender equality is not synonymous with sameness with establishing men, their life-style and conditions as the norm. [...] Gender equality means accepting and valuing equally the differences between women and men and the diverse roles they play in society (Council of Europe 1998: 7-8).

It seems to be generally recognized nowadays that gender roles, norms and expectations are constructed in a culturally specific way. At least in the Western world there is a growing agreement that gender expectations should not have any negative impact on personal or public spheres of life. This cannot be taken for granted, however, since social contexts usually assume a certain universality and neutrality of current gender norms. Especially gender analysis, gender sensitive research and women's movements contribute to questioning the supposed self-evidence of associated social processes and power relations. These approaches help to create the necessary conditions for critical comments, political action and the development of equal policies, sometimes realized in legal regulations and mainstreaming. In this context economic independence, equal access to the labor market and good quality education are recognized as the most important targets to avoid gender hierarchies, to remove imbalances and to ensure shared responsibility and social solidarity in society.

Already in 2010, the *International Network of Women with Disabilities* tried to figure out whether gender mainstreaming ensured their civil and political rights. Given women's movement policies usually refer to healthy, normal and nondisabled women (Waldschmidt 1997: 52), it is hardly surprising that the living conditions and prospects of women with disabilities stayed largely unnoticed at the Fourth World Conference on Women. Neither the social relevance of their concerns, nor the essential political contribution of disability perspectives were recognized, and the same happened to political statements and the increasing demand for international networking (Arnade/Häfner 2005: 4). This clearly shows to what extent different senses of identities and hierarchical power relations within social groups affect possibilities to gain political influence and participate. Moreover, mainstreaming policies usually fail to accommodate different living conditions. The International Network of Women with Disabilities noted that in most societies severe discrimination based on gender and disabilities are ongoing problems and that

> [t]here is an enormous gap in the legal system between the effort to provide for fundamental human rights and the reality for women with disabilities. (International Network of Women with Disabilities 2010: 9)

Gender mainstreaming, which regards political and social implications of any planned action in all political, economic and societal spheres, is directly linked to a legal framework. As the *World Development Report on Gender Equality and Development* (2012) highlights, law and justice are essential factors in achieving equality. Associated regulations specify political goals and support – but also prevent – the implementation of concrete equality strategies. Even if legal systems should be recognized as agents of change and social transformation, basic understandings of equality are developed against the background of social norms and cultural values. Therefore, it seems to be evident that a narrow, legalistic perspective is not able to challenge social inequality. Following Thompson's (2016) reflections, antidiscrimination policies need a wide approach, including all dimensions of diversity and incorporating sociological, political and economic concerns above and beyond the law.

Aiming to reduce the wide gender gaps in society and organizations, mainstreaming in general focuses on structural causes of social inequality. It anticipates the future consequences of existing policies and tries to prevent undesired developments and their future reproduction (Squires 2007: 45f). As a component of organizational transformation, gender mainstreaming strategies and guidelines are currently applied as key components of a new management culture. Trendsetting innovations, however, often reach their limits when encountering the stability of institutional structures and routines. Not only do mainstreaming policies not always seek to achieve the most efficient use of financial resources, reality shows that power relations and hierarchies – in society and organizations – remain surprisingly stable. Business interests and the external representation of organizations might sometimes be in conflict with the concrete extent of implementing equality policies. Therefore, critical voices underline that mainstreaming could be seen more as an administrative and technocratic instrument of organizational development than as a political strategy that ensures social change and gender equality (Emmerich/Hormel 2013: 187f). Life choices and opportunities are determined by various factors, therefore social inequalities are as specific as the life experiences of marginalized people (Verloo 2006: 222). Recognizing the interdependency of all dimensions of social difference, equality policies and associated strategies like mainstreaming must be re-visited. Especially in view of multiple discrimination, intersectional approaches and political concepts as well as action plans need further development.

Intersectionality

Starting from the premise that female lives and experience are comparable with each other, feminist-oriented policies until the 1990s usually claimed to speak in the name of *all* women. Women of color as well as women with disabilities, however, could frequently not identify with the demands of mainstream feminism and criticized generalizing political statements. They experienced being regarded as *the others* – whose concerns were not listened to and trivialized as special interests (Walgenbach 2007: 38). Making their specific living conditions, social localizations and political standpoints visible, they distanced themselves from identity-political concepts of representation and started a broad discussion about social differences and power relations *between* women. Nowadays, intersectional approaches that also try to make hidden social inequalities visible are regarded as one of the most important outcomes of these controversies. Aiming to specify the effects of interlocking social power relations, intersectionality emphasizes primarily interdependences between social inequalities and various axes of difference. Kimberlé Crenshaw took up this notion in 1989, criticizing the fact that antidiscrimination laws ensure legal protection only to a limited extent. Referring specifically to the interrelations between race and gender, Crenshaw underlined that neither the gender aspects of racial discrimination nor the racial aspects of gender discrimination are fully comprehended within human rights and social movement approaches (Crenshaw 1991). Conceptualizing intersectionality, she tries

> […] to capture both the structural and dynamic consequences of the interaction between two or more axes of subordination. It specifically addresses the manner in which racism, patriarchy, class oppression and other discriminatory systems create background inequalities that structure the relative positions of women, races, ethnicities, classes, and the like. Moreover, it addresses the way that specific acts and

> policies create burdens that flow along these axes constituting the dynamic or active aspects of disempowerment. (Crenshaw 2000: no page)

Focusing on social categories like race, class and gender, Crenshaw puts legal criteria in the center of her approach and underlines that specific acts and policies might strengthen asymmetrical power distributions and intensify social inequality and injustice. Critically, the question arises if the problem of social discrimination can be addressed in an appropriate manner with continuous reference to abstract social categories and the generalizations related to them.

It is essential to consider concrete social arrangements and interdependencies between culture, politics, economy and law, Katharina Walgenbach (2007) points out. Viewed from this perspective it is particularly important to recognize the significance of social relations of dominance as well as impacts arising from social positions and status. Winker and Degele (2009), however, set different priorities. Starting from a critique of neoliberal policy development in capitalist societies, their concept of multilevel analysis relates to interdependencies between social structures, the symbolic order of society and identity formations that influence power relations to a high degree. Thus, their interest is primarily focused on economic, political and cultural dimensions of intersectionality, so that research can answer the question how social inequality is (symbolically) reproduced, represented and legitimized. Critical reflections on social norms, ideologies and hegemonic social habits are used as central points in these discussions, which try to understand how oppression might overlap at different levels in society (Winker/Degele 2009).

In intersectionality research the question arises if people with multiple assignments to marginalized social groups experience more disadvantages than others. If this occurs, power effects multiply and produce a different and particularly new, complex quality of privilege or discrimination, which is different from what each of the single categories would produce separately. Against this background one must assume that our senses of identity in fact are multiple, marked by various dimensions of social difference like gender, race, class and ability. But intersectionality considers more than that. Approaches remind us "that oppression cannot be reduced to one fundamental type, and that oppressions work together in producing injustice" (Collins 2000: 18). Aiming to clarify in which ways social regulations contribute to inequality, high priority should be given to critical reflections of structural power relations, legal systems, politics and the economy. Moreover, it is very important to consider institutionalized sociocultural habits, contextual value systems, processes of embodiment and related senses of identities.

Questioning whether disability can be interpreted as a master category is a precondition for intersectional research and development. Associated simplifications and generalizations, which assume a separate way of life, similar identity concepts and shared interests of "the disabled", have come under severe criticism. Furthermore, it should be recognized that disability is part of the stable, ableist and paternalistic relations in society and culture, reproduced in different social fields such as education, employment, social protection and health care. Heike Raab (2007) defines this social category as a multiple concept and social practice, embedded in culture as well as associated with social power relations and inequality. Highly affected by racism, class, sexism and heteronormativity, disability can – from her point of view – be interpreted as an interdependent category of social differentiation, associated with economy, law, social policies and identities.

Nowadays, the political and legal frameworks connected to disability frequently refer to multiple forms of discrimination, whereas intersectionality considers interdependencies between race, class, gender and disability. Searching to understand associated social challenges, it seems clear that we first need to develop an increased awareness of personal privileges and disadvantages, which would possibly enable more nuanced discussions about interlocking dimensions of social inequality. What we need to clarify, as Meike Verloo suggests, is "a clear conceptualization of how intersectionality operates, a theory of the power dynamics of a specific inequality, as well as a choice for a clear political goal" (Verloo 2006: 222). As such, intersectional approaches should be able to expand existing knowledge about the specifics and particularities of social differences and to refine explanations of mutual interdependences. Analyzing legal, economic, social and cultural conditions of social inequality might help to reflect power dynamics, to identify inhibiting effects of social and institutional habits and to make the social backgrounds of identity concepts understandable.

It is important to recognize, however, that there are no (political) goals for all. This interest in avoiding homogenization might help to understand the complexity of interdependent social regulations that mark privilege and oppression. In this way intersectionality contributes to changing concepts of social disadvantages by making marginalized social experiences and hidden discrimination visible (Murphy et al. 2009: 7f). In this context, it seems to be indispensable to stand up for a more balanced distribution of resources, for public recognition and institutional commitment and – above all – it is crucial to develop concepts that allow critical objection as well as concrete action.

Conclusion

Particularly because we should recognize disability rights as a universal claim in society, it is necessary to clarify the specific aspects of associated inequalities and to demand more specific responses to related social and political challenges. It is important to pay full attention to personal experiences, which are – now or in the future – associated with vulnerabilities, limitations and disabling social environments. In this context, it is necessary to examine to what extent and in what respects social locations, based on categories like race, class and gender, lead to social inequalities and to different access to valued social goods and services. Equality, access and full participation in society undoubtedly are the most relevant guiding goals related to disadvantaged social groups. Discussing the effects of rights-based approaches, antidiscrimination policies and strategies of mainstreaming show that public representation of political analyses, interests and goals differ significantly depending on the specific dimensions of diversity that they are dealing with (Verloo 2006). The resulting power relations and dominance in *and* between social groups demonstrate that a fundamental re-thinking of diversity policies, mainstreaming and political alliances is required. At a political level – as Jahan (1996) stresses – we need an agenda that includes the transformation and reorientation of existing political paradigms, new approaches for decision-making processes, a clear prioritization of equality objectives and a consideration of policy ends.

Economic, legal, cultural, social and personal influences contribute to inequalities and act in combination, so that some social groups require specific protection under the law. Aiming to point out the conceptual implications and concrete effects of interdependences and power relations, intersectional approaches contribute to a completely different understanding of social inequality. Making also hidden discrimination visible, intersectionality recognizes that persons have different access to resources and social influence, resulting from their social location. Even if a high risk of poverty and social inclusion of disabled persons exists, life opportunities have changed and multiplied. Only if we succeed in opening political, scientific and everyday discourses can we recognize the plurality of social conditions and different dimensions of social inequality. To develop differentiated perspectives, however, needs more than appreciating and recognizing diversity. Efforts associated with intersectionality always aim at social change, at questioning dominant norms and at a fundamental rethinking of institutionalized actions and attitudes. Neither human rights instruments, antidiscrimination laws, mainstreaming nor intersectional research will necessarily work within common principles of the existing political and scientific agenda. Therefore, far reaching cultural changes and structural shifts, connected with reflections about political goals and research interests, are necessary to achieve social improvements that relate – for example – to persons with disabilities.

List of Abbreviations

EU	European Union
CRPD	Convention on the Rights of Persons with Disabilities
SPC	Social Protection Committee

References

Adams, Maurianne/Blumenfeld, Warren J./Castañeda, Rosie/Hackman/Heather W., Peters/Madeline L./Zúñiga, Ximena (eds.) (2000): Readings for diversity in social justice: an anthology on racism, anti-semitism, sexism, heterosexism, ableism, and classism. New York.

Alcoff Martin, Linda/Hames-García/Michael, Mohanty/Satya P./Moya, Paula M. L. (eds.) (2006): Identity Politics Reconsidered. New York.

Albrecht, Gary L./Seelman, Katherine D./Bury, Michael (eds.) (2001): Handbook of disability studies. Thousand Oaks, London and New Delhi.

Andersen, Margaret L. (1996): Foreword. Chow, Esther Ngan-ling/ Wilkinson, Doris/ Zinn, Maxine Baca. Race, class and gender: Common bonds, different voices. Thousand Oaks, London and New Delhi, ix-xii.

Andersen, Margaret L. (2005): Thinking about women: A quarter century's view, in: Gender & Society, 19, 437-455.

Arnade, Sigrid/Häfner, Sabine (2005): "Towards Visibility of Women with Disabilities in the UN Convention". Available at: www.nw3.de/un-konv/doku/draftend.pdf (19.11.2019).

Campbell, Fiona A. Kumari (2008): Exploring internalized ableism using critical race theory, in: Disability & Society, 23: 2, 151-162.

Cermi (2008): “European Conference. Recognizing the Rights of Girls and Women with Disabilities. An added Value for Tomorrow’s Society. Cermi collection 32”. Available at: www.cedro.org (19.11.2019).

Chebout, Lucy (2012): “Back to the roots! Intersectionality und die Arbeiten von Kimberlé Crenshaw“. Available at: http://portal-intersektionalitaet.de/theoriebildung/ueberblickstexte/chebout/ (19.11.2019).

Collins, Patricia (2000): Black feminist thought: Knowledge, consciousness, and the politics of empowerment. New York.

Commission of the European Communities (1996): “Incorporating equal opportunities for women and men into all community policies and activities”. Available at: http://aei.pitt.edu/3991/1/3991.pdf (19.11.2019).

Committee on the Rights of Persons with Disabilities (2015): “Concluding observations on the initial report of the European Union”. Available at: https://ec.europa.eu (19.112019).

Council of Europe (1998): “Gender mainstreaming. Conceptual framework, methodology and presentation of good practices”. Available at: www.gendermainstreaming-planungstool.at/_lccms_/downloadarchive/00003/Europarat.pdf (19.11.2019).

Crenshaw, Kimberlé (1991): Mapping the margins: Inter, Identity, Politics and Violence against Women of Color. Albertsen Fineman, Martha/Mykitiuk, Roxanne. The public nature of private violence. New York, 93-118.

Crenshaw, Kimberlé (2000): Background Paper for the Expert Meeting on the Gender-Related Aspects of Race Discrimination. Zagreb.

Crow, Liz (1996): Including all of our lives: Renewing the social model of Disability. Barnes, Colin/ Merver, Geoffrey. Exploring the Divide. Leeds, 55-72.

Degener, Theresia (2009): Die UN-Behindertenrechtskonvention als Inklusionsmotor, in: Recht der Jugend und des Bildungswesens, 2, 200-219.

Emmerich, Markus and Hormel, Ulrike (2013): Heterogenität Diversity Intersektionalität. Zur Logik sozialer Unterscheidungen in pädagogischen Semantiken der Differenz. Wiesbaden.

Fraser, Nancy (1998): “Social justice in the age of identity politics: redistribution, recognition, participation“. Available at: www.ssoar.info/ssoar/handle/document/12624 (19.11.2019).

Garland Thomson, Rosemarie (2004): Integrating Disability, Transforming Feminist Theory. Smith, Bonnie G./ Hutchison, Beth. Gendering Disability. New Brunswick, New Jersey and London, 73-103.

Handicap International (2012): “Inclusive Development. Principles of disability-inclusive developement”. Available at: https://pdfslide.net/download/link/inclusive-development-principles-of-disability-inclusive-development (19.11.2019).

International Network of Women with Disabilities (2010): “15-Year review of the Beijing Declaration and Platform for Action. Comments from the International Network of Women with Disabilities (INWWD)”. Available at: https://inwwd.files.wordpress.com/2010/11/final19february2010beijing15.doc (19.11.2019).

Jahan, Rounaq (1996): The Elusive Agenda: Mainstreaming Women in Development, in: The Pakistan Development Review, 35: 4, 825-834.

Klinger, Cornelia and Knapp, Gudrun-Axeli (2007): Achsen der Ungleichheit – Achsen der Differenz. Verhältnisbestimmungen von Klasse, Geschlecht, ‚Rasse'/Ethnizität. Klinger, Cornelia/Axeli-Knapp, Gudrun/Sauer, Birgit. Achsen der Ungleichheit. Zum Verständnis von Klasse, Geschlecht und Ethnizität. Frankfurt am Main, 19-41.

Link, Jürgen (1998): Versuch über den Normalismus. Wie Normalität produziert wird. Opladen and Wiesbaden.

Makkonen, Timo (2002): "Multiple, Compound and Intersectional Discrimination: Bringing the Experiences of the Most Marginalized to the Fore". Available at: www.abo.fi/wp-content/uploads/2018/03/2002-Makkonen-Multiple-compound-and-intersectional-discrimination.pdf (19.11.2019).

Murphy, Yvette/Hunt, Valerie/Zajicek, Anna M./Norris, Adele N./Hamilton, Leah (eds.) (2009): Incorporating Intersectionality in Social Work Practice, Research, Policy and Education. Washington.

O'Tool Corbett, Joan (2004): The sexist Inheritance of the Disability Movement. Smith, Bonnie G./ Hutchison, Beth. Gendering Disability. New Brunswick, New Jersey and London, 294-300.

Raab, Heike (2007): Intersektionalität in den Disability Studies. Zur Interdependenz von Behinderung, Heteronormativität und Geschlecht. Waldschmidt, Anne/Schneider, Werner. Disability Studies, Kultursoziologie und Soziologie der Behinderung. Erkundigungen in einem Forschungsfeld. Bielefeld, 127-148.

Shakespeare, Tom/Watson, Nicholas (2002): The social model of disability: an outdated ideology?, in: Research in Social Science and Disability, 2, 9-28.

Social Protection Committee (2016): "Annual Report 2016. Review of the Social Protection Performance, Monitor and Developments in Social Protection Policies". Available at: www.ec.europa.eu/social/main.jsp?catId=738&langId=en&pubId=7936&furtherPubs=yes (19.11.2019).

Squires, Judith (2007): Diversity Mainstreaming: Moving Beyond Technocratic and Additive Approaches, in: Femina Politica, 1, 45-56.

Thomas, Carol (1999): Narrative Identity and the disabled self. Corker, Mairian/French, Sally. Disability Discourse. Philadelphia and Buckingham, 47-55.

Thompson, Neil (2016): Anti-Discriminatory Practice. Equality, Diversity and Social Justice. London.

Uccellari, Paola (2008): Multiple Discrimination: How Law can Reflect Reality, in: The Equal Rights Review, 1, 24-49.

United Nations (2006): "Convention on the Rights of Persons with Disabilities". Available at: www.un.org/disabilities/documents/convention/convoptprot-e.pdf (19.11.2019).

Verloo, Mieke (2006): Multiple Inequalities, Intersectionality and the European Union, in: European Journal of Women's Studies, 13: 3, 211-228.

Waddington, Lisa/Broderick, Andrea/Poulus, Anne (2016): "Disability law and reasonable accommodation beyond employment. A legal analysis of the situation in the EU Member States". Available at: https://op.europa.eu/en/publication-detail/-/publication/154560d2-d494-4080-90b5-dacfc1b83094 (19.11.2019).

Waldschmidt, Anne (1997): Interessensvertretung und politische Partizipation von Frauen mit Behinderungen: Forschungsdefizite – Forschungsperspektiven. Warzecha, Birgit. Geschlechterdifferenz in der Sonderpädagogik: Forschung Praxis Perspektiven. Münster, Hamburg and London, 49-66.

Waldschmidt, Anne (2005): Disability Studies: Individuelles, soziales und/oder kulturelles Modell von Behinderung?, in: Psychologie und Gesellschaftskritik, 1: 113, 9-31.

Walgenbach, Katharina (2007): Gender als interdependente Kategorie. Walgenbach, Katharina/Dietze, Gabriele/Hornscheidt, Antje/Palm, Kerstin. Gender als interdependente Kategorie. Neue Perspektiven auf Intersektionalität, Diversität und Heterogenität. Opladen and Farmington Hills, 23-64.

Wendell, Susan (1996): The Rejected Body. Feminist philosophical reflections on Disability. New York and London.

Windisch, Monika (2014): Behinderung Geschlecht Soziale Ungleichheit. Intersektionelle Perspektiven. Bielefeld.

Winker, Gabriele/Degele, Nina (2009): Intersektionalität. Zur Analyse sozialer Ungleichheit. Bielefeld.

Wolbring, Gregor (2014): „Ability Privilege: A Needed Addition to Privilege Studies". Available at: www.ucalgary.ca/crds/research/faculty/icasjustmine.pdf (19.11.2019).

Yeo, Rebecca (2005): "Disability, poverty and the new development agenda". Available at: http://hpod.org/pdf/Developmentagenda.pdf (19.11.2019).

Yuval-Davis, Nira (2006): Intersectionality and feminist politics, in: European Journal of Women's Studies, 13: 3, 193-209.

About the Authors

Sarah Böllinger

Sarah Böllinger is a Ph.D. candidate and Junior Fellow of the Bayreuth International Graduate School of African Studies (BIGSAS). She ist the director of becks, the administrative department for disabled and chronically ill students at University of Bayreuth. Her research interests comprise contemporary arts in East Africa, Disability Aesthetics, Disability Studies, Curatorial Studies as well as Visual Culture with a main research focus on Kenya. Within her dissertation Sarah Böllinger currently works on the "visual representation of disability in the Iwalewahaus collection". This project is set up as an aesthetic-visual studies reflection of artworks that have been either neglected to be studied to date or have not been analyzed with a focus on disability aesthetics. Her goal within her dissertation is to develop a new aesthetic cast on the discourse of disability in artworks.

sarah.boellinger@uni-bayreuth.de

Katharina Fink

Katharina Fink is a curator and works at Iwalewahaus, a place for the production and presentation of modern and contemporary art. Her particular concern is the power of aesthetics in art practice and museum work, especially regarding inclusion and diversity. Together with friends and colleagues, she runs two festivals, the Sophiatown Arts Festival in Johannesburg/South Africa; and the inclusive literature festival, Bayreuth blättert. She's a visiting researcher to the Wits Centre of Diversity Studies (WiCDS) at the University of the Witwatersrand in Johannesburg, South Africa. Her main research interests are popular culture, aesthetics, museum, memory, heritage, feminism and gender. Together with Nadine Siegert, she founded and runs a publishing house featuring art and discourse, with a focus on publications from the Global South: iwalewabooks (www.iwalewabooks.com).

katharina.fink@uni-bayreuth.de

Ann Fox

Ann M. Fox is a Professor of English at Davidson College, where she specializes in modern and contemporary dramatic literature and disability studies. Her scholarship on disability and theater has been supported by an AAUW postdoctoral fellowship, a Boswell Family Faculty Fellowship and has been published widely. She has also cocurated disability-related visual arts exhibitions including *RE/FORMATIONS: Disability, Women, and Sculpture*, *STARING*, and *Re/Presenting HIV/AIDS*. Ann Fox earned a B.S. in Management as well as a BA in English from the State University of New York at Buffalo, and a M.A. and Ph.D. in English from Indiana University at Bloomington.
anfox@davidson.edu

Thomas Hughes

Thomas Scott Hughes earned a Ph.D. at Copenhagen University's Department of Anthropology. His Ph.D. project investigates ethnicity and disability in the Danish Welfare State. He is a medical anthropologist with a strong interest in the social aspects of immigrant health and healthcare. His master's dissertation focused on non-western immigrants with mental illness at a support center in Copenhagen. He now works as an applied anthropologist, consulting for industry, NGOs, and governments.
thomashughes1319@gmail.com

Ras-I Mackinzeph

Zephyrinus Ghong Ndum a.k.a. Ras-I Mackinzeph was born in Wum, Menchum Division of the North West Region of Cameroon on August 24, 1968 and was later infected by the polio virus at the age of 18 months, paralyzing his right leg. He is a holder of a B.A. in Philosophy obtained in 1991 from the University of Yaounde 1. Already a reggae artist, Ras-I joined Cameroon's public service in 2000 as a Philosophy lecturer, served as head of the Philosophy Department at Government Bilingual High School Etoug-Ebe in Yaounde from 2006 to November 2017 when he was appointed Regional Pedagogic Inspector of Philosophy for the Centre Region based in Yaounde. He is currently a master's degree research fellow in the Department of Curriculum and Evaluation, Faculty of Education at the University of Yaounde 1. He has also been a philosophy examiner at the Cameroon General Certificate of Education Board (CGCEB) for the past sixteen years.
mackinzeph@gmail.com

Carsten Mildner

Carsten Mildner graduated with a Master of Science in Anthropology from Copenhagen University and was a Fulbright grantee at the Department for Comparative Human Development at the University of Chicago. He has done disability related research in Northern Mali, Germany and Uganda and has worked in inclusive public culture and higher education in Germany. Carsten is currently finishing his Ph.D. project at the chair for Social Anthropology on being deaf in Benin as a junior fellow at the Bayreuth International Graduate School of African Studies.

carsten.mildner@uni-bayreuth.de

Kevin Mwachiro

Kevin Mwachiro is a broadcaster with 18 years of experience in the media sector. He is now building a career for himself as a writer, podcaster and is an LBGTQ+ activist. He produces the storytelling podcast called *Nipe Story*. His first book *Invisible: Stories from Kenya's Queer Community* was published by the Goethe Institut in Nairobi in 2014. Kevin is a contributor to the recently launched anthology *Nairobi Noir* and he was also part of the editorial team that produced the Hivos supported journal *Boldly Queer* and is a cofounder of the *Out Film Festival*, East Africa's first queer film festival. Kevin lives in the coastal Kenyan town of Kilifi.

kmwachiro@yahoo.co.uk

Dieter Neubert

Dieter Neubert (born 1952), studied sociology, education and social anthropology in Mainz. He holds a degree in education, (University of Mainz 1978) a PhD in sociology (University of Mainz 1986) and a habilitation in sociology (Free University of Berlin 1995). He was a visiting professor for development research at University of Hohenheim (1999-2000). Since 2000 he has been professor of development sociology at the University of Bayreuth; he retired in 2018. His research areas include sociology of Africa (including social structure), sociology of violent conflicts, social change, and development policy. His regional research focus is Africa, particularly East Africa. He has also conducted research in Southeast Asia (Vietnam and Thailand).

dieter.neubert@uni-bayreuth.de

Emmanuel Sackey

Emmanuel Sackey holds a Ph.D. in Development Sociology from the University of Bayreuth, Germany. He successfully completed his Ph.D. program at the Bayreuth International Graduate School of African Studies (BIGSAS) in January 2018. His Ph.D. research focused on the internal governance dynamics of the disability rights movement in Ghana. His research interest comprises disability inclusive development, disability and politics, civil society and development and related topics in political sociology.

emmanuel.sackey@gmail.com

Florian Stoll

Florian Stoll is a postdoc researcher at University of Bayreuth where he is writing his habilitation thesis. The habiliation has the working title "Cultural Milieus in the middle-income strata of Nairobi and Mombasa. A framework of milieu study and Cultural Sociology". From May 2013 to September 2018 he was part of the Project "Middle Classes on the Rise: Concepts of the Future among Freedom, Consumption, Tradition and Moral" at the Bayreuth Academy of Advanced African Studies. From October 2016 to September 2017, Florian was a visiting scholar at the Center of Cultural Sociology, Yale University where he works on his project "Understanding the Diversity of Middle Classes in 21st Century Kenya: Social Milieus, Lifestyles and Meanings in Nairobi", founded by the Volkswagen Foundation. In 2011, he received his Ph.D. from Albrecht-Ludwigs-University in Freiburg with a study on social milieus and their use of time in Recife, Brazil. He holds a Magister in philosophy and sociology as well.

Geographically Florian Stoll focusses especially on Kenya and Brazil. His thematic research interest includes Sociology of the Global South and Cultural Sociology, social stratification, social milieus, Urban Studies and the sociology of space.

florian.stoll@uni-bayreuth.de

Ulf Vierke

Ulf Vierke has been director of Iwalewahaus since 2010 and commissioner for disabled and chronically ill students since 2014. His major focus as researcher and curator is on modern and contemporary art from Africa as well as on the archive. Under his directorate, Iwalewahaus has become a prototype and laboratory for bridging museum praxis, academic research, and inclusion (BayFinK). His interest in disability politics connects with questions of sensual and aesthetic experience and expression of art. His regional focus is on East Africa (Kenya, Uganda and Tanzania), Lusophone Africa (Angola and Mozambique), Namibia, Nigeria, Ivory Coast and Morocco.
ulf.vierke@uni-bayreuth.de

Monika Windisch

Monika Windisch worked as a teacher of students with special needs for many years and has been traning teachers at the University of Education in Innsbruck. Currently she works as a counseling teacher and as supervisor and psychotherapist. She studied educational science at Leopold Franzens University and graduated with a doctorate. In recent years she has been involved in the planning and implementation of inclusive teacher training. She has done research on disability, gender, social inequality, intersectionality and inclusive school development.
office@monika-windisch.at

Index

Bereits erschienen in der Reihe „Bayreuther Studien zu Politik und Gesellschaft in Afrika“

Already published in the series “Bayreuth Studies in African Politics and Societies”

Diversity Gains
Stepping Stones and Pitfalls
hrsg. von Sarah Böllinger, Carsten Mildner und Ulf Vierke,
2020, Band 6

Medialisierungen Afrikas
hrsg. von Valerie Hänsch, Johanna Rieß, Ivo Ritzer und Heike Wagner,
2018, Band 4

Local State Institutional Reforms in Ghana
Actors, Legitimacy and the Unfulfilled Promise of Participatory Development
von Matthew Sabbi,
2017, Band 3

Mittelklassen, Mittelschichten oder Milieus in Afrika?
Gesellschaften im Wandel
hrsg. von Antje Daniel, Sebastian Müller, Florian Stoll und Rainer Öhlschläger,
2016, Band 2

Globale Krisen – Lokale Konflikte?
Soziale Bewegungen in Afrika
hrsg. von Bettina Engels, Melanie Müller und Rainer Öhlschläger,
2015, Band 1